ISBN 978-1-330-68206-7
PIBN 10091620

1 MONTH OF
FREE
READING

at

www.ForgottenBooks.com

---◆---

By purchasing this book you are eligible for one month membership to ForgottenBooks.com, giving you unlimited access to our entire collection of over 700,000 titles via our web site and mobile apps.

To claim your free month visit:
www.forgottenbooks.com/free91620

English
Français
Deutsche
Italiano
Español
Português

www.forgottenbooks.com

Mythology Photography **Fiction**
Fishing Christianity **Art** Cooking
Essays Buddhism Freemasonry
Medicine **Biology** Music **Ancient
Egypt** Evolution Carpentry Physics
Dance Geology **Mathematics** Fitness
Shakespeare **Folklore** Yoga Marketing
Confidence Immortality Biographies
Poetry **Psychology** Witchcraft
Electronics Chemistry History **Law**
Accounting **Philosophy** Anthropology
Alchemy Drama Quantum Mechanics
Atheism Sexual Health **Ancient History**
Entrepreneurship Languages Sport
Paleontology Needlework Islam
Metaphysics Investment Archaeology
Parenting Statistics Criminology
Motivational

THE GERMS AND DEVELOPMENTS

OF THE

LAWS OF ENGLAND

EMBRACING

THE ANGLO-SAXON LAWS EXTANT

FROM THE SIXTH CENTURY TO A. D., 1066,

AS TRANSLATED INTO ENGLISH UNDER THE ROYAL
RECORD COMMISSION OF WILLIAM IV.,

WITH THE

INTRODUCTION OF THE COMMON LAW

By Norman Judges after the Conquest, and its Earliest Proferts in

MAGNA CHARTA.

WITH NOTES AND COMMENTS

By JOHN M. STEARNS, A.M.,

Counsellor-at-Law.

PRESS OF
SPRINGFIELD PRINTING AND BINDING CO.,
SPRINGFIELD, MASS.

PREFACE.

HISTORICAL research is the genius of this age. Speculations in science, philosophy, and morals have had their day. Investigation and inquiry rest conclusions on facts known, and on facts ascertained to exist as the necessary results of the relations of what is known to the developed phenomena of what is hidden and concealed. Effective powers in nature and in the world of thought are often concealed, and spring from sources far beyond the knowledge of man. Yet the existence of these hidden forces is incontrovertible. The child can read the figures and note the movement of the index finger on the dial plate of the clock. But he knows nothing of the forces within that produce the motion. So the body of human knowledge is made up of what we see, and what things seen prove to exist beyond the limit of vision.

Facts in history are gathered from original records —writings, hieroglyphics, and visible monuments— from whatever makes up the archæology and life of the past.

So, in the legal history we propose in this work, neither inference nor tradition is counted sufficient to establish any facts or principles in law, that do not find a permanent support in the legal developments of the age to which they are ascribed. The legal *status* of England in the ages of the old Saxon laws is better evidence of the principles of the then civil administration than any pretended traditions put forth five hundred to a thousand years later.

Sir Edward Cóke was a notable man for his day; but his pedantry and egotism belonged to the age in which he lived. He would be tolerated even now if his old traditions of the origin of the common law had been true.

And here it is proper to note that this work has had its origin in the inquiry as to the origin, early history, and source of authority of the common law. In its prosecution, we have sought to be guided by what we know of the science of history, and the status and conditions of the English nation in successive ages. In this pursuit, we have inquired how little, if anything, is positively known of the laws of Britain in the old Roman Period. Thus we have done the public, and the law student, a special service, in giving in translation a nearly complete body of the old Anglo-Saxon Laws, from the days of Æthelbirht, the king of Kent, from A. D. 560 to 616, down to and including the laws of Edward the Confessor, A. D. 1066. This translation is copied from the English, in an edition of the Anglo-Saxon Laws translated and published under the direction of the commissioners of the public records of the kingdom appointed by the late King William IV. in 1831 and published in 1840.

The laws of Edward the Confessor were left in that work, in Latin, and I have had them rendered into English, by G. H. Gilman, Esq., a recent graduate and a classical scholar of promise.

The *notes* are chiefly my own. In these I have often supplied untranslated words by what would seem consistent with the scope of the sentences, in which they occur. For my object has been not to present a critical exposition of an ancient writing, but the scope and spirit of legal provisions, so far as they found a record, at the periods of their enactments.

Though these laws are a convenient hand-book of law, as it subsisted with our ancestors a thousand years ago, they have a special purpose in this work—that they may defy the worshiper of the old tradition of unwritten law, as to which the memory of man never ran at all, to find in them a precedent or fragment of a precedent of anything, by custom, beyond and distinct from the laws of nature. The subsequent chapters, showing the source and authority of the common law, will need no further notice here.

JOHN M. STEARNS.

CONTENTS.

INTRODUCTION.

LAW is the growth of centuries. It is the counterpart or indication of human civilization. To understand it, as a science, its history becomes a key to its objects and purposes, and the conditions precedent that have given it shape and force are essential incidents in its construction. He is but a sciolist in the law, who is only familiar with the last acts of the legislature or the latest decisions of the court of appeals—or who knows only tricks by which he can circumvent an adversary and get advantages which are against law and justice. Unless the lawyer who cites an authority can give an intelligent exposition of the mental process by which the court comes to its conclusions, an analysis of the law involved, by his opponent, may divert the precedent from the point to support which it was relied on. Where the sense of justice of remote antiquity accords with our own notions of right, we are strengthened in our convictions, and courts follow the same process of reasoning in their judgments.

This is an age when fossil antiquity is sought to be resuscitated, and made to answer inquiries, in every department of human knowledge; and, while the law has a history from the remote past, its origin and growth show precedent forces that have shaped its provisions and given it character. The *syllabus* of text-books are but meager developments of the science of law. The living, breathing world, in which laws operate as the ligatures and joints of society and the body politic, is to be considered as essential to legal science and its illustrations.

We hence go back to prehistoric times, to the days of darkness, and in the shimmer of the early morning of our civil state, we scan the faint shadows of law, as we would scan the features of a new-born child, with all the future, to our prophetic eyes, as dark as Egypt. Still, the law has lit its feeble flame within the closet or domicile of its foster father, Christianity, that has been the nurturing agency of law and of civilization. How has law grown upon the world!

In the vast cycles of time there is developed the slow but certain changes in the condition of man, and the way points of civilization. "The mills of the gods grind slowly; but they grind exceeding fine." The precession of the equinoxes and the motions of fixed stars are all unseen by mortal eyes; yet the facts of such perpetual changes are demonstrated science. So, to know what Christianity has done for humanity, we must go far back of its existing power as an active force in our intellectual and moral progress. We go back and analyze the condition and character of our remote ancestors in our fatherland for more than two thousand years—beyond the age of fable, to prehistoric darkness, and fetch up in the dark woods of a forest-clad land, where ogres, giants, and specter kings had reigned supreme for uncounted centuries!

To know what Christianity has done for us, we look on this old, old picture, in its darkness and horrors, and then, in contrast, on Christianity and law as they are to-day, as an affirmative, demonstrated power in the world—the force that develops man in the instincts of his spirit life—the great facts and experiences that constrain his acts, create his joys, and inspire his songs—the laws that have been a guiding hand in all his fortune.

THE CREED OF THE DRUIDS AS THE LAWS OF THE LAND.

The earliest authentic history shows us the Britons clad in the skins of animals, and roaming as herdsmen, from place to place, for the sustenance of their flocks, and living in cabins and tents without regard for government or order. They had chieftains to lead them in military encounters, but the real power of their government was vested in the Druid priesthood, and enforced by the superstitions of the Druid religion. A Burgundian writer of the Middle Ages gives us the Druid creed, in which, among others, are the following propositions:—

"None must be instructed but in the Sacred Grove."

"Mistletoe must be gathered with reverence, and if possible in the sixth moon. It must be cut with a golden bill."

"Everything derives its origin from Heaven."

"The arcana of science must not be committed to writing, but to the memory."

"Great care is to be taken of the education of children."

"The powder of mistletoe makes women fruitful."

"The disobedient are to be shut out from the sacrifices."

"Souls are immortal. The soul, after death, goes into other bodies."

" If the world is destroyed, it will be by fire and water."

" Upon extraordinary emergencies a man must be sacrificed. According as the body falls, or moves after it has fallen; according as the blood flows, or the wound opens, future events are foretold."

" Prisoners of war are to be slain upon the altars, or burned alive, enclosed in wicker in honor of the gods."

"All commerce with strangers must be prohibited."

" He that comes last to the assembly of the states ought to be punished with death."

" Children are to be brought up apart from their parents till they are fourteen years of age."

" Money lent in this world will be repaid in the next."

" There is another world, and those who kill themselves, to accompany their friends, will live with them there."

" Letters given to dying persons or thrown on the funeral pile of the dead will faithfully be delivered in the other world."

" The moon is a sovereign remedy for all things."

" Let the disobedient be excommunicated; let him be deprived of the benefits of the law; let him be avoided by all, and rendered incapable of any employ."

"All masters of families are kings in their own houses. They have the power of life and death over their wives, children, and slaves.

It was under these institutes of the Druid religion, and we may say government, that history found our ancient forefathers. These propositions cover the civil

rights and relations of citizens, as well as their relig-
ous faith.

The Druid religion was, in fact, a religion of
church and state. Though the proferts set forth of
this religion were written on the continent, they were,
nevertheless, the Druid creed in Britain.

The character of the Druid religion is indicated by
the creed we have copied. Its priesthood was a veri-
table hierarchy, with a thorough organization, from a
high priest, or pontiff, to the lower order of priests,
having the conduct and consciences of the masses of
people under strict surveillance.

There were terrible ordeals and punishments for
ecclesiastical offenses—among them, excommunica-
tions, with cursings, social ostracisms that were fitting prototypes of the anathemas pronounced by modern priests in persecuting churches. In fine, the
Druids had a terrible religion ; darker in its superstitions and more refined in its cruelties than any
other that has cursed the world.

Still, its union of civil and ecclesiastical order is
in being in the English church and state of to-day.
If ideas govern the world for the hour they perpetuate institutions through the ages.

And in the proposition, " The arcana of science
must not be committed to writing but to the memory," is set forth the policy of professional mystery
that has pleaded its prerogative in law and jurisprudence and theology to the present hour.

The ancient Britons, oppressed, subordinated, and
enslaved by the forms and spirit of paganism, matured under the reign of the Druid priesthood,
scarcely developed in their history, aside from their

superstitions, the first elements of a civil state or of
secular law, much less of human rights. Whatever
restraints, through the fears of the people, might
have grown out of the Druid superstitions, the civilization of the people could not have been raised
above the religious ideas of a bloody creed coupled
with the conceived necessity of controlling opinions
by inflicting tortures.

When the Romans conquered Britain the Druid
hierarchy sunk to insignificance; save here and there
it attracted the attention of the conquerors, as it
seemed a hidden instigator of military resistance.
Where the true merit lay, between the paganism
of Britain and that of Rome, it is difficult to say.
In Rome religion was developed in more varied
forms, and was more affected by state policy, through
the conviction of the rulers, " that an empire embracing so many tribes or nationalities could not
afford to create religious tests against the scarcely
subdued remote provinces."

It was only when the religion of these border
lands developed antagonisms against the Roman authority, that the conquerors disturbed them, in religious matters. But the Druids were a concen-
trated paramount authority over the people, and when
instigating resistance to foreigners were a terrible
power in the land where they ruled. Hence, the
Romans soon became convinced that the suppression
of the Druids was a military necessity. So the
strongholds of this bloody superstition were destroyed,
and their ogres in that forest land became the myths
of tradition and gradually faded out from the tablets
of time, and a few rough stones at Stonehenge is

all that lives of this once reigning power in that country.

With such a picture in the background we can indeed rejoice in the light of Christian civilization, as shed over the world to-day. These adherents of the Druid faith were among our remote forefathers. Who and what has caused us to differ from them? In this so marked difference is seen the office and work of Christianity and law among men—what they have done and what is the divine economy of their work. We may, indeed, rejoice that our lot is cast, not only in a goodly land, but under the influence of a true, beneficent, and benevolent religion. And why should we not adore and worship the power that has brought us out of a terrible wilderness to the light of life?

WHENCE CAME THE DRUIDS?

But where and whence came the subjects of this old, cruel superstition to our father-land?

The islands of Britain and Ireland in prehistoric ages were the furthest bourne of wild, uncultured countries. Dwelling amidst the clouds and storms of an unknown and angry ocean, the roving brigands of the Continent had often looked through the mists around the coast with covetous and longing eyes, for the land which nature had so protected as a safe home for those who should become its people. Those who had theretofore found protection in mountain caves or had constructed dwellings on piles in the lakes that the surrounding waters might protect them from hostile or mercenary enemies, conceived that these islands in the sea would afford them a better protection than their rude domiciles, hid in the mountains forests and lakes of the Continent. But how or when these adventurers made their primitive advent to the land is all unknown. They brought their Druid religion with them from the Continent we know, for in both countries civilization in its earliest traditions found the people subject to this pagan *régime*.

THE ROMAN PERIOD DEVELOPED NO SYSTEM OF LAW.

About fifty years before Christ, Britain was invaded by the Romans under Julius Cæsar. The conqueror wrote an account of his campaign, and of the condition of the country, it then being very wild and barbarous. When the Roman power in the island declined, new invasions took place; some obscure fragmentary accounts of the Roman rule were preserved in the archives of the Roman empire. But the Roman archives in Britain were neither in language nor writing. Portions of the old Roman wall in London are still there, and so of architectural structures in various parts of the island, including the wall across the island as a defense against the fierce tribes of what is now Scotland. But learning or science beyond what was necessary to produce the structures remaining there did not follow the conquerors. In fact, after four hundred years of occupation, we scarcely find an historical record of the events that transpired, and a picture of the state and condition of the country, and the people outside of the writings of Romans at home. As to the towns erected, the commerce established, or the civil or political institutions growing up, we are left mainly to conjecture. The Druid religion arraying itself in antagonism to the Roman rule in Britain

was suppressed by military power. Excavations in the
bed of the Thames have brought up to the light of
day old Roman coins and a few specimens of Penates
or household images that were once the shrines of the
pagan Romans. But letters were scarcely known as
local archives in Britain. During the Roman period
what was written of its local history was done at
Rome or by authors of the empire. It is alleged that
Christianity was preached in Britain during the Roman
period, and that three or four bishops were there at
the coming of the Saxons. Such may have been the
case. But the presence and influence of Christianity
was but obscurely certified in the lack of those beneficent benefits which it has ever borne with it, in all
ages and throughout the world, to wit:—

THE INTRODUCTION AND CULTURE OF LETTERS

as the means of development and civilization of rude
and barbarous peoples. There was scarcely a local
historian in the Roman period. If scholars from the
empire came there they soon departed to their homes
and left no impress of their knowledge or influence on
the people. They might as well have gone as pil-
grims to the tomb of Confucius as to have thought of
refining the people in this barbarous land.

Yet a residence of over four hundred years must
have impressed much of the Roman character and
something of Roman laws on the minds of the people.
But there were no historians to record the acts of the
governors or governed during all that long period.

The rudeness of the people, destitute of letters except perhaps with the few, at that early day, would
give permanence and stability to few legal principles;

and these only the most simple, incident to the passions, necessities, and interests of the most rude and uncultivated.

Still crime, in that rude age, had its distinguishing features. Boadicea, the queen of Mercia, regarded the brutal treatment of herself and her daughter, by a brutal Roman general, as a just cause of war.

But law does not develop itself to any settled forms without letters, nor perpetuate itself without a record. And the proferts of positive law are wanting to such an extent, in the old Roman days, in Britain, that the alternative rule of natural law, or the despotic orders of military governors, made up an often conflicting code, that from its variableness and uncertainty would scarcely produce a rationale of either authority or right.

While the growth of law and civilization are the counterparts of human progress in any age, the pretended existence of ancient English law would have been a greater miracle than has yet taxed our faith in any other department of knowledge. It is not contended that laws might not have existed; but it is doubted if their forms or principles were preserved to any other extent than natural law will find a natural development and application to human conduct, among mankind in any state or condition.

As a presumption against the existence of a settled code of laws during the Roman *régime* in England, we are to note the fact that from the first invasion of the Romans and afterwards, the country, with but brief intervals, was engaged in foreign and domestic wars—in repelling invasions, or in subduing internal strifes and contentions.

CONQUEST AND FOREIGN RULE HOSTILE TO THE GROWTH OF LAW.

England was conquered not in the spirit of modern conquests, that limit their demands to the exercise of government over the people, left unmolested in their persons, rights, and property. But these early invaders of England came with the purpose of pirates and brigands, not only to seize the government, but to appropriate to themselves all the property in the realm. During these violent changes in the government and the people, it is to be presumed that the chief authority was the dominant military authority for the time being. For each succeeding conqueror ignored existing laws affecting rights of persons or property, and set up his own arbitrary will, in the place of all prior customs and laws; so the people lived on in slavery and barbarism, attaching themselves to their immediate oppressors for life and protection.

THE SAXON LAWS.

The Saxon laws as written are an index if not a record of the habits, conditions, and character of the people. They are facts in legal history, superseding all the logic, inferences, and speculations of law writers as to *laws unwritten* in those rude and barbarous ages. Customs they might have had, but no living mortal can tell what they were. The laws of nature would settle customs, to meet emergencies in the conditions, relations, and progress of a people; but these customs would be changing and ambulatory, to meet new conditions, realized from time to time. Writers have labored to show that settled customs obtained among the Britons and the early Saxons, derived from

the old Roman law of the republic and empire. But
these attempts utterly fail, when they go beyond the
developments of natural law, to be realized under prescribed conditions, among any people that never heard
of Rome or its government.

But the historical fact is noted, that the Romans
were in occupation of England for four centuries.
Yes, but, though some of the leaders were posted in
literature and letters at Rome, they did not plant
them in Britain. ·The most obscure monuments of
Roman learning are not found in Britain. The archives of the Roman age are limited to the foundations
of parts of the London wall, the great wall between
Caledonia and Britain, and a few Roman coins and
household gods, fished up from the bottom of the
Thames. But these are no more significant, in fixing
a body of facts in law or science, than the arrow-heads
and other relics of the prehistoric age dug from the
chalk hills of Britain, or the caves on the continent.

But the principles of natural law, applied to the
conditions of the ancient Britons, would develop un-
derstandings and customs between neighbor and neighbor, that would, under the pressure of necessity, have
the force of law. These might not differ from customs
having resulted from like conditions among other
nations, as early Greece and Rome, when Britain was
to them unknown.

As we have intimated, at the coming of Julius
Cæsar, the Britons were mere herders, dressing in
the skins taken from their slaughtered sheep and cattle, with scarcely a semblance of houses for domiciles. So long as such a population was sparse and
the spontaneous growth on the land furnished suf-

ficient forage for all, no division or enclosure of the land would be thought of; no royal demesnes would be located or claimed, as against the common use of the people. But, as soon as tillage of the soil or agriculture became a necessity to the growing population, then at least a possessory located title to the soil would become a necessity, as without it, at least for the season, no matured crop could be realized unless the rights of the husbandman to gather it were respected. That improvements made this year might inure to the benefit of the person making them, prudent political economy would seek to give a perpetuity to the possession of the land. So property in land would become fixed and defined, and the relation of neighbor to neighbor, in land holding, would become a matter of comity, and the land and its fruits would become fixed in the rights of their owners. Then the betterments and improvements made by the father would be sought by way of descent by his children, and the law of successions would be developed, rude and imperfect and uncertain as might be the tenure of the estates. Then the relation of husband and wife would develop their relative rights in the common property of the family. And the duties of morality in this relation would come to be recognized and respected; or, if not respected, their violation would come within the rationale of crime.

So far, we note the development of natural law in convenient customs, in rude states of society, where men are supposed to sojourn together, as a common brotherhood. But, where violent and disturbing forces produce abnormal conditions of human society and human relations, consequences therefrom may determine themselves by force of natural law. Such violent precedent conditions are realized from foreign invasions and conquests. The conquerors assume a violent domain over the lands of a kingdom, and levy unnatural contributions on the labor and gains of those who till them. But, though this may modify and limit the tenure of the cultivator, natural law will still obtain in defining the relation of neighbor to neighbor in the possession of adjacent lands, and the influential force of the laws of descent and successions would obtain, within the restrictions of the military aristocracy. The condition of absolute bond slaves, in the cultivators of the soil, is so against natural law that all its beneficial economies would be excluded.

The natural results of conquests are restrictions on liberty, and the dominating of a military aristocracy over the lands and the people of the conquered country. So the Romans might have parceled out the lands of Britain, or such of them as they subdued, among the Roman chieftains, and thereafter allowed the Britons to eke out a scanty living by sharing the fruits of their labors with their oppressors. Great manor estates might have been created, after the style and organization prevailing in Rome and its vicinity. But, if such estates existed, and whatever they might have been called, the relation of the aggregate invaders and domestic population varied little from like conditions under the conquests of the Saxons, the Danes, and that of the Normans. One result was the natural law of human selfishness, that the masses should be compelled, by the force of circumstances, to work for and support the aristocracy. The Norman conquest brought in the full-fledged feudal system that turned Europe into a great military camp. But the condition of the tillers of the soil was scarcely made better or worse under this system, unless as to those subject to military conscription.

Having so considered whatever acquired the prescription of a custom under the Romans and their successors, to understand to what a limited extent such customs prevailed among the Saxons, we produce the Saxon laws to indicate the condition of the people for whom they were enacted.

PREFATORY NOTE TO ÆTHEL-BIRHT'S LAWS.

To analyze the provisions of the old Saxon laws and to develop system out of the mixed record of them extant, it is needful to define certain terms and distinctions that were of common use in the proferts of these old statutes.

A fine is designated as *bot*, doubtless, an untranslated Saxon term; the payment of fines as "making bot." This word, *bot*, implied something more than the modern idea of a legal penalty; it embraced the payment of damages to the injured party, as well as, if the case might require, a penalty to the king or bishop or other special ruling power offended or contemned by the event suffered or transaction wrought. The term was used both in secular and ecclesiastical laws.

In the days of Æthelbirht's reign, noted as the first Christian Saxon king, who reigned in Kent from A. D. 560 to 616, all offenses, even capital crimes, were compensated for in the payment of bot, or money-fines. There were some offenses where the life of the culprit was in the mercy of the king; yet the price of such pardon was fixed and defined. No doubt people in offending the government were often put to death; but such executions took place more as military emergencies than as the result of a civil judgment and conviction. They were summary and without trial. To render such a system practicable, it was necessary to fix a schedule of values to everything that was likely to come within the scope of legal cognizance, the life of the king, the bishop, the ealderman, the eorl, the freeman, the ceorl, and esne.

The value of a freeman seems to have been the basis of comparative values; so, advancing according to rank or depreciating in the subordinate classes, this valuation was called the *wer* or worth of a man. A slave, however, was valued according to the worth of his services to his master, who received the *wer* in case he was slain. Property was valued according to the rank or class of its possessor by way of penalty in case of its wanton destruction. The property of the church if destroyed was to be compensated for by its destroyer twelvefold its intrinsic value. A bishop's property was to be compensated for with eleven-fold its value, a priest's ninefold, a deacon's property sixfold, a clerk's property threefold; property in church frith or protection, twofold. Every crime varied in its money penalty or fine, by the rank of the party injured. The *bot* or compensation went to the persons or class or guild injured. The *wer* was the greater forfeiture fixed by the value of a life of the class with respect to whom such penalty was incurred. The *wite* was a fine to be paid by the offenders to the king. This corresponded more strictly with a modern fine.

The chief office of the statutes of Æthelbirht was to fix a schedule of *bot*, fines, compensations, or penalties, or *wite*, for the known offenses of the times. From these laws the status of the people as to civilization and progress is shown with some obscurity, yet with considerable clearness. The crimes enumerated were doubtless of frequent occurrence, or they would not have been made the subject of law.

The scale of valuations and damages and fines rose in subsequent reigns, increased when money became more plenty, and hence of less specific value. Then the emergencies arising from the increase of crime, as the population increased, called for greater severity in the laws.

As to the secular members of the Saxon state in the days of Æthelbirht, A. D. 600, the lowest class were the *theows*, slaves by birth. Then there were *wite* theows, those reduced to slavery from their inability to pay fines or penalties pronounced by the magistrate.

The *esne* was sometimes ranked as a slave, but seems to have been a hireling in a servile condition.

The *ceorl* was a freeman of ignoble rank, a churl, a two hynd man, 'a villain.

The *freeman* was doubtless what the name signifies; though under duty to the lord or the king from whom he might hold lands in the limited tenure then known or allowed.

A *læt* was one of a class between servile and free. The value put on his life in Æthelbirht, 26, shows he was a person of higher consequence than even a freeman, which has led to the inference that he was an alien residing in the country under the protection of the government. There being different penalties shows that these might have been of different qualities or rank, but either class of no established rank in England.

Eorls had an office of honor and came at length to the exercise of power in the administration of the government. But there is nothing in the laws of Æthelbirht showing anything in their enactment beyond the simple power of the king.

Ealdormen were vested with the powers of government in the other Saxon kingdoms as viceroys of the Bretwelda, or chief king over the other kingdoms of the Heptarchy. The powers of the Ealdormen at a later date passed to the eorls, whose office represented that of compts on the continent.

THE LAWS OF KING ÆTHELBIRHT.

THESE ARE THE DOOMS WHICH KING ÆTHELBIRHT ESTABLISHED IN THE DAYS OF AUGUSTINE.

1. The property of God and of the church, twelve-fold; a bishop's property, eleven-fold; a priest's property, nine-fold; a deacon's property, six-fold; a clerk's property, three-fold; "church-frith," two-fold; "m. . . . frith," two-fold.

2. If the king calls his "leod" to him, and any one there do them evil, [let him compensate with] a two-fold "bot," and L. shillings to the king.

3. If the king drink at any one's home, and any one there do any "lyswe," let him make two-fold "bot."

4. If a freeman steal from the king, let him pay nine-fold.

5. If a man slay another in the king's "tun," let him make "bot" with L. shillings.

6. If any one slay a freeman, L. shillings to the king, as "drihtin-beah."

7. If the king's "ambiht-smith," or "laad-rinc," slay a man, let him pay a half "leod-geld."

8. The king's "mund-byrd," L. shillings.

---

2. *Leod*, men, people.

3. *Lyswe*, small offense—petit larceny.

7. *Ambiht-smith* or *laad-rinc*, kings-smith or carpenter. *Leod-geld*, value of a life.

8. *Mund-byrd*, one under protection or guardianship.

9. If a freeman steal from a freeman, let him make three-fold "bot"; and let the king have the "wite" and all the chattels.

10. If a man lie with the king's maiden, let him pay a "bot" of L. shillings.

11. If she be a grinding slave, let him pay a "bot" of xxv. shillings. The third [class] xii. shillings.

12. Let the king's "fed-esl" be paid for with xx. shillings.

13. If a man slay another in an "eorl's" "tun," let make "bot" with xii. shillings.

14. If a man lie with an "eorl's" "birele," let him make "bot" with xii. shillings.

15. A "ceorl's" "mund-byrd," vi. shillings.

16. If a man lie with a "ceorl's" "birele," let him make "bot" with vi. shillings; with a slave of the second [class], L. "scætts"; with one of the third, xxx. "scætts."

17. If any one be the first to make an inroad into a man's "tun," let him make "bot" with vi. shillings; let him who follows, with iii. shillings; after, each, a shilling.

18. If a man furnish weapons to another where there is strife, though no evil be done, let him make "bot" with vi. shillings.

19. If "weg-reaf" be done, let him make "bot" with vi. shillings.

20. If the man be slain, let him make "bot" with xx. shillings.

---

12. *Fed-esl*, supposed one feeding or fed, a menial servant.

16. *Birele*, a superior slave. *Scætts*, a small coin, of which there were 250 in a pound of silver.

19. *Weg-reaf*, highway robbery.

21. If a man slay another, let him make "bot" with a half "leod-geld" of C. shillings.

22. If a man slay another at an open grave, let him pay XX. shillings, and pay the whole "leod" within XL. days.

23. If the slayer retire from the land, let his kindred pay a half "leod."

24. If any one bind a freeman, let him make "bot" with XX. shillings.

25. If any one slay a "ceorl's" "hlaf-æta," let him make "bot" with VI. shillings.

26. If [any one] slay a "læt" of the highest class, let him pay LXXX. shillings; if he slay one of the second, let him pay LX. shillings; of the third, let him pay XL. shillings.

27. If a freeman commit "edor"-breach, let him make "bot" with VI. shillings.

28. If any one take property from a dwelling, let him pay a three-fold "bot."

29. If a freeman pass over an "edor," let him make "bot" with IV. shillings.

30. If a man slay another, let him pay with his own money, and with any sound property whatever.

31. If a freeman lie with a freeman's wife, let him pay for it with his "wer-geld," and provide another wife with his own money, and bring her to the other.

32. If any one thrust through the "riht ham-scyld," let him adequately compensate.

---

25. *Hlaf-æta,* loaf-eater, menial servant.

27. *Edor-breach,* breaking in by violence.

29. *Edor,* an enclosure.

33. If there be "**feax-fang**," let there be L. scætts for "bot."

34. If there be **an exposure** of the bone, let "bot" be made with III. shillings.

35. If there be an injury of the bone, let "bot" be made with IV. shillings.

36. If the outer "hion" be broken, let "bot" be made with X. shillings.

37. If it be both, let "bot" be made with XX. shillings.

38. If a shoulder be lamed, let "bot" be made with XXX. shillings.

39. If an ear be struck off, let "bot" be made with XII. shillings.

40. If the other ear hear not, let "bot" be made with XXV. shillings.

41. If an ear be pierced, let "bot" be made with III. shillings.

42. If an ear be mutilated, let "bot" be made with VI. shillings.

43. If an eye be [struck] out, let "bot" be made with L. shillings.

44. If the mouth or an eye be injured, let "bot" be made with XII. shillings.

45. If the nose be pierced, let "bot" be made with IX. shillings.

46. If it be one "ala," let "bot" be made with III. shillings.

47. If both be pierced, let "bot" be made with VI. shillings.

---

33. *Feax-fang*, a taking hold by the hair.
36. *Hion*, a membrane.

48. If the nose be otherwise mutilated, for each let " bot " be made with VI. shillings.

49. If it be pierced, let " bot " be made with VI. shillings.

50. Let him who breaks the chin-bone pay for it with XX. shillings.

51. For each of the four front teeth, VI. shillings; for the tooth which stands next to them, IV. shillings; for that which stands next to that, III. shillings; and then afterwards, for each a shilling.

52. If the speech be injured, XII. shillings. If the collar-bone be broken, let " bot " be made with VI. shillings.

53. Let him who stabs [another] through an arm, make " bot " with VI. shillings. If an arm be broken, let him make " bot " with VI. shillings.

54. If a thumb be struck off, XX. shillings. If a thumb nail be off, let " bot " be made with III. shillings. If the shooting (i. e. fore) finger be struck off, let " bot " be made with VIII. shillings. If the middle finger be struck off, let " bot " be made with IV. shillings. If the gold (i. e. ring) finger be struck off, let " bot " be made with VI. shillings. If the little finger be struck off, let " bot " be made with XI. shillings.

55. For every nail, a shilling.

56. For the smallest disfigurement of the face, III. shillings; and for the greater, VI. shillings.

57. If any one strike another with his fist on the nose, III. shillings.

58. If there be a bruise, a shilling; if he receive a right hand bruise, let him [the striker] pay a shilling.

59. If the bruise be black in a part not covered

by the clothes, let "bot" be made with XXX. "scætts."

60. If it be covered by the clothes, let "bot" for each be made with XX. "scætts."

61. If the belly be wounded, let "bot" be made with XII. shillings; if it be pierced through, let "bot" be made with XX. shillings.

62. If any one be "gegemed," let "bot" be made with XXX. shillings.

63. If any one be "cear-wund," let "bot" be made with III. shillings.

64. If any one destroy [another's] organ of generation, let him pay him with III. "leod-gelds": if he pierce it through, let him make "bot" with VI. shillings; if it be pierced within, let him make "bot" with VI. shillings.

65. If a thigh be broken, let "bot" be made with XII. shillings; if the man become halt, then the friends must arbitrate.

66. If a rib be broken, let "bot" be made with III. shillings.

67. If a thigh be pierced through, for each stab VI. shillings; if (the wound be) above an inch, a shilling; for two inches, II.; above three, III. shillings.

68. If a sinew be wounded, let "bot" be made with III. shillings.

69. If a foot be cut off, let L. shillings be paid.

70. If a great toe be cut off, let X. shillings be paid.

71. For each of the other toes, let one-half be paid, like as it is stated for the fingers.

---

62. *Gegemed*, the Saxon translator finds no definite meaning for this word.

72. If the nail of a great toe be cut off, xxx. "scætts" for "bot"; for each of the others, make " bot" with x. "scætts."

73. If a freewoman "loc-bore" commit any "leswe," let her make a "bot" of xxx. shillings.

74. Let "maiden-bot" be as that of a freeman.

75. For the "mund" of a widow of the best class, of an "eorl's" degree, let the "bot" be L. shillings; of the second, xx. shillings; of the third, xii. shillings; of the fourth, vi. shillings.

76. If a man carry off a widow not in his own tutelage, let the "mund" be two-fold.

77. If a man buy a maiden with cattle, let the bargain stand, if it be without guile; but if there be guile, let him bring her home again, and let his property be restored to him.

78. If she bear a live child, let her have half the property, if the husband die first.

79. If she wish to go away with her children, let her have half the property.

80. If the husband wish to have them, [let her portion be] as one child.

81. If she bear no child, let her paternal kindred have the "fioh" and the "morgen-gyfe."

82. If a man carry off a maiden by force, let him pay L. shillings to the owner, and afterwards buy [the object of] his will of the owner.

83. If she be betrothed to another man in money, let him make "bot" with xx. shillings.

---

76. *Mund*, guardianship, protection.

81. *Morgen-gyfe*, gifts of the husband to the wife the morning after marriage. *Fioh*, gifts of her father or kindred.

3

84. If she become "gængang," xxxv. shillings;
and xv. shillings to the king.

85. If a man lie with an "esne's" wife, her husband still living, let him make two-fold "bot."

86. If one "esne" slay another unoffending, let
him pay for him at his full worth.

87. If an "esne's" eye and foot be struck out or
off, let him be paid for at his full worth.

88. If any one bind another's "esne," let him make
"bot" with vi. shillings.

89. Let the "weg-reaf" of a "theow" be iii. shillings.

90. If a "theow" steal, let him make two-fold
"bot."

Hume says, "The Anglo-Saxons were a nation of drunkards"—
and if their laws were enacted against existing evils, the results of
brawls and fighting contests among the people such as usually result
from drunkenness, Hume's judgment seems to have been just.

And he says further: "With regard to the manners of the Anglo-
Saxons, we can say little. But they were in general a rude, uncultivated people, ignorant of letters, unskilled in the mechanic arts,
untamed to submission under law and government, addicted to in-
temperance, riot, and disorder. Their best quality was their military
courage, which, yet, was not supported by discipline or conduct.
Their want of fidelity to the prince or to any trust reposed in them
appears strongly in the history of their later period, and their
want of humanity in all their history."

Bede says, "Among other benefits which he [Æthelbirht] conferred
on the nation, he also by the advice of wise persons introduced *judicial decrees* after the Roman model; which being then in English
are still kept and observed by them; among which he in the first
place set down what satisfaction should be given by those who
should steal anything belonging to the church, the bishop, or the
other clergy; resolving to give protection to those whose doctrines
he had embraced."

THE TEXT OF THE LAWS OF KINGS HLOTHHÆRE AND EADRIC.

THESE ARE THE DOOMS WHICH HLOTHHÆRE AND EADRIC, KINGS OF THE KENTISH-MEN, ESTABLISHED.*

Hlothhære and Eadric, kings of the Kentish-men, augmented the laws, which their elders had before made, by these dooms, which hereafter say.

1. If any one's " esne " slay a man of an " eorl's " degree, whoever it be, let the owner pay with three hundred shillings, give up the slayer, and add three " man-wyrths " thereto.

2. If the slayer escape, let him add a fourth " man-wyrth," and let him prove, with good " æwdas," that he could not obtain the slayer.

3. If any one's " esne " slay a freeman, whoever it be, let the owner pay with a hundred shillings, give up the slayer, and a second " man-wyrth " thereto.

4. If the slayer escape, let the owner pay for him with two " man-wyrths " ; and let him prove, with good " æwdas," that he could not obtain the slayer.

---

*Æthelbirht died in **A. D. 616**, and the sixteen laws of HLOTHHÆRE and *Eadric*, styling themselves kings of Kentish-men, are dated near sixty years after. In these laws we find the recognition of local courts and judicial officers.

2. *Man-wyrth*, the value of a man.

5. If a freeman steal a man; if the man return, and denounce him before the "stermelda"; let him clear himself, if he be able, and let him have the number of free "æwda"-men, and one with (himself) in the oath, each at the "tūn" to which he belongs; if he be unable, let him pay as he "gono hage."

6. If a husband die, wife and child yet living, it is right that the child follow the mother; and let there be sufficient "borh," given to him from among his paternal kinsmen, to keep his property till he be x. years of age.

7. If one man steal property from another, and the owner afterwards lay claim to it; let him vouch to warranty at the king's hall, if he can, and let him bring thither the person who sold it him; if he cannot do that, let him give it up, and let the owner take possession of it.

8. If one man make plaint against another in a suit, and he cite the man to a "methel" or to a "thing," let the man always give "borh" to the other, and do him such right as the Kentish judges prescribe to them.

9. But if he refuse to give "borh," let him pay XII. shillings to the king, and let the suit be as open as it before was.

---

5. *Stermelda,* a local court or magistrate like the reeve or sheriff of later times.

6. *Borh,* security-pledge.

8. *Methel,* or a *thing,* courts, or Gemot, of the hundred, or tithing. A making of a complaint and a citing to a *methel* are set out and to be determined as the *Kentish judges* prescribe to them; showing that *magistrates* were then charged with the duty of adjudicating under the laws.

10. If one man make plaint against another; after he has given him " borh," and then after three days let them seek for themselves an arbitrator, unless a longer period be desired by him who carries on the suit: after the suit is settled, let the man do justice to the other within seven days; let him satisfy him either in money or with an oath, whichever be desired by him; but if he will not do this, then let him pay c. without an oath: within one day after, let them settle.

11. If one man call another perjurer, in another's " flet," or shamefully bespeak him with abusive words, let him pay a shilling to him who owns the " flet," and VI. shillings to him to whom he said the words, and XII. shillings to the king.

12. If a man " steop asette " to another, where men are drinking unoffendingly; according to ancient usage, let him pay a shilling to him who owns the " flet," and VI. shillings to him to whom he the " steop aset," and XII. shillings to the king.

13. If a man draw a weapon where men are drinking, and no harm be done there; a shilling to him who owns the " flet," and XII. shillings to the king.

14. If the " flet " be stained with blood, let him pay to the man his " mund-byrd," and L. shillings to the king.

15. If a man entertain a stranger for three nights at his own home, a chapman or any other who has come over the march, and then feed him with his own

---

10. This was a judicial proceeding before the king or such as were acting as his judges in a place appointed.

11. *Flet*, cottage or house; sometimes a drinking saloon.

food, and he then do harm to any man, let the man bring the other to justice, or do justice for him.

16. If any Kentish-man buy a chattel in "Lunden-wic," let him then have two or three true men to witness, or the king's "wic"-reeve. If it be afterwards claimed of the man in Kent, let him then vouch the man who sold it him to warranty, in the "wic" at the king's hall, if he know him, and can bring him to the warranty; if he cannot do that, let him prove at the altar, with one of his witnesses or with the king's "wic"-reeve, that he bought the chattel openly in the "wic," with his own property, and then let him be paid its worth: but if he cannot prove that by lawful averment, let him give it up, and let the owner take possession of it.

---

16. A money compensation for offenses is retained in all the sixteen laws preserved from this reign with additions in the nature of fines to the king.

THE LAWS OF KING WIHTRÆD.

In the reign of the most clement king of the Kentish-men, Wihtræd, in the fifth year of his reign, the ninth indiction, the sixth day of Rugern, in the place which is called Bergham-styde, where was assembled a deliberative convention of the great men; there was Birhtwald, archbishop of Britain, and the fore-named king; also the bishop of Rochester, the same was called Gybmund, was present; and every degree of the Church of that province spoke in unison with the obedient people. There the great men decreed, with the suffrages of all, these dooms, and added them to the lawful customs of the Kentish-men, as it hereafter saith and declareth.

1. To the Church freedom from imposts, and that the king be prayed for, and that they revere him of their own will, without command.

2. That the " mund-byrd " of the Church be L. shillings, as the king's.

3. That men living in illicit intercourse take to a righteous life, with repentance of their sins; or that they be separated from communion with the Church.

4. That foreigners, if they will not correct their fornication, depart from the land, with their goods

and with their sins. Let natives among the people forfeit communion with the Church, without expulsion.

5. If it happen that a "gesithcund" man, after this "gemot," take to illicit intercourse, contrary to the king's command, and the bishop's and the books' doom; let him make a "bot" for it to his lord of c. shillings, according to ancient usage. If it be a "ceorlish" man, let him make a "bot" of L. shillings; and let either with penitence desist from his fornication.

6. If a priest allow of illicit intercourse; or neglect the baptism of a sick person, or be drunk to that degree that he cannot do it; let him abstain from his ministry until the doom of the bishop.

7. If a shorn man go wandering about for hospitality, let it be given him once; and, unless he have leave, let it not be that any one entertain him longer.

8. If any one give freedom to his man at the altar, let him be folk-free; let the freedom-giver have his heritage, and "wer-geld," and the "mund" of his family, be he over the march wherever he may be.

9. If an "esne" do any servile labor, contrary to his lord's command, from sunset on Sunday-eve till sunset on Monday-eve, let him make a "bot" of LXXX. shillings to his lord.

10. If an "esne" so do of his own accord on that day, let him make a "bot" of VI. to his lord, or his hide.

---

5. Wihtræd about the year 700 refers to gesithcund men who were military followers of the Saxon kings; some had lands, some had none; at the subsequent times the name went out of use, and thane was applied to them in common with other retainers of the kings.

11. But if a freeman [so do] at the forbidden time, let him be liable in his "heals-fang"; and the man who detects him, let him have half the "wite," and the work.

12. If a husband, without his wife's knowledge, make an offering to devils, let him be liable in all his substance and his "heals-fang." If both make offering to devils, let them be liable in their "heals-fang," and all their substance.

13. If a "theow" make an offering to devils, let him make a "bot" of VI. shillings, or his hide.

14. If a man during a fast give flesh-meat to his family, let him redeem, free or bond, with his "heals-fang."

15. If a "theow" eat of his own will, VI. shillings, or his hide.

16. Let the word of a bishop and of the king be, without an oath, incontrovertible.

17. Let the "aldor" of a "minster" clear himself with a priest's "canne."

18. Let a priest clear himself by his own sooth, in his holy garment before the altar, thus saying: "Veritatem dico in Christo, non mentior." In like manner, let a deacon clear himself.

19. Let a clerk clear himself with four of his fellows, and he alone with his hand on the altar, let the others stand by, make the oath.

20. Let a stranger [clear himself] with his own oath at the altar: in like manner, a king's thane.

21. Let a "ceorlish" man clear himself with four of his fellows at the altar; and let the oath of all

---

11. *Heals-fang,* composition in money, for punishment by pillory.

these be incontrovertible: then is the Church "canne"
right.

22. If any one make plaint against a bishop's "esne"
or the king's, let him clear himself by the person of the
reeve; either let the reeve clear him, or give him up
to be scourged.

23. If any one make plaint against a priest's "esne"
in their congregation, let his lord clear him with his
sole oath, if he be a communicant; if he be not a
communicant, let him have with him in the oath another good "æwda"; or let him pay, or give him up
to be scourged.

24. If a layman's "esne" make plaint against a
churchman's "esne," or a churchman's "esne" make
plaint against a layman's "esne"; let his lord clear
him with his sole oath.

25. If any one slay a layman while thieving; let
him lie without "wer-geld."

26. If a man seize a freeman with stolen goods upon
him, then let the king have power of one of three
things: either that he be slain, or sold beyond sea, or
redeemed with his "wer-geld." Whoever shall seize
and secure him, let him have half of him; if any one
slay him, let him be paid LXX. shillings.

27. If a "theow" steal, and he be redeemed, LXX.
shillings as the king may choose; if any one slay him,
let half his value be paid to the owner.

28. If a man come from afar, or a stranger, go out
of the [high] way, and he then neither shout nor blow
a horn; he is to be accounted a thief, either to be
slain, or to be redeemed.

OF THE DOOMS OF INE.

I, Ine, by God's grace, king of the West-Saxons, with the counsel and with the teaching of Cenred my father, and of Hedde my bishop, and of Eorcenwold my bishop, with all my "ealdormen," and the most distinguished " witan " * of my people, and also with a large assembly of God's servants, have been considering of the health of our souls, and of the stability of our realm; so that just law and just kingly dooms might be settled and established throughout our folk; so that none of the "ealdormen," nor of our subjects, should hereafter pervert these our dooms.

OF THE RULE OF GOD'S SERVANTS.

1. First, we command that God's servants rightly hold their lawful rule. After that, we command that the law and dooms of the whole folk be thus held.

---

* This sort of Parliament appears to have been assembled on the summons of the king seemingly by. the advice of the bishops and the secular nobility, as the result of a conviction that the arbitrary will of the sovereign was not sufficient to give force and effect to a body of laws without the concurrence and support of the representative men of the kingdom. And this in that rude age indicated political necessities in giving a liberal government to the state. No matter how this *witan* or council were chosen, they had their constituencies in those they were expected to influence in giving strength and permanence to law and a beneficial government.

1. The first principle asserted in these laws, was, that God's servants rightly hold their lawful rule. After that, that the law and judgments of the whole people be thus held. In other words that the law should be in permanence.

OF CHILDREN.

2. Let a child, within thirty days, be baptized. If it be not so, let him make "bot" with xxx. shillings. But if it die without baptism, let him make "bot" for it with all that he has.

OF SUNDAY WORKINGS.

3. If a "theowman" work on Sunday by his lord's command, let him be free; and let the lord pay xxx. shillings as "wite." But if the "theow" work without his knowledge, let him suffer in his hide, or in "hide-gild." But if a freeman work on that day without his lord's command, let him forfeit his freedom, or sixty shillings: and be a priest doubly liable. ·

OF CHURCH–SCOTS.

4. Let church-scots be rendered at Martinmas. If any one do not perform that, let him forfeit LX. shillings, and render the church-scot twelvefold.

OF CHURCH–"SOCNS."

5. If any one be guilty of death, and he flee to a church, let him have his life, and make "bot" as the law may direct him. If any one put his hide in peril, and flee to a church, be the scourging forgiven him.

OF FIGHTING.

6. If any one fight in the king's house, let him be liable in all his property, and be it in the king's doom whether he shall or shall not have life. If any one

---

4. *Church-scot*, a certain measure of grain given to the church for its support. *Scot-free*, free from taxes.

5. This mode of escaping punishment being abused and compensations paid corrupting to the clergy, in subsequent ages penalties for crimes were enacted to be without benefit of clergy.

fight in a minster, let him make "bot" with one hundred and twenty shillings. If any one fight in an "ealdorman's" house, or in any other distinguished "wita's," let him make "bot" with LX. shillings, and pay a second LX. shillings as "wite." But if he fight in a "gafol-gelda's" house, or in a "gebur's," let him pay CXX. shillings as "wite," and to the "gebur" VI. shillings. And though it be fought on mid-field, let one hundred and twenty shillings be given as "wite." But if they have altercation at a feast, and one of them bear it with patience, let the other give XXX. shillings as "wite."

OF STEALING.

7. If any one steal, so that his wife and his children know it not, let him pay LX. shillings as "wite." But if he steal with the knowledge of all his household, let them all go into slavery. A boy of X. years may be privy to a theft.

OF PRAYING FOR JUSTICE.

8. If any one demand justice before a "scir-man" or other judge, and cannot obtain it, and a man [the defendant] will not give him "wed"; let him make "bot" with XXX. shillings, and within VII. days do him justice.

OF HIM WHO TAKES REVENGE BEFORE HE DEMANDS JUSTICE.

9. If any one take revenge before he demand jus-

---

8. The demand of justice, before a *scir-man* (an inferior judge or magistrate). Justice through the courts, instead of taking the law into one's own hands, was thus made the duty of the citizen, at that early day as well as in later times. Thus a conservative principle of civil government was recognized and established. *Wed*, pledge, security.

tice; let him give up what he has taken to himself, and pay [the damage done], and make " bot " with xxx. shillings.

OF " REAF–LAC."

10. If any one within the limits of our realm commit " reaf-lac " and " nyd-næme "; let him give up the " reaf-lac," and pay LX. shillings as " wite."

OF THOSE MEN WHO SELL THEIR COUNTRYMEN.

11. If any one sell his own countryman, bond or free, though he be guilty, over sea, let him pay for him according to his " wer."

OF THIEVES SEIZED.

12. If a thief be seized, let him perish by death, or let his life be redeemed according to his " wer."

OF THOSE WHO BELIE THEIR TESTIMONIES BEFORE A BISHOP.

13. If any one before a bishop belie his testimony and his " wed," let him make " bot" with CXX. shillings.

Thieves we call as far as VII. men; from VII. to XXXV. a " hloth "; after that it is a " here."

OF " HLOTH."

14. He who is accused of " hloth," let him clear himself with CXX. hides; or make " bot " accordingly.

OF " HERGE."

15. He who is accused of " hereteam," let him redeem himself with his " wer-gild," or clear himself

---

10. *Reaf-lac, nyd-næme,* robbery, spoliation; disseisin of land.

12. *Theft* was punished by death, unless the life of the culprit should be redeemed, according to his *wer* or legal value, by his rank.

15. *Hereteam,* assembling a mob or band of armed men.

according to his "wer." The oath shall be half of communicants. A thief, after he is in the king's custody, shall not have the clearance.

OF THIEF–SLAYING.

16. He who slays a thief must declare on oath that he slew him offending; not his gild-brethren.

OF STOLEN FLESH.

17. He who finds stolen flesh and keeps it secret, if he can, he may prove on oath that he owns it. He who traces it out, he shall have the information money.

OF A "CEORLISH" THIEF SEIZED.

18. A "ceorlish" man, if he have often been accused, if he at last be seized, let his hand or foot be cut off.

OF A KING'S "GENEAT."

19. A king's "geneat," if his "wer" be twelve hundred shillings, he may swear for sixty hides, if he be a communicant.

---

17. It seems that informers in matters of crime were recognized as favored in the law, as in modern times.

18. If a servant or man in servitude be often accused of thefts and at last be caught, let his hand or foot be cut off. (Barbarity of slavery.) The enslavement of men, and their control when so enslaved, involves the necessity for such barbarous laws. He has no property, no services, no wife and no children he can call his own out of which to answer for crime. Hence the mutilation and scourging for the slave, while the master could buy his peace with money. And the spirit and necessities of slavery are the same whether its victims be black or white, our kindred or strangers. This is the oldest instance in these laws in which mutilation of the body is enacted as a legal punishment. Other instances subsequently appear, indicating an element of barbarism in the constitution of the laws.

OF A MAN COMING FROM AFAR FOUND OUT OF THE HIGHWAY.

20. If a far-coming man, or a stranger, journey through a wood out of the highway, and neither shout nor blow his horn, he is to be held for a thief, either to be slain or redeemed.

OF A MAN'S "WER" THUS SLAIN.

21. If a man demand the "wer" of the slain, he must declare that he slew him for a thief; not the associates of the slain, nor his lord: but if he conceal it, and after a time it become known, then makes he room for an oath on behalf of the dead man, that his kindred may exculpate him.

IN CASE A MAN'S "GENEAT" STEAL.

22. If thy "geneat" steal, and run away from thee, if thou have a "byrgea," admonish him of the "angylde": if he have it not, pay thou the "angylde," and be it to him, therefore, not the more settled.

OF SLAYING A FOREIGNER.

23. If a foreigner be slain, the king has two parts of the "wer," a third part his son or kinsmen. But if he be kinless, half the king, half the "gesith." If,

---

19. A king's *geneat*, a person holding lands of the king not by nobility, but by base tenure, if his *wer* be 1200 shillings, he may swear for sixty hides, if he be a communicant. That is, his oath as a compurgator or æwda should count for that of sixty poor men; suggesting an idea that has grown up to be a part of public opinion in England to-day, that property is a conservative element in the state, that virtue rests with the nobility and men of property, that villains and vagabonds are synonymous.

22. *Geneat*, sub-tenant. *Byrgea*, same as bohr, security. *Angylde*, price of cattle.

however, it be an abbot or an abbess, let them divide
in the same wise with the king.

A " Wealh gafol-gelda," CXX. shillings ; his son,
C. ; a " theow," LX. ; some with fifty : a " Wealh's "
hide with twelve.

OF SLAYING A " WITE-THEOW."

24. If a " wite-theow," an Englishman, steal himself away, let him be hanged ; and nothing paid to his
lord. If any one slay him, let nothing be paid to his
kindred, if they have not redeemed him within twelve
months.

A " Wealh," if he have five hides, he shall be as a
six-" hynde " man.

OF THE JOURNEYING OF CHAPMEN UP THE COUNTRY.

25. If a chapman traffic up among the people, let
him do it before witnesses. If stolen property be attached with a chapman, and he have not bought it before good witnesses, let him prove, according to the
" wite," that he was neither privy [to the theft] nor
thief ; or pay as " wite " XXXVI. shillings.

OF FOSTERING A FOUNDLING.

26. Let VI. shillings be paid for the fostering of a
foundling for the first year : XII. shillings the second ;
XXX. shillings the third ; afterwards, according to its
appearance.

---

23. *Gesith* here seems to be the host by whom the foreigner was
entertained, or, if there was a traveling companion of the dead man,
the term might refer to him. *Gafol-gelda*, one paying rent. *Wealh*,
or a Welchman or any foreigner, but resident in the country.

26. Showing the value then put on money, or its purchasing
power.

IN CASE A MAN BEGET A CHILD CLANDESTINELY.

27. He who clandestinely begets a child, and conceals it, shall not have the "wer" for its death; but his lord and the king.

OF SEIZING A THIEF IN A THEFT.

28. He who seizes a thief shall have **x.** shillings, and the king the thief; and let the kindred swear to him oaths of "unfæhthe." But if he run away, and become "orige," then shall he be liable in the "wite." If he will deny it, let him do so according to the property, and according to the "wite."

IN CASE A MAN LEND A SWORD TO ANOTHER'S "THEOW."

29. If a man lend a sword to another's "esne," and he run away, let him pay a third part of his value. If a man give a spear, half: if he lend a horse, let him pay his whole value.

IN CASE A "CEORLISH" MAN HARBOR A FUGITIVE.

30. If a man accuse a "ceorlish" man of harboring a fugitive, let him clear himself according to his own "wer." If he cannot, let him pay for him according to his own "wer": and the "gesithman" in like manner according to his "wer."

IN CASE A MAN BUY A WIFE, AND THEN THE MARRIAGE TAKE NOT PLACE.

31. If a man buy a wife, and the marriage take not place; let him give the money, and compensate and

---

27. The *wer* or damage for the death of an illegitimate child should be paid not to the father, but to the lord and the king. (How about the mother?)

make "bot" to his "byrgea," as his "borg-bryce" may be.

OF A "WILISC"-MAN'S LANDED ESTATE.

32. If a "Wylisc"-man have a hide of land, his "wer" shall be CXX. shillings; but if he have half a hide, LXXX. shillings; if he have none, LX. shillings.

OF THE KING'S "HORSE-WEALH."

33. The king's "horse-wealh," who can do his errands, his "wer-gild" shall be CC. shillings.

OF MAN-SLAYING.

34. He who has been in a foray where a man has been slain, let him prove himself innocent of the slaying, and make "bot" for the foray, according to the "wer-gild" of the slain. If his "wer-gild" be CC. shillings, let him make "bot" with L. shillings; and let the like justice be done with respect to the dearerborn.

OF SLAYING A THIEF; THAT HE MUST PROVE ON OATH.

35. He who slays a thief must prove on oath that he slew him fleeing for a thief; and the kinsmen of the dead swear to him an "unceas"-oath. But if he conceal it, and it afterwards become known, let him pay for him.

If any one vouch a man to the warranty of goods who had before denied it on oath, and again is willing to deny it on oath; let him deny it on oath, according to the "wite" and the worth of the goods. If he will

---

34. This is in reverse of the common law rule that one is to be presumed innocent till proved guilty.

not deny it on oath, let him make "bot" for the false oath twofold.

OF TAKING A THIEF, AND THEN LETTING HIM GO.

36. Let him who takes a thief, or to whom one taken is given, and he then lets him go, or conceals the theft, pay for the thief according to his "wer." If he be an "ealdorman," let him forfeit his shire, unless the king is willing to be merciful to him.

OF ACCUSING A "CEORLISH" MAN OF THEFT.

37. The "ceorlish" man who has been oft accused of theft, and then at last is taken offending, whether in the fact or otherwise in open guilt, let his hand or foot be cut off.

IN CASE LAWFULLY MARRIED PERSONS HAVE A CHILD, AND THEN THE HUSBAND DIE.

38. If a "ceorl" and his wife have a child between them, and the "ceorl" die, let the mother have her child and feed it: let VI. shillings be given her for its fostering; a cow in summer, an ox in winter. Let the kindred take care of the "frum-stol" until it be of age.

OF GOING FROM HIS LORD WITHOUT LEAVE.

39. If any one go from his lord without leave, or steal himself away into another shire, and he be discovered, let him go where he was before, and pay to his lord LX. shillings.

---

36. To avoid duplicate claims for detecting thieves it was enacted that the allowing the escape of a thief, if arrested by one or committed to his care, or his concealment, was punished by imposing a fine on one thus careless or corrupt, equal to the legal value of the thief. If an earl did this let him forfeit his shire, unless the king is willing to be merciful to him.

OF A "CEORL'S" CLOSE.

40. A "ceorl's" close ought to be fenced winter and summer. If it be unfenced, and his neighbor's cattle stray in through his own gap, he shall have nothing from the cattle: let him drive it out, and bear the damage.

OF DENIAL OF "BORH."

41. A man may make denial of "borh," if he know that he does right.

OF A "CEORL'S" MEADOW.

42. If "ceorls" have a common meadow, or other partible land to fence, and some have fenced their part, some have not, and eat up their common corn or grass; let those go who own the gap, and compensate to the others, who have fenced their part, the damage which there may be done, and let them demand such justice on the cattle as it may be right. But if there be a beast which breaks hedges and goes in everywhere, and he who owns it will not or cannot restrain it; let him who finds it in his field take it and slay it, and let the owner take its skin and flesh, and forfeit the rest.

OF WOOD–BURNING.

43. When any one burns a tree in a wood, and it be found out against him who did it, let him pay the full "wite"; let him give LX. shillings, because fire is a thief. If any one fell in a wood a good many trees, and it be afterwards discovered; let him pay for III.

---

40. A ceorl seems to mean here a tenant of the soil or serf, or a vassal of sufficient standing or capacity to be entrusted with the care and culture of the soil. A rural herder of cattle.

trees, each with XXX. shillings. He need not pay for more of them, were there as many of them as might be ; because the axe is an informer, not a thief.

OF TAKING WOOD WITHOUT LEAVE.

44. But if any one cut down a tree under which XXX. swine may stand, and it be discovered, let him pay LX. shillings.

A " gafol-hwitel " from a " hiwisc " shall be worth VI. pence.

OF " BURG–BRYCE."

45. " Bot" shall be made for the king's " burg-bryce," and a bishop's, where his jurisdiction is, with CXX. shillings ; for an ealdorman's, with LXXX. shillings ; for a king's thane's, with LX. shillings ; for a " gesithcund " man's having land, with XXXV. shillings : and according to this make the legal denial.

OF THEFT–CHARGE.

46. When a man charges another that he steals, or harbors stolen cattle, then shall he deny the theft with LX. hides, if he be oath-worthy. If, however, an English " onstal " come forward, let him then deny it with twice as many. But if it be a " Wilisc " " onstal," the oath shall not be the greater.

Every man may deny " frymth " and " wer-fæhthe," if he can or dare.

---

45. *Burg-bryce* was an offense somewhat like burglary, meaning the breaking of a castle. Such an offense against the king's castle incurred the penalty of 120 shillings. The same as to a bishop's palace. As to an ealdorman, 70 shillings ; another landholder, 35 shillings.

46. It seems doubtful if the sixty hides means one person owning sixty hides of land, or sixty persons owning one hide each were the necessary compurgators.

IN CASE A MAN ATTACH STOLEN CATTLE.

47. If a man attach stolen cattle, the party may not vouch a " theowman " to the warranty of it.

OF " WITE-THEOWMEN."

48. If any man be a ." wite-theow " newly made a "theow," and he be accused that he had before thieved, ere he was made a " theow," then may the accuser have one scourging at him : let him follow him to the scourging according to his value.

OF TAKING UNALLOWED MAST.

49. If a man among his mast find unallowed swine, then let him take a " wed " of VI. shillings value. If, however, they have not been there oftener than once, let the owner pay a shilling, and let him prove that they came there not oftener, according to the value of the beasts. If they have been there twice, let him pay two shillings.

If pannage be taken for swine, of those three fingers thick in fat, the third ; of those two fingers, the fourth ; of those a thumb thick, the fifth.

OF A " GESITHCUND " MAN'S COMPOUNDING A SUIT.

50. If a " gesithcund " man compound a suit with the king or with the king's " ealdorman " for his household, or with his lord for bond or for free ; he, the " gesith," shall not there have any " witeræden,"

---

47. If a man attach stolen cattle, a party may not vouch a bond servant to the warranty of title.

48. This punishment seems to have been without any trial or judicial inquiry as to the facts, illustrating the natural and necessary brutality of slavery.

because he would not correct him before of his evil deeds at home.

IN CASE A "GESITHCUND" MAN NEGLECTS THE "FYRD."

51. If a "gesithcund" man, owning land, neglect the "fyrd," let him pay CXX. shillings and forfeit his land; one not owning land, LX. shillings; a "ceorlish" man, XXX. shillings; as "fyrd-wite."

OF PRIVATE COMPOSITION.

52. Let him who is accused of secret compositions clear himself of those compositions with CXX. hides, or pay CXX. shillings.

OF SEIZING A STOLEN MAN.

53. If any one attach a stolen man in another's possession, and the hand be dead which sold him to the man in whose possession he is attached; then let him vouch the tomb of the dead to warranty of the man, in like manner with other property whatsoever it may be; and with the oath of LX. hides let him declare that the dead hand sold him to him. Then has he abated the "wite" with that oath: and let him give up the man to the owner. But if he know who has the property of the dead, let him then vouch the

---

50. *Gesithcund* men were military aids or followers, afterwards known as *thagnes* or *comptes*.

52. This is still a misdemeanor punishable as for the compounding a felony; both on the score of public policy, or on the assumption that a party accepting private compensation for an offense against him becomes in a manner privy to the crime; at least interested in concealing it. But the reason given for such a law at that time was that the income of the court and the crown was affected disadvantageously by such compositions.

property to warranty, and demand of the hand which has that property, that he make the chattel uncontestable to him; or prove that the dead man never owned that property.

OF CHARGE OF "WER-FÆHTHE."

54. He who is charged with "wer-fæhthe," and he is willing to deny the slaying on oath; then shall there be in the "hynden" one king's oath of XXX. hides, as well for a "gesithcund" man as for a "ceorlish" man, whichsoever it may be. If he be found guilty, then may he give to any one of the "hyndens," a man and a coat of mail and a sword, in the "wer-gild," if he need.

A "Wylisc wite-theowman" shall be followed up with twelve hides, like a "theow," to the scourging; an English, with four and thirty hides.

OF A EWE'S WORTH.

55. A ewe with her young sheep shall be worth a shilling, until XIV. days after Easter.

OF THE "ANGYLDE" OF ALL KINDS OF CATTLE.

56. If a man buy any kind of cattle, and he then discover any unsoundness in· it within XXX. days; then let him throw the cattle on his hands, or let him swear that he knew not of any unsoundness in it when he sold it to him.

OF A "CEORLISH" MAN'S STEALING.

57. If a "ceorl" steal a chattel, and bear it into his dwelling, and it be attached therein; then shall he be guilty for his part, without his wife, for she must obey her lord. If she dare to declare by oath

that she tasted not of the stolen property, let her take her third part.

OF AN OXES HORN.

58. An oxes horn shall be worth x. pence.

OF A COW'S HORN.

59. A cow's horn shall be worth two pence; an oxes tail shall be worth a shilling; a cow's shall be five pence; an oxes eye shall be worth five pence; a cow's shall be worth a shilling.

There shall always be given as barley-rent from one " wyrhta " six pounds.

OF A HIRED YOKE.

60. The " ceorl " who has hired another's yoke, if he have to pay wholly in fodder, let that be looked to, let him give it wholly. If he have not, let him pay half in fodder, and half in other goods.

OF CHURCH—SCOT.

61. Church-scot shall be rendered according to the " healm " and to the hearth that the man is at at mid-winter.

IN CASE A MAN COMPEL [ANOTHER] TO GIVE PLEDGE.

62. When a man is charged with an offense, and is compelled to give pledge, but has not himself aught

---

57. " If she dare to declare by oath that she tasted not of the stolen property let her take her third part," obviously as a reward for her integrity.

60. *Ceorl,* generally meaning slave, seems here to imply a serf or tenant of the soil, vested with some responsibility in working a farm.

61. Thatch roof of a cottage and hearth are here made the basis of church taxation.

to give for pledge; then goes another man, [and] gives his pledge for [him], as he may be able to arrange, on the condition that he give himself into his hands, until he can make good to him his pledge. Then again, a second time, he is accused and compelled to give pledge; if he will not continue to stand for him who before gave pledge for him, and he [the last accuser] then imprison him; let him then forfeit his pledge, who had before given it for him.

OF A "GESITHCUND" MAN'S GOING AWAY.

63. If a "gesithcund" man go away, then may he have his reeve with him, and his "smith," and his child's fosterer.

OF HIM WHO HAS XX. HIDES OF LAND.

64. He who has xx. hides, shall show xii. hides of cultivated land, when he wishes to go away.

OF X. HIDES.

65. He who has x. hides, shall show vi. hides of cultivated land.

OF III. HIDES.

66. He who has three hides, let him show one and a half.

OF A YARD OF LAND.

67. If a man agree for a yard of land, or more, at a fixed rent, and plough it; if the lord desire to raise the land to him to service and to rent, he need not take it upon him, if the lord do not give him a dwelling: and let him lose the crop.

---

67. If the lord make a demand of increased advantage to himself—that is, of service in addition to the rent previously agreed upon—he may do so, provided at the same time he give an equivalent, to wit,

OF DRIVING A "GESITHCUND" MAN OFF THE LAND.

68. If a "gesithcund" man be driven off, let him be driven from the dwelling, not from the stock.

OF A SHEEP'S GOING WITH ITS FLEECE.

69. A sheep shall go with its fleece until mid-summer, or let the fleece be paid for with two pence.

OF A "TWY–HYNDE'S WER."

70. With a "twy-hynde" man's "wer" shall be given, as "man-bot," XXX. shillings; with a six-"hynde's," LXXX. shillings; with a twelve-"hynde's," CXX. shillings.

With X. hides, as "foster," X. vessels of honey, CCC. loaves, XII. "ambers" of "Wilisc" ale, XXX. of clear; two full-yeared oxen or X. wethers, X. geese, XX. hens, X. cheeses, an "amber" full of butter, V. salmons, XX. pounds of fodder, and a hundred eels.

OF "WER–TYHTLE."

71. If a man be accused of "wer-tyhtle," and he then confess it before the oath, and had previously denied it; let the "wite-ræden" abide until the "wer" be paid.

OF THE CAPTION OF A "WER–GILD" THIEF.

72. If a man seize a "wer-gild" thief, and he escape that day from the men who seize him; though he be seized again by night, they shall have no more from him than full "wite."

---

a botl; for to this, as a tenement, service shall be incident. If he do not give the botl, and still choose to determine the tenure by enhancing the terms, let him lose the crop; that is to say, his proportion of it. It is still a principle of our law, that if the landlord of a tenant at will determine the tenancy by ejecting the tenant, the latter shall have the crop without paying any rent.

OF A DAY–OLD THEFT.

73. If it be a theft of a day old, let those make "bot" for the offense who seized him, as they can agree with the king and his reeve.

IN CASE A "THEOW–WEALH" SLAY A FREEMAN.

74. If a "theow-wealh" slay an Englishman, then shall he who owns him deliver him up to the lord and the kindred, or give LX. shillings for his life. But if he will not give that sum for him, then must the lord enfranchise him; afterwards let his kindred pay the "wer," if he have a free "mæg-burh": if he have not, let his foes take heed to him. The free need not pay "mæg-bot" with the "theow," unless he be desirous to buy off from himself the "fæhthe"; nor the "theow" with the free.

OF THE ATTACHMENT OF STOLEN PROPERTY.

75. If a man attach stolen property, and the person with whom it is attached then vouch another man to warranty; if then the man will not accept it, and says that he never sold him that, but sold him other; then must he prove who vouches it to that person, that he sold to him none other, but that same.

IN CASE A MAN SLAY ANOTHER'S GODSON OR HIS GODFATHER.

76. If any one slay another's godson or his god-father, let the "mæg-bot" and the "man-bot" be alike. Let the "bot" increase according to the

---

74. The reason of this case was : That the free were not bound for the offenses of a slave. And this law seemed to look more for the fine, than the punishment of the slave-criminal.

" wer," in like manner as the "man-bot" does, which
is due to the lord.   But if it be a king's godson, let
him make "bot" to the king according to his "wer,"
in like manner as to the kindred.   If, however, he
strive against him who slew him, then let the "bot"
to the godfather decrease in like manner as the
"wite" to the lord does.   If it be a bishop's son, let
it be half of this.

---

76. " If it be a bishop's son, let it be half of this."   This exception,
while it was unequal and unjust, shows the influence of the clergy on
the character of these laws.

INTRODUCTION TO ALFRED'S LAWS.

Three hundred and seventy-eight years after the first landing of Hengist, the Saxon leader in England, the country, or most of it, became united under one government with Egbert for its king or bretwelda. In the year 800 of the Christian era, Egbert commenced his reign over the West Saxons, but his kingdom was enlarged to embrace other parts of England by 828. After ten years reign over England he died in 838, having evinced in his life distinguished military capacity, which seems to have been used with wisdom for the benefit of his country. Nor was he destitute of capacity as a politician and a statesman. Historians tell us that some portion of his early life was spent at the court of Charles the Great, or Charlemagne, in France, and his skill in government is attributed to the knowledge acquired in such a school. Next to Æthelbirht, the first Christian Kentish king, he seems to have been the best of the Saxon kings. His reign was not, however, without disturbance.

It was during this reign that the Danish pirates and brigands made their first appearance in England in force ; though, in 789, a small band had destroyed the town of Portland, and in 832 another band had laid waste the island of Pepey. In 833 they came with thirty-five vessels to Charmouth, and landed and laid the country waste. And more, they defeated Egbert in a pitched battle, and then gathered up their plunder and departed with their ships. Two years later the Danes returned, but were now defeated by Egbert with a signal victory.

At Egbert's death, his son, Ethelwulph, succeeded him on the throne, who first divided his power between himself and his natural son, Athelstan, whom he made king of Kent. Between these was perfect accord; they fought together, and won a great victory over the Danes, who continued their raids upon the country. Shortly after Athelstan died, and his kingdom reverted again to his father. Ethelbald, his legitimate son, insisted on being put in the place of Athelstan. But Ethelwulph, knowing his son's disposition and character, declined this request. It is not said that he considered the bad policy of such a measure, or that it was cited as a reason. But shortly after, the turbulent son, through the intrigues of one of the bishops, took advantage of Ethelwulph's absence on a religious journey to Rome, and sought to prevent his return to England, which, the king learning, he hastened home before the son's plans were matured. But such a turbulence was raised as threatened civil war, and, for the sake of peace, Ethelwulph yielded a part of his dominions to his unnatural son, saying he would, as heir to the throne, presently attain to them, at his death. But during the two subsequent years of his life the king was noted for his acts of charity, while the son gave himself to vice and debauchery, and ended his days two years after the death of his father.

Ethelwulph settled the succession, by his will, first

to his son Ethelbert, then to his son Ethelred, and then to his youngest son, Alfred; who in this order succeeded to the throne. Though Ethelbert left sons, they were excluded from the succession by his father's will.

Ethelbert reunited the kingdom, at the death of his brother Ethelbald in 860, and lived six years, when he left the throne to Ethelred. The reign of Ethelred was in the midst of turbulence and strife from the incursions of the Danes, who overran considerable portions of the kingdom. This troubled reign ended, in six years, in 872, when Alfred succeeded to the throne under the will of Ethelwulph, his father, to the exclusion of the sons of the two brothers who preceded him. Alfred at this time was twenty-two years of age.

Alfred found the kingdom in a deplorable condition. The Danes were established in some of the old Saxon counties, and had a ready will to plunder anywhere, where they were not opposed. In his first battle at Wilton, he was beaten, and was forced to make peace and stipulate not to interfere in their ravages of other portions of the country, not then under his immediate control.

THE LAWS OF KING ALFRED.

The Lord spake these words to Moses, and thus said: I am the Lord thy God. I led thee out of the land of the Egyptians, and of their bondage.

1. Love thou not other strange gods above me.

2. Utter thou not my name idly, for thou shalt not be guiltless towards me if thou utter my name idly.

3. Remember that thou hallow the rest-day. Work for yourselves six days, and on the seventh rest. For in six days Christ wrought the heavens and the earth, the seas, and all creatures that are in them, and rested on the seventh day: and therefore the Lord hallowed it.

4. Honor thy father and thy mother whom the Lord hath given thee, that thou mayst be the longer living on earth.

5. Slay thou not.

6. Commit thou not adultery.

7. Steal thou not.

8. Say thou not false witness.

9. Covet thou not thy neighbor's goods unjustly.

10. Make thou not to thyself golden or silver gods.

11. These are the dooms which thou shalt set for them. If any one buy a Christian "theow," let him serve VI. years; the seventh he shall be free without purchase. With such raiment as he went in, with such go he out. If he have a wife of his own, go she

out with him. If, however, the lord have given him
a wife, be she and her child the lord's. But if the
" theow" should say : " I will not from my lord, nor
from my wife, nor from my child, nor from my goods ; "
let his lord then bring him to the door of the Temple,
and bore his ear through with an awl, in token that he
ever after shall be a " theow."

12. Though any one sell his daughter to servitude,
let her not be altogether such a " theowu " as other
female slaves are. He ought not to sell her away
among a strange folk. But if he who bought her reck
not of her ; let her go free among a strange folk. If,
however, he allow his son to cohabit with her, let him
marry her: and let him see that she have raiment, and
that which is the worth of her maid-hood, that is, the
dowry ; let him give her that. If he do unto her none
of these things, then let her be free.

13. Let the man who slayeth another willfully perish
by death. Let him who slayeth another of necessity
or unwillingly or unwillfully, as God may have sent
him into his hands, and for whom he has not lain in
wait, be worthy of his life, and of lawful "bot," if he
seek an asylum. If, however, any one presumptuously
and willfully slay his neighbor through guile, pluck
thou him from my altar, to the end that he may perish by death.

14. He who smiteth his father or his mother, he
shall perish by death.

15. He who stealeth a freeman, and selleth him, and
it be proved against him so that he cannot clear himself ; let him perish by death. He who curseth his
father or his mother, let him perish by death.

16. If any one smite his neighbor with a stone or

with his fist, and he nevertheless can go out with a staff; let him get him a leech, and work his work the while that himself may not.

17. He who smiteth his own "theow-esne" or his female slave, and he die not on the same day; though he live [but] two or three nights, he is not altogether so guilty, because it was his own property; but if he die the same day, then let the guilt rest on him.

18. If any one, in strife, hurt a breeding woman, let him make "bot" for the hurt, as the judges shall pre-scribe to him. If she die, let him give soul for soul.

19. If any one thrust out another's eye, let him give his own for it; tooth for tooth, hand for hand, foot for foot, burning for burning, wound for wound, stripe for stripe.

20. If any one smite out the eye of his "theow" or of his "theowen," and he then make them one-eyed; let him free them on this account. And if he smite out a tooth, let him do the like.

21. If an ox gore a man or a woman, so that they die, let it be stoned, and let not its flesh be eaten. The lord shall not be liable, if the ox were wont to push with its horns for two or three days before, and the lord knew it not; but if he knew it, and he would not shut it in, and it then shall have slain a man or a woman, let it be stoned; and let the lord be slain, or the man be paid for, as the "witan" decree to be right. If it gore a son or a daughter, let him be sub-ject to the like judgment. But if it gore a "theow" or a "theow-mennen," let xxx. shillings of silver be given to the lord, and let the ox be stoned.

22. If any one dig a water-pit, or open one that is shut up, and close it not again; let him pay for what-

ever cattle may fall therein; and let him have the dead [beast].

23. If an ox wound another man's ox, and it then die, let them sell the [live] ox, and have the worth in common, and also the flesh of the dead one. But if the lord knew that the ox hath used to push, and he would not confine it, let him give him another ox for it, and have all the flesh for himself.

24. If any one steal another's ox, and slay or sell it, let him give two for it; and four sheep for one. If he have not what he may give, be he himself sold for the cattle.

25. If a thief break into a man's house by night, and he be there slain; the slayer shall not be guilty of manslaughter. But if he do this after sunrise, he shall be guilty of manslaughter; and then he himself shall die, unless he were an unwilling agent. If with him living that be found which he had before stolen, let him pay for it twofold.

26. If any one injure another man's vineyard, or his fields, or aught of his lands; let him make "bot" as it may be valued.

27. If fire be kindled to burn "ryht," let him who kindled the fire make "bot" for the mischief.

28. If any one entrust property to his friend, if he steal it himself, let him pay for it twofold. If he know not who hath stolen it, let him clear himself that he hath therein committed no fraud. If, however, it were live cattle, and he say, that the "here" hath taken it, or that it perished of itself, and he have witness; he needeth not to pay for it. But if he have no witness, and he believe him not, then let him swear.

29. If any one deceive an unbetrothed woman, and

sleep with her; let him pay for her, and have her afterwards to wife. But if the father of the woman will not
give her, let him render money according to her dowry.

30. The women who are wont to receive enchanters,
and workers of phantasms, and witches, suffer thou not
to live.

31. And let him who lieth with cattle perish by
death.

32. And let him who sacrificeth to gods, save unto
God alone, perish by death.

33. Vex thou not comers from afar, and strangers;
for ye were formerly strangers in the land of the
Egyptians.

34. Injure ye not the widows and the step-children,
nor hurt them anywhere: for if ye do otherwise, they
will cry unto me, and I will hear them, and I will then
slay you with my sword; and I will do so that your
wives shall be widows, and your children shall be
step-children.

35. If thou give money in loan to thy fellow who
willeth to dwell with thee, urge thou him not as a
"niedling," and oppress him not with the increase.

36. If a man have only a single garment wherewith
to cover himself, or to wear, and he give it [to thee]
in pledge; let it be returned before sunset. If thou
dost not so, then shall he call unto me, and I will hear
him; for I am very merciful.

37. Revile thou not thy Lord God: nor curse thou
the Lord of the people.

38. Thy tithes, and thy first-fruits of moving and
growing things, render thou to God.

39. All the flesh that wild beasts leave, eat ye not
that, but give it to the dogs.

40. To the word of a lying man reck thou not to hearken, nor allow thou of his judgments; nor say thou any witness after him.

41. Turn thou not thyself to the foolish counsel and unjust desire of the people, in their speech and cry, against thine own reason, and according to the teaching of the most unwise; neither allow thou of them.

42. If the stray cattle of another man come to thy hand, though it be thy foe, make it known to him.

43. Judge thou very evenly: judge thou not one doom to the rich, another to the poor; nor one to thy friend, another to thy foe, judge thou.

44. Shun thou ever leasings.

45. A just and innocent man, him slay thou never.

46. Receive thou never meed-monies; for they blind full oft the minds of wise men, and pervert their words.

47. To the stranger and comer from afar behave thou not unkindly, nor oppress thou him with any wrongs.

48. Swear ye never by heathen gods, nor cry ye unto them for any cause.

49. These are the dooms which the Almighty God himself spake unto Moses, and commanded him to keep: and after the only begotten son of the Lord, our God, that is, our Saviour Christ, came on earth, he said that he came not to break nor to forbid these commandments, but with all good to increase them: and mercy and humility he taught. Then after his Passion, before his Apostles were dispersed throughout all the earth, teaching, and while they were yet together, many heathen nations they turned to God. When they were all assembled, they sent messengers

to Antioch and to Syria, to teach the law of Christ.
But when they understood that it speeded them not,
then sent they a letter unto them.   Now this is the letter which all the Apostles sent to Antioch, and to Syria,
and to Cilicia, which now from heathen nations are
turned to Christ.

" The Apostles and the elder brethren wish you
health: and we make known unto you, that we have
heard that some of our fellows have come to you with
our words, and have commanded you to observe a
heavier rule than we commanded them, and have too
much misled you with manifold commands, and have
subverted more of your souls than they have directed.
Then we assembled ourselves concerning that; and it
then seemed good to us all that we should send Paul
and Barnabas, men who desire to give their souls for
the name of the Lord.   With them we have sent
Judas and Silas, that they might say the same to you.
It seemed to the Holy Ghost and to us, that we
should set no burthen upon you above that which it
was needful for you to bear: now that is, that ye for-
bear from worshiping idols, and from tasting blood or
things strangled, and from fornications: and that
which ye will that other men do not unto you, do ye
not that to other men."

From this one doom a man may remember that he
judge every one righteously; he need heed no other
doom-book.   Let him remember that he adjudge to
no man that which he would not that he should
adjudge to him, if he sought judgment against him.

After this, then happened it that many nations received the faith of Christ; then were many synods
assembled throughout all the earth, and also among

the English race, after they had received the faith of
Christ, of holy bishops, and also of other exalted
" witan." They then ordained, out of that mercy
which Christ had taught, that secular lords, with
their leave, might, without sin, take for almost every
misdeed, for the first offense, the money-" bot" which
they then ordained ; except in cases of treason against
a lord, to which they dared not assign any mercy, because God Almighty adjudged none to them who despised him, nor did Christ the Son of God adjudge
any to him who sold him to death: and he commanded that a lord should be loved as one's self.
They then in many synods ordained a " bot " for
many human misdeeds ; and in many synod-books
they wrote, at one place one doom, at another another.

I, then, Alfred, king, gathered these together, and
commanded many of those to be written which our
forefathers held, those which to me seemed good ; and
many of those which seemed to me not good I rejected them, by the counsel of my " witan," and in
other wise commanded them to be holden ; for I durst
not venture to set down in writing much of my own,
for it was unknown to me what of it would please
those who should come after us. But those things
which I met with, either of the days of Ine, my kinsman, or of Offa, king of the Mercians, or of Æthelbirht, who first among the English race received
baptism, those which seemed to me the rightest,
those I have here gathered together, and rejected the
others.

I, then, Alfred, king of the West-Saxons, shewed
these to all my " witan," and they then said that it
seemed good to them all to be holden.

OF OATHS AND OF "WEDS."

1. At the first we teach, that it is most needful that every man warily keep his oath and his "wed." If any one be constrained to either of these wrongfully, either to treason against his lord, or to any unlawful aid; then is it juster to belie than to fulfill. But if he pledge himself to that which it is lawful to fulfill, and in that belie himself, let him submissively deliver up his weapon and his goods to the keeping of his friends, and be in prison forty days in a king's "tun": let him there suffer whatever the bishop may prescribe to him; and let his kinsmen feed him, if he himself have no food. If he have no kinsmen, or have no food, let the king's reeve feed him. If he must be forced to this, and he otherwise will not, if they bind him, let him forfeit his weapons and his property. If he be slain, let him lie uncompensated. If he flee thereout before the time, and he be taken, let him be in prison forty days, as he should before have been. But if he escape, let him be held a fugitive, and be excommunicate of all Christ's churches. If, however, there be another man's " borh," let him make "bot" for the "borh-bryce," as the law may direct him, and the " wed-bryce," as his confessor may prescribe to him.

---

1. [So the church became not only a co-lawgiver but a hand of punishment in its execution.] If, however, there be another man's surety, let him make compensation for the broken security as the law may direct him and the broken pledge as his confessor may prescribe to him. [In this paragraph we have the framework of the civil administration under Alfred the Great. Provisions so open to abuse and corruption, and putting the power of increasing the punishment even to death in the hand of the clergy, find no precedent in prior enactments.] That every man warily keep his oath and his

OF CHURCH-"SOCNS."

2. If any one, for whatever crime, seek any of the "mynsterhams" to which the king's "feorm" is incident, or other "free-hired" which is worthy of reverence, let him have a space of three days to protect himself, unless he be willing to come to terms. If during this space, any one harm him by blow, or by bond, or wound him, let him make "bot" for each of these according to regular usage, as well with "wer" as with "wite": and to the brotherhood one hundred and twenty shillings, as "bot" for the church-"frith": and let him not have "forfongen" his own.

OF "BORH-BRYCE."

3. If any one break the king's "borh," let him make "bot" for the plaint, as the law shall direct him; and for the "borh-bryce" with v. pounds of "mærra" pence. For an archbishop's "borh-bryce," or his "mund-byrd," let him make "bot" with three pounds: for any other bishop's or an "earldorman's" "borh-bryce," or "mund-byrd," let him make "bot" with two pounds.

OF PLOTTING AGAINST A LORD.

4. If any one plot against the king's life, of himself, or by harboring of exiles, or of his men; let him be liable in his life and in all that he has. If he desire to prove himself true, let him do so according to the

---

wed (pledges). But if pledged to do wrong, to commit treason or other crimes; it is juster to belie his pledges than to fulfill them. [So is stated a principle that law and sound morals forbid the keeping of an unlawful oath binding one to the commission of crime.]

3. *Borh-bryce*, breaking the king's protection.

king's "wer-gild." So also we ordain for all degrees, whether "ceorl" or "eorl." He who plots against his lord's life, let him be liable in his life to him and in all that he has; or let him prove himself true according to his lord's "wer."

OF CHURCH-"FRITH."

5. We also ordain to every church which has been hallowed by a bishop, this "frith": if a "fah-man" flee to or reach one, that for seven days no one drag him out. But if any one do so, then let him be liable in the king's "mund-byrd" and the church-"frith"; more if he there commit more wrong, if, despite of hunger, he can live; unless he fight his way out. If the brethren have further need of their church, let them keep him in another house, and let not that have more doors than the church. Let the church-"ealdor" take care that during this term no one give him food. If he himself be willing to deliver up his weapons to his foes, let them keep him xxx. days, and let them give notice of him to his kinsmen. It is also church-"frith": if any man seek a church for any of those offenses, which had not been before revealed, and there confess himself in Gód's name, be it half forgiven. He who steals on Sunday, or at Yule, or at Easter, or on Holy Thursday, and on Rogation days; for each of these we will that the "bot" be twofold, as during Lent-fast.

---

4. The life and property of any innocent man might have been put in jeopardy under this statute. The commission of an act is one thing, but a charge of plotting to accomplish it might as well be made against the innocent as the guilty.

5. King's *mund-byrd*, protection. The price of such protection as penalty. *Church-frith*, privilege of granting protection. *Notice to*

OF STEALING IN A CHURCH.

6. If any one thieve aught in a church, let him pay the "angylde," and the "wite," such as shall belong to the "angylde"; and let the hand be struck off with which he did it. If he will redeem the hand, and that be allowed him, let him pay as may belong to his "wer."

IN CASE A MAN FIGHT IN THE KING'S HALL.

7. If any one fight in the king's hall, or draw his weapon, and he be taken; be it in the king's doom, either death, or life, as he may be willing to grant him. If he escape, and be taken again, let him pay for himself according to his "wer-gild," and make "bot" for the offense, as well "wer" as "wite," according as he may have wrought.

OF FORNICATION WITH A NUN.

8. If any one carry off a nun from a minster, without the king's or the bishop's leave, let him pay a hundred and twenty shillings, half to the king, half to the bishop and to the church-"hlaford" who owns the nun. If she live longer than he who carried her

---

kinsmen. Presumed that they might redeem him from the penalty of his crime. *Theft on fast days.* The reason of this seems to have been that during the public occasions property would be less vigilantly watched, and more exposed. But beyond this the government regarded religious sanctions of binding obligations on the conscience of the citizen, and the punishment to be inflicted was not only for theft, etc., but for the sacrilege in its commission on a sacred day.

6. And let *the hand be struck off* with which he did it. [A barbarism not creditable to the Christianity of the period.] If he will redeem the hand and that be allowed him, let him pay as may belong to his *wer* [value].

off, let her not have aught of his property. If she bear a child, let not that have of the property more than the mother. If any one slay her child, let him pay to the king the maternal kindred's share; to the paternal kindred let their share be given.

OF SLAYING A CHILD-BEARING WOMAN.

9. If a man kill a woman with her child, while the child is in her, let him pay for the woman her full "wer-gild," and pay for the child half a "wer-gild," according to the "wer" of the father's kin.

Let the "wite" be always LX. shillings, until the "angylde" rise to XXX. shillings. After the "angylde" has risen to that let the "wite" be CXX. shillings. Formerly there was [a distinct "wite"] for a gold-thief, and a mare-thief, and a bee-thief, and many "wites," greater than others; now are all alike, except for a man-thief, CXX. shillings.

---

8. *Church-hlaford,* church corporation. None of the damage for carrying off a nun was given to the nun, but half to the king and half to the bishop and church-hlaford. Here is a law that in some sense is obsolete in our civil administration, but in some of its incidents has survived to these later years. Illegitimate children are made to suffer for the sins of their parents within what is claimed to be the benevolent sentiments of Christianity. The authors of such a law might claim to be promoters of virtue by rendering most drear and desolate the path of the transgressor. But there was obviously ecclesiastical policy in this law. The superstitions in the church had enacted laws in restraint of marriage and in contravention of the laws of nature, and those laws could only be enforced by extraordinary penalties. Hence the law in question. It seems that between the parties so brought together the relation of husband and wife might have subsisted in all honor during the lives of the parties, and the offense punished was simply a rebellion against ecclesiastical orders.

9. [Abortionists would have lost instead of gaining fortunes in those days.] Rules of fines or damages were these: The wite-fine

OF THE ADULTERY OF A TWELVE-"HYNDE" MAN'S WIFE.

10. If a man lie with the wife of a twelve-"hynde" man, let him make "bot" to the husband with one hundred and twenty shillings. To a six-"hynde" ·man, let him make "bot" with one hundred shillings. To a "ceorlish" man, let him make "bot" with forty shillings.

OF SEIZING HOLD OF A "CEORLISH" WOMAN.

11. If a man seize hold of the breast of a "ceorlish" woman, let him make "bot" to her with v. shillings. If he throw her down and do not lie with her, let him make "bot" with x. shillings. If he lie with her, let him make "bot" with LX. shillings. If another man had before lain with her, then let the "bot" be half that. If she be charged [therewith], let her clear herself with sixty hides, or forfeit half the "bot." If this befall a woman more nobly born, let the "bot" increase according to the "wer."

OF THE BURNING OF WOODS.

12. If a man burn or hew another's wood without leave, let him pay for every great tree with v. shillings, and afterwards for each, let there be as many of them as may be, with v. pence; and XXX. shillings as "wite."

---

to the king was sixty shillings, until the value of property in question arose to 30 shillings. Then the fine arose to 120 shillings. Formerly fines varied as for a gold-theft, and a mare-theft, and a bee-theft, and many fines were greater than others; now are they all alike, except a man-theft, 120 shillings.

IF ONE MAN SLAY ANOTHER AT THEIR COMMON WORK.

13. If at their common work one man slay another unwillfully, let the tree be given to the kindred, and let them have it off the land within xxx. days; or let him take possession of it who owns the wood.

OF DUMB MEN'S DEEDS.

14. If a man be born dumb or deaf, so that he cannot acknowledge or confess his offenses, let the father make "bot" for his misdeeds.

OF THOSE MEN WHO FIGHT BEFORE A BISHOP.

15. If a man fight before an archbishop or draw his weapon, let him make "bot" with one hundred and fifty shillings. If before another bishop or an ealdorman this happen, let him make "bot" with one hundred shillings.

IN CASE ANY ONE DRIVE OFF A MARE'S FOAL OR A COW'S CALF.

16. If a man steal a cow or a stud-mare, and drive off the foal or the calf, let him pay with a shilling, and for the mothers according to their worth.

IN CASE ANY ONE COMMIT A MINOR TO ANOTHER'S KEEPING.

17. If any one commit his infant to another's keeping, and he die during such keeping, let him who feeds him prove himself innocent of treachery, if any one accuse him of aught.

OF SEIZING HOLD OF A NUN.

18. If any one, with libidinous intent, seize a nun either by her raiment or by her breast without her

leave, let the "bot" be twofold, as we have before
ordained concerning a laywoman. If a betrothed
woman commit adultery, if she be of "ceorlish" degree, let "bot" be made to the "byrgea" with LX.
shillings, and let it be in live stock, cattle goods, and
in that let no human being be given: if she be of
six-"hynde" degree, let him pay one hundred shillings to the "byrgea": if she be of XII. "hynde"
degree, let him make "bot" to the "byrgea" with
CXX. shillings.

OF THOSE MEN WHO LEND THEIR WEAPONS FOR MAN-SLAYING.

19. If any one lend his weapon to another that he
may kill some one therewith, they may join together
if they will in the "wer." If they will not join together, let him who lent the weapon pay of the
"wer" a third part, and of the "wite" a third part.
If he be willing to justify himself, that he knew of no
ill-design in the loan; that he may do. If a sword-
polisher receive another man's weapon to furbish, or
a smith a man's material, let them both return it
sound as either of them may have before received it:
unless either of them had before agreed that he should
not hold it "angylde."

OF THOSE WHO ENTRUST THEIR CATTLE TO MONKS WITHOUT LEAVE.

20. If a man entrust cattle to another man's monk,

---

18. The compensation or penalty of such offenses against morality
increased or diminished according to the rank of the participant. If
the woman were betrothed the penalties were the same, only to be
paid to the surety (byrgea). In such case it might be paid in cattle
but not in slaves.

without leave of the monk's lord, and it escape from him, let him forfeit it who before owned it.

OF THE FIGHTING OF PRIESTS.

21. If a priest kill another man, let all in his home that he had bought be delivered up, and let the bishop secularize him; then let him be given up from the minster, unless the lord will compound for his " wer."

OF CONFESSION OF DEBT.

22. If any one at the folk-mote make declaration of a debt, and afterwards wish to withdraw it, let him charge it on a righter person, if he can; if he cannot, let him forfeit his " angylde " [and take possession of the " wite "].

OF TEARING BY A DOG.

23. If a dog tear or bite a man, for the first misdeed let VI. shillings be paid; if he [the owner] give him food; for the second time, XII. shillings; for the third, XXX. shillings. If, after any of these misdeeds, the dog escape, let this " bot " nevertheless take place. If the dog do more misdeeds, and he keep him; let him make " bot " according to the full " wer," as well wound-" bot " as for whatever he may do.

OF MISDEEDS BY CATTLE.

24. If a neat wound a man, let the neat be delivered up or compounded for.

OF THE RAPE OF A "CEORL'S" FEMALE SLAVE.

25. If a man commit a rape upon a " ceorl's " female slave, let him make " bot " to the " ceorl " with V. shillings, and let the " wite " be LX. shillings.

If a male "theow" commit a rape upon a female "theow," let him make "bot" with his testicles.

OF THE RAPE OF A WOMAN UNDER AGE.

26. If a man commit a rape upon a woman under age, let the "bot" be as that of a full-aged person.

[OF KINLESS MEN.]

27. If a man, kinless of paternal relatives, fight, and slay a man, and then if he have maternal relatives, let them pay a third of the "wer"; his guild-brethren a third part; for a third let him flee. If he have no maternal relatives, let his guild-brethren pay half, for half let him flee.

OF SLAYING A MAN THUS CIRCUMSTANCED.

28. If a man kill a man thus circumstanced, if he have no relatives, let half be paid to the king; half to his guild-brethren.

OF "HLOTH"-SLAYING OF A "TWY-HYNDE" MAN.

29. If any one with a "hloth" slay an unoffending "twy-hynde" man, let him who acknowledges the death-blow pay "wer" and "wite"; and let every one who was of the party pay xxx. shillings as "hloth-bot."

OF A SIX-"HYNDE" MAN.

30. If it be a six-"hynde" man, let every man pay LX. shillings as "hloth-bot"; and the slayer, "wer" and full "wite."

OF A TWELVE-"HYNDE" MAN.

31. If he be a twelve-"hynde" man, let each of them pay one hundred and twenty shillings; and the slayer, "wer" and "wite." If a "hloth" do this, and

afterwards will deny it on oath, let them all be accused, and let them then all pay the " wer " in common ; and all, one " wite," such as shall belong to the " wer."

OF THOSE WHO COMMIT "FOLK-LEASING."

32. If a man commit "folk-leasing," and it be fixed upon him, with no lighter thing let him make " bot " than that his tongue be cut out ; which must not be redeemed at any cheaper rate than it is estimated at according to his " wer."

OF "GOD-BORHS."

33. If any one accuse another on account of a "god-borh," and wish to make plaint that he has not fulfilled any of those [" god-borhs "] which he gave him, let him make his " fore-ath " in four churches ;

---

31. In the reign of Alfred the twelve-hynde man is said to have been of the highest rank in the Saxon aristocracy, his value being 1200 shillings, while the two-hynde man ranked as the lowest class of freemen, a ceorl. But in all the old Saxon councils or witan, while the ealdormen are mentioned with other principal men, none of them are named as were the archbishops and bishops, and hence, while making up a part of the government, they have left no figure of civil life in its history. They seem to have been only distinguished in the domestic and foreign wars that preyed on the nation during all these centuries.

32. Fines, though varied by the rank of one or both of the parties, are the only punishment for murder in these laws unless the dignity and safety of the king are brought into jeopardy, though mutilations in case of slaves were to be inflicted in several instances. *Folk-leasing*, a crime not well-defined, was to be punished by cutting out his tongue. The law adding, which must not be redeemed at any cheaper rate than is estimated according to his *wer*. This offense seems to have been slander and evil speaking, hence the tongue as its instrument was the primary subject of punishment.

33. *God-borhs*, pledge of one's baptismal vow, or of Christian duties for payment of a debt or other obligation.

and if the other will prove himself innocent, let him do so in XII. churches.

OF CHAPMEN.

34. It is also directed to chapmen, that they bring the men whom they take up with them before the king's reeve at the folk-mote, and let it be stated how many of them there are; and let them take such men with them as they may be able afterwards to present for justice at the folk-mote; and when they have need of more men up with them on their journey, let them always declare it, as often as their need may be, to the king's reeve, in presence of the "gemot."

OF BINDING A "CEORLISH" MAN.

35. If any one bind an unoffending "ceorlish" man, let him make "bot" with X. shillings. If any one scourge him, let him make "bot" with twenty shillings. If he lay him in prison, let him make "bot" with XXX. shillings. If, in insult, he shave his head like a "homola," let him make "bot" with X. shillings. If, without binding him, he shave him like a priest, let him make "bot" with XXX. shillings. If he shave off his beard, let him make "bot" with XX. shillings. If he bind him, and then shave him like a priest, let him make "bot" with LX. shillings.

OF HEEDLESSNESS WITH A SPEAR.

36. It is moreover decreed: if a man have a spear over his shoulder, and any man stake himself upon it, that he pay the "wer" without the "wite." If he

---

34. The purchases being so made before witnesses, these witnesses in case of false charges could vouch for the honest title of chapmen to their goods.

stake himself before his face, let him pay the "wer." If he be accused of willfulness in the deed, let him clear himself according to the "wite"; and with that let the "wite" abate. And let this be if the point be three fingers higher than the hindmost part of the shaft; if they be both on a level, the point and the hindmost part of the shaft, be that without danger.

OF A "BOLD–GETÆL."

37. If a man from one "bold-getæl" wish to seek a lord in another "bold-getæl," let him do it with the knowledge of the "ealdorman" whom he before followed in his shire. If he do it without his knowledge, let him who entertains him as his man pay CXX. shillings as "wite"; let him, however, deal the half to the king in the shire where he before followed, half in that into which he comes. If he has done any wrong where he before was, let him make "bot" for it who has then received him as his man; and to the king CXX. shillings as "wite."

IN CASE A MAN FIGHT BEFORE AN "EALDORMAN" IN THE "GEMOT."

38. If a man fight before a king's "ealdorman" in the "gemot," let him make "bot" with "wer" and "wite," as it may be right; and before this, CXX. shillings to the "ealdorman" as "wite." If he disturb the folk-mote by drawing his weapon, one hundred and twenty shillings to the "ealdorman" as "wite." If aught of this happen before a king's "ealdorman's" junior, or a king's priest, XXX. shillings as "wite."

---

37. *Bold-getœl,* supposed to be a roll of the subjects of a lord.

OF FIGHTING IN A "CEORLISH" MAN'S "FLET."

39. If any one fight in a "ceorlish" man's "flet," with six shillings let him make "bot" to the "ceorl." If he draw his weapon and fight not, let it be half of that. If, however, either of these happen to a six-"hynde" man, let it increase threefoldly, according to the "ceorlish" "bot": to a twelve-"hynde" man, twofoldly, according to the six-"hynde's" "bot."

OF "BURH-BRYCE."

40. The king's "burh-bryce" shall be cxx. shillings. An archbishop's, ninety shillings. Any other bishop's, and an "ealdorman's," LX. shillings. A twelve-"hynde" man's, XXX. shillings. A six-"hynde" man's, XV. shillings. A "ceorl's edor-bryce," V. shillings. If aught of this happen when the "fyrd" is out, or in Lent fast, let the "bot" be twofold. If any one in Lent put down holy law among the people without leave, let him make "bot" with cxx. shillings.

OF BOC-"LANDS."

41. The man who has "boc-land," and which his kindred left him, then ordain we that he must not give it from his "mægburg," if there be writing or witness that it was forbidden by those men who at first acquired it, and by those who gave it to him, that he should do so; and then let that be declared in the presence of the king and of the bishop, before his kinsmen.

---

40. *Burh-bryce,* breaking the king's protection.
41. *Boc-land,* book-land title by charter.

OF FEUDS.

42. We also command: that the man who knows his foe to be home-sitting fight not before he demand justice of him. If he have such power that he can beset his foe, and besiege him within, let him keep him within for VII. days, and attack him not, if he will remain within. And then, after VII. days, if he will surrender, and deliver up his weapons, let him be kept safe for XXX. days, and let notice of him be given to his kinsmen and his friends. If, however, he flee to a church, then let it be according to the sanctity of the church; as we have before said above. But if he have not sufficient power to besiege him within, let him ride to the "ealdorman," and beg aid of him. If he will not aid him, let him ride to the king before he fights. In like manner also, if a man come upon his foe, and he did not before know him to be home-staying; if he be willing to deliver up his weapons, let him be kept for XXX. days, and let notice of him be given to his friends; if he will not deliver up his weapons, then he may attack him. If he be willing to surrender, and to deliver up his weapons, and any one after that attack him, let him pay as well "wer" as wound, as he may do, and "wite," and let him have forfeited his "mæg"-ship. We also declare, that with his lord a man may fight "orwige," if any one attack the lord: thus may the lord fight for his man. After the same wise, a man may fight with his born kinsman, if a man attack him wrongfully, except against his lord; that we do not allow. And a man may fight "orwige," if he find another with his lawful wife, within closed doors, or under one covering, or with his lawfully-born daughter, or

with his lawfully-born sister, or with his mother, who was given to his father as his lawful wife.

OF THE CELEBRATION OF MASS–DAYS.

43. To all freemen let these days be given, but not to "theow-"men and "esne"-workmen: XII. days at Yule, and the day on which Christ overcame the devil, and the commemoration day of St. Gregory, and VII. days before Easter and VII. days after, and one day at St. Peter's tide and St. Paul's, and in harvest the whole week before St. Mary-mass, and one day at the celebration of All-Hallows and the IV. Wednesdays in the IV. Ember weeks. To all "theow"-men be given, to those to whom it may be most desirable to give, whatever any man shall give them in God's name, or they at any of their moments may deserve.

OF HEAD–WOUND.

44. For head-wound, as "bot": if the bones be both pierced, let XXX. shillings be given him. If the outer bone be pierced, let XV. shillings be given as "bot."

OF HAIR–WOUND.

45. If within the hair there be a wound an inch long, let one shilling be given as "bot." If before the hair there be a wound an inch long, two shillings as "bot."

OF STRIKING OFF AN EAR.

46. If his other ear be struck off, let XXX. shillings be given as "bot." If the hearing be impaired, so that he cannot hear, let LX. shillings be given as "bot."

---

43. The absolute rights of freeman are herein accorded by ecclesiastical law, while the slave may or may not be favored on special merits in the judgment of his master, but religious or secular rights he has none.

OF A MAN'S EYE—WOUND AND OF VARIOUS OTHER LIMBS.

47. If a man strike out another's eye, let him pay him LX. shillings, and VI. shillings and VI. pennies and a third part of a penny, as "bot." If it remain in the head, and he cannot see aught therewith, let one third part of the "bot" be retained.

48. If a man strike off another's nose, let him make "bot" with LX. shillings.

49. If a man strike out another's tooth in the front of his head, let him make "bot" for it with VIII. shillings: if it be the canine tooth, let IV. shillings be paid as "bot." A man's grinder is worth XV. shillings.

50. If a man smite another's cheeks so that they be broken, let him make "bot" with XV. shillings.

A man's chin-bone, if it be cloven, let XII. shillings be paid as "bot."

51. If a man's wind-pipe be pierced, let "bot" be made with XII. shillings.

52. If a man's tongue be done out of his head by another man's deeds, that shall be like as eye-" bot."

53. If a man be wounded on the shoulder so that the joint-oil flow out, let "bot" be made with XXX. shillings.

54. If the arm be broken above the elbow there shall be XV. shillings as "bot."

55. If the arm-shanks be both broken, the "bot" is XXX. shillings.

56. If the thumb be struck off, for that shall be XXX. shillings as "bot."

If the nail be struck off, for that shall be V. shillings as "bot."

57. If the shooting [*i. e.* fore] finger be struck off, the "bot" is XV. shillings; for its nail it is IV. shillings.

58. If the middlemost finger be struck off, the "bot" is XII. shillings; and its nail's "bot" is II. shillings.

59. If the gold [*i. e.* ring] finger be struck off, for that shall be XVII. shillings as "bot"; and for its nail IV. shillings as "bot."

60. If the little finger be struck off, for that shall be as "bot" IX. shillings; and for its nail one shilling, if that be struck off.

61. If a man be wounded in the belly, let XXX. shillings be paid him as "bot": if it be thorough-wounded, for either orifice twenty shillings.

62. If a man's thigh be pierced, let XXX. shillings be paid him as "bot"; if it be broken, the "bot" is likewise XXX. shillings.

63. If the shank be pierced beneath the knee, there shall be twelve shillings as "bot"; if it be broken beneath the knee, let XXX. shillings be paid him as "bot."

64. If the great toe be struck off, let XX. shillings be paid him as "bot"; if it be the second toe, let XV. shillings be paid as "bot"; if the middlemost toe be struck off, there shall be IX. shillings as "bot"; if it be the fourth toe, there shall be VI. shillings as "bot"; if the little toe be struck off, let V. shillings be paid him.

65. If a man be so severely wounded in the genitals that he cannot beget a child, let "bot" be made to him for that with LXXX. shillings.

66. If a man's arm, with the hand, be entirely cut

off before the elbow, let "bot" be made for it with LXXX. shillings.

For every wound before the hair, and before the sleeve, and beneath the knee, the "bot" is two parts more.

67. If the loin be maimed, there shall be LX. shillings as "bot"; if it be pierced, let XV. shillings be paid as "bot"; if it be pierced through, then shall there be XXX. shillings as "bot."

68. If a man be wounded in the shoulder, let "bot" be made with LXXX. shillings, if the man be alive.

69. If a man maim another's hand outwardly, let XX. shillings be paid him as "bot," if he can be healed; if it half fly off, then shall be XL. shillings as "bot."

70. If a man break another's rib within the whole skin, let X. shillings be paid as "bot"; if the skin be broken, and bone be taken out, let XV. shillings be paid as "bot."

71. If a man strike out another's eye, or his hand or his foot off, there goeth like "bot" to all; VI. pennies and VI. shillings and LX. shillings and the third part of a penny.

72. If a man's shank be struck off near the knee, there shall be LXXX. shillings as "bot."

73. If a man fracture another's shoulder, let XX. shillings be paid him as "bot."

74. If it be broken inwardly, and bone be taken out, let XV. shillings [in addition] be paid as its "bot."

75. If a man rupture the great sinew, if it can be healed so that it be sound, let XII. shillings be paid as "bot." If the man be halt on account of the wounded

sinew, and he cannot be cured, let xxx. shillings be paid as " bot."

76. If the small sinew be ruptured, let vi. shillings be paid him as " bot."

77. If a man rupture the tendons on another's neck, and wound them so severely that he has no power of them, and nevertheless live so maltreated; let c. shillings be given him as "bot," unless the " witan " shall decree to him one juster, and greater.

Rapin, the French historian of England, says: " The laws during the wars had been very much trampled upon, and were become almost unknown to the people. Alfred laid out his pains, for some time, in making a collection of the best laws he could find. He inserted some of the judicial laws of the Old Testament, and several of those formerly enacted by Ina, King of

---

Alfred's laws from number 44 to 77 both inclusive, are mainly transcripts from the laws of Æthelbirht, excepting the amount of the penalties imposed for various injuries to the person to which these laws relate. The penalties call for larger sums of money, showing that the increase of the currency had diminished the purchasing power of a particular species of money.

There might have been another consideration on which this increase of money penalties is to be accounted for. The population subject to these laws had become more dense in particular localities; but all England was united in a single kingdom, with a heterogeneous population of Britons, Saxons, Danes, Welshmen, and others, and an effective government required a more severe and thorough code of laws.

In these laws we find marked evidence of the growth of the country in civilization and material development. Ranks among the people are better defined and the domestic life and its surroundings present less obscure pictures than in the earlier times.

Several distinct courts are noticed, but the extent of their jurisdiction and the methods of their procedure are left quite obscure. The

Wessex, and Offa, King of Mercia, in their respective
[Saxon] kingdoms. To these he added many of his
own, adapted to the circumstances of his people.
Throughout these laws may easily be observed an ar-
dent zeal for justice, and a sincere desire of rooting
out oppression and violence. . . . They were
indeed mild, if compared with those of later ages,
since, like the older Saxon laws, they punished most
offenses by fines."

"In addition to these laws, Alfred divided the kingdom into shires, hundreds, and tithings, and made
every tithing responsible for the conduct of its people as well as for sojourners with them. And every
hundred was responsible for what took place in each
and every of the tithings within its limits, answering

---

ealdormen seem to hold courts within their shires, either by themselves or the gemot over which they presided. Then, there was the
folk-mote, that seems to have had about the same jurisdiction as the
modern justices of the peace. Then there were ecclesiastical courts
presided over by the bishops, that took cognizance of matters of conscience and of the conduct and duties of the clergy. There is no
doubt but the judicial functions of the king were performed by him
in person in the court at the king's hall or by judges appointed to
represent him in these duties, and the king's reeves in the several
counties, as in later ages, held courts of criminal jurisdiction, and of
matters affecting the king's revenues. It would seem that the organization of the kingdom, of which Alfred has the credit, into shires,
hundreds, and tithings, must have embraced also a judicial organization that would have given force to a responsible government.
The division of the kingdom into estates and counties and parishes,
as shown in Doomsday-book, must have suggested means of administering a government, thus elaborated to overspread the kingdom.
We can gather more clearly the holdings of the lands at that age.
The king in his demesnes, while he was sovereign over all the lands
of the kingdom, was vested with the absolute title of all crown lands,
that had not been granted by him or his predecessors. Lands held
by prescription by the nobles or commonalty were only subject to

to the shires for the enforcement of the laws over all the people subject to its supervision."

Thus, by gradations of responsibility, coming up through intermediate officials, from the individual to the king, a responsible and peaceful government was established among a warlike and barbarous people. Alfred also had a doom-book, in which the records of the titles of the principal estates of the realm were recorded. This is said to be in existence at the present day. Laws granting tithes to the religious establishments of the kingdom are noted as originating with Ethelwulph, the father of Alfred. Learning and science were chiefly confined in that age to the monks and religious houses, which accounts for the fact that the Church and its rights and privileges were much better defined than mere secular institutions, and, what is perhaps better, their records are much more elaborate and better preserved. The canons passed by ecclesiastical councils required the payment of tithes, required the *magistrates* to execute judgments

---

the general royal authority, and only answered to the obligations of their holders to the crown for relief in emergencies and in times of great public danger. There were lands held by the people in common for pasturage or cultivation called folc-lands, and other lands called boc-lands held by title by book or survey in fee simple. These lands descended in families to heirs at law. Such lands were alienable or might be entailed to heirs by a public declaration, as before described.

Alfred, like some of his predecessors, seems to have made the archbishop and high functionaries of the church his chief counselors. It is to be noted that in these laws of Alfred no traces appear of what has since been known as the common law. The force of his government and obviously limited ability among his judges were not favorable to judicial legislation, out of which the common law has grown in later times.

on trials by ordeal, condemned witchcraft, and established mints for the coining of money. At Canterbury were to be seven mints—four for the king, two for the archbishop, and one for the abbot of St. Augustine. Rochester had three mints—two for the king and one for the bishop. These ordinances forbade the people to buy and sell on Sunday, enacted penalties against perjury, and ordered the bishops to sit with the judges, to assist them in administering the laws. A subsequent council enacted other laws, relating chiefly to priests and the administration of the ordinances, which it would be a digression here to notice.

Alfred gathered together all the laws known in his age and compiled his laws on the most complete system that could then be produced. There is something to be said on the whole in favor of the humanity of these laws of Alfred as compared to some of later ages. In fact, civilization and progress found a footing under Alfred's government that had not been realized before in England. True, he rehearses from the old Mosaic code the provisions of an eye for an eye and a tooth for a tooth. But the real intent of these Mosaic citations is not so clear, since in his laws he has provided a *bot*, or compensation, for the injury or destruction of these members.

A state of war succeeded the death of Alfred in 901 of the Christian era. Though Edward the Elder appears to have been an able prince, yet the Danes renewed their incursions into England and continued to disturb the public peace.

ALFRED AND GUTHRUM'S PEACE.[*]

This is the peace that King Alfred, and King Guthrum, and the "witan" of all the English nation, and all the people that are in East-Anglia, have all ordained and with oaths confirmed, for themselves and for their descendants, as well for born as for unborn, who reck of God's mercy or of ours.

1. First, concerning our land-boundaries: up on the Thames, and then up on the Lea, and along the Lea unto its source, then right to Bedford, then up on the Ouse unto Watling-street.

2. Then is this: if a man be slain, we estimate all equally dear, English and Danish, at VIII. half-marks of pure gold; except the "ceorl" who resides on "gafol-land," and their "liesings": they also are equally dear, either at CC. shillings.

3. And if a king's thane be accused of man-slaying, if he dare to clear himself, let him do that with XII. king's thanes. If any one accuse that man who is of less degree than the king's thane, let him clear him-

---

[*]In the terms of peace between Alfred and the invading Danes in 878, Guthrum, the Danish leader or king, having embraced Christianity and been baptized, entered into a treaty by which he was to withdraw from the rest of the kingdom and locate in East-Anglia, and there govern his countrymen, who were probably the bulk of the population. That there might be uniformity in the government and laws of the two sections, Alfred and Guthrum entered into treaty stipulations.

self with xi. of his equals, and with one king's thane.
And so in every suit which may be for more than iv.
"mancuses." And if he dare not, let him pay for it
threefold, as it may be valued.

OF WARRANTORS.

4. And that every man know his warrantor for men,
and for horses, and for oxen.

5. And we all ordained on that day that the oaths
were sworn, that neither bond nor free might go to
the host without leave, no more than any of them to
us. But if it happen, that from necessity any of them
will have traffic with us, or we with them, with cattle
and with goods, that is to be allowed in this wise; that
hostages be given in pledge of peace, and as evidence
whereby it may be known that the party has a clean
back.

NOTE ON LAWS OF EDWARD THE ELDER.

Edward, distinguished as the Elder, was the son of Alfred; succeeded his father on the throne in 901, and died in 924.

Edward established a few ordinances that scarcely enlarged the scope of statutory enactments or developed any new principles in civil jurisprudence.

He commands all his reeves to fidelity in their judicial functions. That their judgments should be without fear. That every suit should have a term when it shall be brought forward and judgment be pronounced.

The warrantee of title to goods bought and sold was specially required; and that every man should know his own warrantor (that is, the person from whom he bought the goods). In his default he incurred the penalty of contempt for the king. Then follows the forms of proceeding in vouching to warranty nearly corresponding to that which was formerly practiced.

The denial of justice in matter of folc-land and boc-land incurred a penalty of thirty shillings to the king by the party in the wrong; a second offense a like penalty; and a third the king's *oferhyrnes*, that is, one hundred and twenty shillings, unless he desists from his course (oferhyrnes, contempt for the king or penalty for).

Perjurers proved as such should not thereafter be oath-worthy, but ordeal-worthy.

King Edward exhorted his "witan" when they were at Exeter, in the interest of the king's peace, cited his own example on sea and land, and exhorted their following.

The reeve who does not lawfully exact justice should pay 120 shillings.

A party recommending another, who was afterwards detected as a thief, should become security for him.

The harboring of willful offenders was forbidden. Every land-holder required to have men on his land who would aid any searching for stolen cattle, etc. Those who protected a willful offender must answer to the laws according to the judgment book.

The old law of forfeiting freedom for theft was continued—so of the harboring of a fugitive slave.

Each reeve was required to hold a (gemot) council or court, once in four weeks, and so do that every man be worthy of folk-right, and that every suit have an end and a term when it shall be brought forward. If that any one disregard, let him pay as we before ordained.

The only point made in these few laws is a special interest in behalf of justice and the public peace—and as showing the first instance of regular terms of the reeves' gemot or local courts.

THE LAWS OF KING EDWARD.

EDWARD'S ORDINANCES.

OF DOOM AND SUIT.

King Edward commands all the reeves: that ye judge such just dooms as ye know to be most righteous, and it in the doom-book stands. Fear not on any account to pronounce folk-right; and that every suit have a term when it shall be brought forward, that ye then may pronounce.

OF BUYING.

1. And I will that every man have his warrantor; and that no man buy out of port, but have the portreeve's witness, or that of other unlying men whom one may believe. And if any one buy out of port, then let him incur the king's "oferhyrnes," and let the warranty nevertheless go forward, until it be known where it shall stop. Also we have ordained: that he who should vouch to warranty should have unlying witness to the effect that he rightfully vouched it; or should bring forward an oath which he might believe who made the claim. So we have ordained the same respecting ownership; that he should adduce unlying witness thereof, or bring forward the oath, if he could, of persons unchosen, by which the claimant should be bound. But if he could not, then should be named to him six men of the same neighborhood wherein he was resiant, and of the six let him get one

for one ox, or for that cattle which may be the worth of
this, and afterwards let it increase, according to the
value of the property, if there ought to be more.
Also we have ordained: if there were any evil-minded
man who would put another's property in "borh" for
"wither-tihtle," that he should then declare on oath
that he did it not "from any knavery, but with full
right, without fraud and guile," and that he then
should there do as he durst with whom it is attached:
"like as he it owned, so he it vouched to warranty."

OF HIM WHO DENIES JUSTICE TO ANOTHER.

2. Also we have ordained of what he were worthy
who denied justice to another, either in "boc-land" or
in "folc-land," and that he should give him a term
respecting the "folc-land" when he should do him
justice before the reeve. But if he had no right either
to the "boc-land" or to the "folc-land," that he who
denied the right should be liable in xxx. shillings to
the king; and for the second offense, the like : for the
third offense, the king's "oferhyrnes," that is, cxx.
shillings, unless he previously desist.

OF PERJURERS.

3. Also we have ordained concerning those men
who were perjurers; if that were made evident, or an
oath failed to them, or were out-proved, that they
afterwards should not be oath-worthy, but ordeal-
worthy.

OF "FRITH."

4. King Edward exhorted his "witan" when they
were at Exeter, that they all should search out how
their "frith" might be better than it had previously

been: for it seemed to him that it was more indifferently observed than it should be, what he had formerly commanded. He then asked them, who would apply to its amendment, and be in that fellowship that he was, and love that which he loved, and shun that which he shunned, both on sea and on land? That is, then, that no man deny justice to another: if any one do so, let him make "bot" as it before is written; for the first offense, with xxx. shillings; and for the second offense, the like; and for the third, with cxx. shillings to the king.

OF THE REEVE WHO DOES NOT LAWFULLY EXACT.

5. And if the reeve do not lawfully exact it, with the witness of those men who are assigned him to bear witness, then let him make "bot" my "oferhyrnes," with cxx. shillings.

OF THOSE ACCUSED OF THEFT.

6. If any one be accused of theft, then let those take him in "borh" who before commended him to his lord, that he may justify himself thereof; or let other friends, if he have any, do the same. If he know not who will take him in "borh," then let those on whom it is incumbent take an "in-borh" on his property. If he have neither property nor other "borh," then let him be held to judgment.

OF THOSE WHO WILL NOT SEEK THEIR OWN.

7. Also I will that every man have constantly those men ready on his land, who may lead those men who desire to seek their own, and for no meed-monies prevent them, nor anywhere protect or harbor a convicted offender, willfully nor violently.

OF THOSE WHO PROTECT A CONVICTED OFFENDER.

8. If any one disregard this, and break his oath and his "wed," which all the nation has given, let him make "bot" as the doom-book may teach: but if he will not, let him forfeit the friendship of us all, and all that he has. If any one harbor him after that, let him make "bot" as the doom-book may say, and as he ought who harbors a fugitive, if it be here within. If it be in the east-country, if it be in the north-country, let him make "bot" according as the "frith-gewritu" say.

OF HIM WHO FORFEITS HIS FREEDOM.

9. If any one, through a charge of theft, forfeit his freedom, and deliver himself up, and his kindred forsake him, and he know not who shall make "bot" for him; let him then be worthy of the "theow"-work which thereto belongs, and let the "wer" abate from the kindred.

OF HIM WHO RECEIVES ANOTHER MAN'S MAN WITHOUT LEAVE.

10. Let no man receive another man's man without his leave whom he before followed, and until he be blameless towards every hand. If any one so do, let him make "bot" my "oferhyrnes."

OF "GEMOT"-TERMS.

11. I will that each reeve have a "gemot" always once in four weeks; and so do that every man be worthy of folk-right: and that every suit have an end and a term when it shall be brought forward. If that any one disregard, let him make "bot" as we before ordained.

AGAIN HIS, AND GUTHRUM'S, AND EDWARD'S.

These are the dooms which king Alfred and king Guthrum chose.

And this is the ordinance also which king Alfred and king Guthrum, and afterwards king Edward and king Guthrum, chose and ordained, when the English and Danes fully took to peace and to friendship; and the "witan" also, who were afterwards, oft and unseldom that same renewed and increased with good.

This is the first which they ordained: that they would love one God, and zealously renounce every kind of heathendom. And they established worldly rules also for these reasons, that they knew that else they might not many control, nor would many men else submit to divine "bot" as they should: and the worldly "bot" they established in common to Christ and to the king, wheresoever a man would not lawfully submit to divine "bot," by direction of the bishops.

1. And this then is the first which they ordained: that "church-grith" within the walls, and the king's "hand-grith," stand equally inviolate.

2. And if any one violate Christianity, or reverence heathenism, by word or by work, let him pay as well

" wer," as " wite " or " lah-slit," according as the deed may be.

3. And if a man in orders steal, or fight, or forswear, or fornicate, let him make " bot " for it according as the deed may be, as well by " wer," as by " wite " or by " lah-slit "; and, above all things, make " bot " before God as the canon teaches, and find " borh " thereof, or yield to prison. And if a masspriest misdirect the people about a festival or about a fast, let him pay xxx. shillings among the English, and among the Danes three half-marks. If a priest fetch not the chrism at the right term, or refuse baptism to him who has need thereof, let him pay " wite " among the English, and among the Danes " lah-slit "; that is, twelve " ores."

OF INCESTUOUS PERSONS.

4. And concerning incestuous persons, the " witan " have ordained, that the king shall have the upper, and the bishop the nether, unless " bot " be made before God and before the world, according as the deed may be ; so as the bishop may teach. If two brothers or two near kinsmen commit fornication with the same woman, let them make " bot " very strictly, in such wise as it may be allowed, as well by " wer," as by " wite " or by " lah-slit," according as the deed may be.

If a man in orders foredo himself with capital crime, let him be seized and held to the bishop's doom.

5. And if a man guilty of death desire confession, let it never be denied him. And all God's dues let every one zealously further, by God's mercy, and by the " wites " which the " witan " have annexed thereto.

6. If any one withhold tithes, let him pay " lah-slit "

among the Danes, "wite" among the English. If
any one withhold "Rom-feoh," let him pay "lah-slit"
among the Danes, "wite" among the English. If
any one discharge not "light-scot," let him pay "lah-
slit" among the Danes, "wite" among the English.
If any one give not plough-alms, let him pay "lah-slit"
among the Danes, "wite" among the English. If
any one deny any divine dues, let him pay "lah-slit"
among the Danes, "wite" among the English. And
if he fight and wound any one, let him be liable in his
"wer." If he fell a man to death, let him then be an
outlaw, and let every of those seize him with "hearm"
who desire right. And if he so do that any one kill
him, for that he resisted God's law or the king's, if
that be proved true, let him lie uncompensated.

OF WORKINGS ON A FESTIVAL–DAY.

7. If any one engage in Sunday marketing, let him
forfeit the chattel, and twelve "ores" among the
Danes, and xxx. shillings among the English. If a
freeman work on a festival-day, let him forfeit his freedom, or pay "wite" or "lah-slit." Let a "theowman"
suffer in his hide or "hide-gild." If a lord oblige his
"theow" to work on a festival-day, let him pay "lah-
slit" within the Danish law, and "wite" among the
English.

OF FASTS.

8. If a freeman break a lawful fast, let him pay
"wite" or "lah-slit." If a "theowman" do so, let
him suffer in his hide or "hide-gild."

OF ORDEAL AND OATHS.

9. Ordeal and oaths are forbidden on festival-days

and lawful fast-days; and he who shall break that, let him pay "lah-slit" among the Danes, and "wite" among the English.

If it can be so ordered, no one condemned should ever be executed on the Sunday festival, but be secured and held till the festival be gone by.

10. If a limb-maimed man who has been condemned be forsaken, and he after that live three days; after that, any one who is willing to take care of sore and soul may help him, with the bishop's leave.

OF WITCHES, DIVINERS, PERJURERS, ETC.

11. If witches or diviners, perjurers or "morth"-workers, or foul, defiled, notorious adulteresses, be found anywhere within the land; let them then be driven from the country and the people cleansed, or let them totally perish within the country, unless they desist, and the more deeply make "bot."

OF ECCLESIASTICS AND FOREIGNERS.

12. If any one wrong an ecclesiastic or a foreigner, through any means, as to money or as to life, then shall the king or the "eorl" there in the land, and the bishop of the people, be unto him in the place of a kinsman and of a protector, unless he have another; and let "bot" be strictly made, according as the deed may be, to Christ and to the king, as it is fitting; or let him avenge the deed very deeply who is king among the people.

HOW A "TWELVE-HYNDE" MAN SHALL BE PAID FOR.

A "twelve-hynde" man's "wer" is twelve hundred shillings.

A "twy-hynde" man's "wer" is two hundred shillings.

If any one be slain, let him be paid for according to his birth. And it is right that the slayer, after he has given "wed" for the "wer," find, in addition, a "wer-borh" according as shall thereto belong; that is, to a "twelve-hynde's" "wer" twelve men are necessary as "wer-borh," vIII. of the paternal kin, and IV. of the maternal kin. When that is done, then let the king's "mund," be established, that is, that they all of either kindred, with their hands in common upon one weapon, engage to the mediator that the king's "mund" shall stand. In XXI. days from that day let CXX. shillings be paid as "heals-fang" at a "twelve-hynde's" "wer." "Heals-fang" belongs to the children, brothers, and paternal uncles; that money belongs to no kinsman, except to those who are within the degrees of blood. In XXI. days from the day that the "heals-fang" is paid, let the "man-bot" be paid; in XXI. days from this, the fight-"wite"; in XXI. days from this, the "frum-gyld" of the "wer"; and so forth, till it be fully paid, within the time that the "witan" have appointed. After this they may depart with love, if they desire to have full friendship.

All men shall do with regard to the "wer" of a "ceorl" that which belongs to his condition, like as we have said about a "twelve-hynde" man.

OF OATHS.

HOW THE MAN SHALL SWEAR.

THUS SHALL A MAN SWEAR FEALTY OATHS.*

1. By the Lord, before whom this relic is holy, I will be to N. faithful and true, and love all that he loves, and shun all that he shuns, according to God's law, and according to the world's principles, and never, by will nor by force, by word nor by work, do aught of what is loathful to him; on condition that he me keep as I am willing to deserve, and all that fulfill that our agreement was, when I to him submitted and chose his will.

THUS SHALL A MAN SWEAR WHEN HE HAS DISCOV-ERED HIS PROPERTY, AND BRINGS IT IN PROCESS.

2. By the Lord, before whom this relic is holy, so I my suit prosecute with full folk-right, without fraud and without deceit, and without any guile, as was

---

* These oaths and the pieces immediately following are found differently arranged in the different MSS. Their respective dates must therefore be left to some future discovery; though it seems not unreasonable to suppose, from internal evidence, that they cannot have had a later origin than the period in which they here stand. Some of them are probably much earlier.

It is impossible to read the oaths without perceiving at every turn their rhythmical quantity and alliteration. An ear any way accustomed to Anglo-Saxon poetry will easily detect the disjointed members of their poetic formulæ, and instinctively arrange them in the order in which they ought to stand.   [TRANSLATOR.

stolen from me the cattle N. that I claim, and that I have attached with N.

THE OTHER'S OATH WITH WHOM A MAN DISCOVERS HIS CATTLE.

3. By the Lord, I was not at rede nor at deed, neither counselor nor doer, where were unlawfully led away N.'s cattle. But as I cattle have, so did I lawfully obtain it. And: as I vouch it to warranty, so did he sell it to me into whose hand I now set it. And: as I cattle have, so did he sell it to me who had it to sell. And: as I cattle have, so did it come of my own property, and so it by folk-right my own possession is, and my rearing.

THE OATH OF HIM WHO DISCOVERS HIS PROPERTY, THAT HE DOES IT NOT EITHER FOR HATRED OR FOR ENVY.

4. By the Lord, I accuse not N. either for hatred or for envy, or for unlawful lust of gain; nor know I any thing soother; but as my informant to me said, and I myself in sooth believe, that he was the thief of my property.

THE OTHER'S OATH THAT HE IS GUILTLESS.

5. By the Lord, I am guiltless, both in deed and counsel, of the charge of which N. accuses me.

HIS COMPANION'S OATH WHO STANDS WITH HIM.

6. By the Lord, the oath is clean and unperjured which N. has sworn.

OATH IF A MAN FINDS HIS PROPERTY UNSOUND AFTER HE HAS BOUGHT IT.

7. In the name of Almighty God, thou didst en-

gage to me sound and clean that which thou soldest
to me, and full security against after-claim, on the
witness of N., who then was with us two.

HOW HE SHALL SWEAR WHO STANDS WITH ANOTHER IN WITNESS.

8. In the name of Almighty God, as I here for N.
in true ,witness stand, unbidden and unbought, so I
with my eyes oversaw, and with my ears overheard,
that which I with him say.

OATH THAT HE KNEW NOT OF FOULNESS OR FRAUD.

9. In the name of Almighty God, I knew not, in
the things about which thou suest, foulness or fraud,
or infirmity or blemish, up to that day's-tide that I
sold it to thee; but it was both sound and clean,
without any kind of fraud.

10. In the name of the living God, as I money demand, so have I lack of that which N. promised me
when I mine to him sold.

DENIAL.

11. In the name of the living God, I owe not to N.
"sceatt" or shilling, or penny or penny's worth; but
I have discharged to him all that I owed him, so far
as our verbal contracts were at first.

OF THE OATH AND DEGREE—"BOT" OF MEN IN ORDERS.

12. A mass-priest's oath, and a secular thane's, ·are
in English-law reckoned of equal value; and by reason of the seven church-degrees that the mass-priest,
through the grace of God, has acquired, he is worthy
of thane-right.

OF THE MERCIAN OATH.

13. A "twelf-hynde" man's oath stands for six "ceorls'" oaths : because, if a man should avenge a "twelf-hynde" man, he will be fully avenged on six "ceorls," and his "wer-gild" will be six "ceorls'" "wer-gilds."

Bequeathed it, and died, he who it owned, with full folk-right, so as it his elders, with money and with life, lawfully got, and let and left, in power of him, whom they well gifted. And so I it have, as he it gave, who had it to give, without fraud and unforbidden; and I will possess it, as my own property, that that I have; and ne'er for thee design, nor plot nor ploughland, nor turf nor toft, nor furrow nor footmark, nor land nor leasowe, nor fresh nor marsh, nor rough nor plain, by wood nor by field, by land nor by strand, by weald nor by water, but that will maintain, the while that I live; for there is no man alive, who ever heard, that any one made plaint against, or summoned him at the hundred, or anywhere at "gemot," in market-place, or among church-folk, the while that he lived. Sackless he was in life, be he in the grave, so as he may. Do as I teach : be thou with thine, and leave me with mine: I covet not thine, nor "læth" nor land, nor "sac" nor "socn"; nor needest thou mine; nor design I to thee any thing.

WER–GILDS.

1. The North people's king's "gild" is **xxx**. thousand "thrymsas"; fifteen thousand "thrymsas" are for the "wer-gild," and xv. thousand for the "cynedom." The "wer" belongs to the kindred, and the "cyne-bot" to the people.

2. An archbishop's and an ætheling's "wer-gild" is xv. thousand "thrymsas."

3. A bishop's and an "ealdorman's," viii. thousand "thrymsas."

4. A "hold's" and a king's high-reeve's, iv. thousand "thrymsas."

5. A mass-thane's and a secular thane's, ii. thousand "thrymsas."

6. A "ceorl's" "wer-gild" is cc. and lxvi. "thrymsas," that is cc. shillings by Mercian law.

7. And if a "Wilisc"-man thrive so that he have a hide of land, and can bring forth the king's "gafol," then is his "wer-gild" cxx. shillings. And if he thrive not except to half a hide, then let his "wer" be lxxx. shillings.

8. And if he have not any land, and yet be free, let him be paid for with lxx. shillings.

9. And if a "ceorlish" man thrive, so that he have v. hides of land for the king's "ut-ware," and any one

---

1. *Thrymsas.* In money, 266⅔ thrymsas were equal to 200 shillings Mercian money.

slay him, let him be paid for with two thousand "thrymsas."

10. And though he thrive, so that he have a helm and coat of mail, and a sword ornamented with gold, if he have not that land, he is nevertheless a "ceorl."

11. And if his son and his son's son so thrive, that they have so much land; afterwards, the offspring shall be of "gesithcund" race, at two thousand ["thrymsas"].

12. And if they have not that, nor to that can thrive, let them be paid for as "ceorlish."

---

1. Let the king's "wer-gild" be with the English race, by folk-right, thirty thousand "thrimsas," and and of these, let xv. thousand be for the "wer," and the other xv. m. for the "cyne-dom." The "wer" belongs to the kindred of the royal family, and the "cyne-bot" to the people of the country.

2. An archbishop's and an "eorl's" "wer-gild" is xv. m. "thrimsas."

6. A "ceorl's" "wer-gild" is CCLXVII. "thrymsas" by the Danish law.

7. And a "Wylisc"-man's "wer-gild," if he be to that degree enriched that he have a hide of land and property, and can pay "gafol" to the king, it is then CCXX. shillings. But if he be only risen to half a hide, then let his "wer" be LXXX. shillings.

8. If he have no land, but is free, let him be paid for with LXX. shillings.

9. If a "ceorl" be enriched to that degree, that he have v. hides of land, and any one slay him, let him be paid for with II. m. "thrimsas."

10. And if he acquire so that he have a coat of mail and a helmet, and an over-gilded sword, if he have not that land, he is "sithcund."

11. And if his son and the son's son that acquire, that they have so much land, let their successors be of the "sithcund" kin, and let them be paid for with II. M. "thrimsas."

OF MERCIAN LAW.

A "ceorl's" "wer-gild" is by Mercian law CC. shillings. A thane's "wer-gild" is six times as much, that is, XII. hundred shillings. Then is a king's simple "wer-gild" VI. thanes' "wer" by Mercian law, that is, XXX. thousand "sceatts," and that is altogether CXX. pounds. So much is the "wer-gild" in the people's folk-right by Mercian law. And for the "cyne-dom" there is due another such sum as "bot" for "cyne-gild." The "wer" belongs to the kindred, and the "cyne-bot" to the people.

RANKS.

OF PEOPLE'S RANKS AND LAW.

1. It was whilom, in the laws of the English, that people and law went by ranks, and then were the counselors of the nation of worship worthy, each according to his condition, "eorl" and "ceorl," "thegen" and "theoden."

2. And if a "ceorl" thrived, so that he had fully five hides of his own land, church and kitchen, bell-house and "burh"-gate-seat, and special duty in the king's hall, then was he thenceforth of thane-right worthy.

3. And if a thane thrived, so that he served the king, and on his summons, rode among his household; if he then had a thane who him followed, who to the king's "ut-ware," five hides had, and in the king's hall served his lord, and thrice with his errand went to the king; he might thenceforth, with his "fore-oath," his lord represent, at various needs, and his plaint lawfully conduct, wheresoever he ought.

4. And he who so prosperous a vicegerent had not, swore for himself according to his right, or it forfeited.

5. And if a thane thrived, so that he became an " eorl," then was he thenceforth of " eorl "-right worthy.

6. And if a merchant thrived, so that he fared thrice over the wide sea by his own means, then was he thenceforth of thane-right worthy.

7. And if there a scholar were, who through learning thrived, so that he had holy orders, and served Christ; then was he thenceforth of rank and power so much worthy, as then to those orders rightfully belonged, if he himself conducted so as he should; unless he should misdo, so that he those orders' ministry might not minister.

8. And if it happened, that any one a man in orders, or a stranger, anywhere injured, by word or work; then pertained it to king and to the bishop, that they that should make good, as they soonest might.

THE LAWS OF KING ÆTHELSTAN.

I.

[COUNCIL OF GREATANLEA.]

KING ÆTHELSTAN'S ORDINANCE.

I, Æthelstan king, with the counsel of Wulfhelm, archbishop, and of my other bishops, make known to the reeves at each " burh," and beseech you, in God's name, and by all his saints, and also by my friendship, that ye first of my own goods render the tithes both of live stock and of the year's earthly fruits, so as they may most rightly be either meted, or told, or weighed out; and let the bishops then do the like from their own goods, and my " ealdormen " and my reeves the same. And I will, that the bishop and the reeves command it to all those who ought to obey them, that it be done at the right term. Let us bear in mind how Jacob the patriarch spake: " Decimas et hostias pacificas offeram tibi : " and how Moses spake in God's law: " Decimas et primitias non tardabis offerre Domino." It is for us to think how awfully it is declared in the books: If we will not render the tithes to God, that he will take from us the nine parts when we least expect ; and, moreover, we have the sin in addition thereto. And I will also that my reeves so do, that there be given the church-scotts and the soul-scotts at the places to which they rightly belong: and plough-alms yearly, on this condition ; that they shall enjoy it at the holy places who are

willing to serve their churches, and of God and of
me are willing to deserve it : but let him who will
not, forfeit the bounty, or again turn to right.   Now
ye hear, saith the king, what I give to God, and what
ye ought to fulfill by my " oferhirnes."   And do ye
also so that ye may give to me my own what ye for
me may justly acquire.   I will not that ye unjustly
anywhere acquire aught for me ; but I will grant to
you your own justly, on this condition, that ye yield
to me mine ; and shield both yourselves, and those
whom ye ought to exhort, against God's anger and
against my " oferhirnes."

ÆTHELSTAN'S ORDINANCES.

OF THIEVES.

1. First : that no thief be spared, who may be taken
" hand-hæbbende," above XII. years, and above eight
pence.   And if any one so do, let him pay for the
thief according to his " wer," and let it not be the
more settled for the thief, or that he clear himself
thereby.   But if he will defend himself, or flees away,
then let him not be spared.   If a thief be brought into prison : that he be XL. days in prison, and then let
him be released thereout with CXX. shillings, and let
the kindred enter into " borh " for him that he evermore desist.   And if after that he steal, let them pay
for him according to his " wer," or bring him again
therein : and if any one stand up for him, let him pay
for him according to his " wer," as well to the king
as to him to whom it lawfully belongs : and let every
man of those who there stand by him pay to the king
CXX. shillings as " wite."

OF LORDLESS MEN.

2. And we have ordained: respecting those lordless men of whom no law can be got, that the kindred be commanded that they domicile him to folk-right, and find him a lord in the folk-mote; and if they then will not or cannot produce him at the term, then be he thenceforth a "flyma," and let him slay him for a thief who can come at him : and whoever after that shall harbor him, let him pay for him according to his "wer," or by it clear himself.

OF DENIAL OF RIGHT.

3. And the lord who denies justice, and upholds his evil-doing man, and the king be applied to on that account; let him pay the "ceap-gild," and give to the king CXX. shillings : and he who applies to the king before he has prayed for justice, as oft as it shall behove him; let him pay the like "wite" that the other should if he had denied him justice. And the lord who is privy to his "theow's" theft, and it is made manifest against him, let him forfeit the "theow," and be liable in his "wer," for the first time. If he do so oftener, let him be liable in all that he has : and, also, such of the king's "horderes," or of our reeves, as shall be privy to the thieves who have stolen, let him be subject to the like.

OF PLOTTINGS AGAINST A LORD.

4. And we have ordained respecting plottings against a lord: that he should be liable in his life if he could not deny it, or afterwards at the threefold ordeal should be guilty.

OF CHURCH–BREACH.

5. And we have ordained respecting church-breach: if he should be guilty at the threefold ordeal, let him make " bot " according as the doom-book may say.

OF WITCH–CRAFTS.

6. And we have ordained respecting witchcrafts, and "lyblacs," and "morth-dæds": if any one should be thereby killed, and he could not deny it, that he be liable in his life. But if he will deny it, and at the threefold ordeal shall be guilty; that he be cxx. days in prison: and after that let his kindred take him out, and give to the king cxx. shillings, and pay the "wer" to his kindred, and enter into "borh" for him, that he evermore desist from the like.

OF INCENDIARIES.

Let incendiaries, and those who avenge a thief, be worthy of the like law. And he who will avenge a thief, and wounds no man, let him give to the king cxx. shillings, as "wite" for the assault.

OF THE SINGLE ORDEAL.

7. And we have ordained respecting the single ordeal, for those men who have been often accused, and have been found guilty, and they know not who shall take them in "borh"; let them be brought into prison: and let them be delivered out as it here before is ordained.

OF LANDLESS MEN.

8. And we have ordained: if any landless man should become a follower in another shire, and again seek his kinsfolk; that he may harbor him on this

condition, that he present him to folk-right if he there do any wrong, or make "bot" for him.

OF ATTACHING CATTLE.

9. He who attaches cattle, let v. of his neighbors be named to him; and of the v. let him get one who will swear with him that he takes it to himself by folk-right: and he who will keep it to himself, to him let there be named x. men, and let him get two of them, and give the oath that it was born on his property, without the "rim-ath"; and let his "cyre-ath" stand for over xx. pence.

OF EXCHANGE.

10. And let no man exchange any property without the witness of the reeve, or of the mass-priest, or of the land-lord, or of the "hordere," or of other unlying man. If any one so do, let him give xxx. shillings, and let the land-lord take possession of the exchange.

OF WRONGFUL WITNESS.

But if it be found that any of these have given wrongful witness, that his witness never stand again for aught, and that he also give xxx. shillings as "wite."

OF HIM WHO WOULD PRAY OFF A CRIMINAL CHARGE FROM ONE SLAIN.

11. And we have ordained: that he who would pray off a criminal charge from a slain thief, should go with three others, two of the paternal, and the third of the maternal kin, and give the oath that they knew of no theft by their kinsman, so that he were not worthy of his life for that crime: and after that

let some XII. go and charge him with the crime, as it was before ordained; and if the kindred of the dead would not come thither at the term, let every one who had before made suit for it pay CXX. shillings.

THAT A MAN BUY NOT OUT OF PORT.

12. And we have ordained: that no man buy any property out of port over XX. pence; but let him buy there within, on the witness of the port-reeve, or of another unlying man: or further, on the witness of the reeves at the folk-mote.

OF REPAIRING OF "BURHS."

13. And we ordain: that every "burh" be repaired XIV. days over Rogation Days.

Secondly: that every marketing be within port.

OF MONEYERS.

14. Thirdly: that there be one money over all the king's dominion, and that no man mint except within port. And if the moneyer be guilty, let the hand be struck off with which he wrought that offense, and be set up on the money-smithy: but if it be an accusation, and he is willing to clear himself; then let him go to the hot-iron, and clear the hand therewith with which he is charged that fraud to have wrought. And if at the ordeal he should be guilty, let the like be done as is here before ordained.

In Canterbury VII. moneyers; IV. the king's, and II. the bishop's, I. the abbot's.

At Rochester III.; II. the king's, and I. the bishop's.

At Lewes II.

At Hastings I.

Another at Chichester ;
At Hampton II.
At Wareham II.
At Exeter II.
At Shaftesbury II.
Else, at the other "burhs" I.

OF SHIELD-WRIGHTS.

15. Fourthly: that no shield-wright cover a shield
with sheep's skin ; and if he so do, let him pay XXX.
shillings.

16. Fifthly: that every man have to the plough
II. well-horsed men.

OF THOSE WHO TAKE MEED-MONEY OF A THIEF.

17. Sixthly: if any one take meed-money of a
thief, and suppress another's right, let him be liable
in his " wer."

OF HORSES.

18. Seventhly: that no man part with a horse over
sea, unless he wish to give it.

OF A "THEOWMAN" WHO IS GUILTY AT THE ORDEAL.

19. And we have ordained respecting a " theowman": if he were guilty at the ordeal, that the "ceap-
gild" should be paid ; and that he be scourged thrice,
or a second "gild" be given : and be the "wite" of
half value for "theows."

OF HIM WHO FAILS TO ATTEND THE "GEMOT."

20. If any one [when summoned] fail to attend
the "gemot" thrice; let him pay the king's "oferhyrnes," and let it be announced seven days before

the "gemot" is to be. But if he will not do right,
nor pay the "oferhyrnes"; then let all the chief men
belonging to the "burh" ride to him, and take all
that he has, and put him in "borh." But if any one
will not ride with his fellows, let him pay the king's
"oferhyrnes." And let it be announced at the
"gemot," that the "frith" be kept toward all that
the king wills to be within the "frith," and theft be
foregone by his life and by all that he has. And he
who for the "wites" will not desist, then let all the
chief men belonging to the "burh" ride to him, and
take all that he has; and let the king take possession
of half, of half the men who may be in the riding;
and place him in "borh." If he know not who will
be his "borh" let them imprison him. If he will not
suffer it, let him be killed, unless he escape. If any
one will avenge him, or be at feud with any of them,
then be he foe to the king, and to all his friends. If
he escape, and any one harbor him, let him be liable in his "wer"; unless he shall dare to clear himself by the "flyma's" "wer," that he knew not he
was a "flyma."

OF HIM WHO COMPOUNDS FOR AN ORDEAL.

21. If any one compound for an ordeal, let him
compound for the "ceap-gild," as he can, and not for
the "wite"; unless he is willing to grant it to whom
it may belong.

OF HIM WHO RECEIVES ANOTHER MAN'S MAN.

22. And let no man receive another man's man,
without his leave whom he before followed. If any
one so do; let him give up the man, and make "bot"

the king's "oferhyrnes." And let no one dismiss his accused man from him before he has done what is right.

OF HIM WHO GIVES "WED" FOR AN ORDEAL.

23. If any one gives "wed" for an ordeal, then let him come three days before to the mass-priest who is to hallow it; and let him feed himself with bread and with water, and salt, and herbs, before he shall go to it; and let him attend mass each of the three days, and make an oblation, and go to housel on the day that he shall go to the ordeal: and then swear the oath that he is, according to folk-right, guiltless of the charge, before he goes to the ordeal. And if it be water, that he dive an ell and a half by the rope; if it be iron ordeal, let it be three days before the hand be undone. And let every man begin his charge with a fore-oath, as we before ordained: and be each of those fasting, on either hand, who may be there together, by God's command and the archbishop's: and let there not be on either side more men than XII. If the accused man be with a larger company than some twelve, then be the ordeal void, unless they will go from him.

OF HIM WHO BUYS PROPERTY.

24. And he who buys property with witness, and is after obliged to vouch it to warranty, then let him receive it from whom he before had bought it, whether he be free or bond, whichsoever he be.

And that no marketing be on Sundays; but if any one so do, let him forfeit the goods, and pay XXX. shillings as "wite."

OF PERJURERS.

25. And he who shall swear a false oath, and it be made clear against him; that he never after be oath-worthy, nor let him lie within a hallowed burial-place, though he die, unless he have the testimony of the bishop in whose shrift-shire he may be, that he has made such "bot" as his confessor prescribed to him. And let his confessor announce to the bishop, within xxx. days, whether he would turn to the "bot." If he do not so, let him make "bot" in such wise as the bishop shall prescribe to him.

26. But if any of my reeves will not do this, and care less about it than we have commanded; then let him pay my "oferhyrnes," and I will find another who will. And let the bishop exact the "oferhyrnes" of the reeve in whose following it may be. He who goes from this ordinance, let him pay for the first time v. pounds; for the second time, his "wer"; for the third time, let him forfeit all that he has, and the friendship of us all.

All this was established in the great synod at "Greatanlea": in which was the archbishop Wulf-helm, with all the noble men and "witan" whom King Æthelstan . . . . . gather.

II.—(*Untranslated.*)

III.—(*Untranslated.*)

IV.

.Æthelstan king makes known : that I have learned that our "frith" is worse kept than is pleasing to me, or it at "Greatanlea" was ordained; and my

" witan " say that I have too long borne with it. Now
I have decreed with the " witan " who were with me at
Exeter at mid-winter; that they [the " frith "-break-
ers] shall all be ready, in themselves and with wives
and with property and with all things, to go whither
I will, (unless from henceforth they shall desist,) on
this condition, that they never come again to the
country. And if they shall ever again be found in
the country, that they be as guilty as he who may be
taken " hand-habbende." And he who shall entertain them or any one of their men, or send any man
to them, be he liable in himself and in all things that
he has: now that is, because that the oaths, and the
" weds," and the " borhs " are all disregarded and
broken which there were given; and we know of no
other things to trust in except it be this.

OF HIM WHO RECEIVES ANOTHER MAN'S MAN.

1. And he who receives another man's man, whom
he for his evil conduct turns away from him, and
whom he cannot clear of his evil, let him pay for him
to him whom he before followed, and give to the king
cxx. shillings. But if the lord will foredo the man
wrongfully; then let him clear himself, if he can, at
the folk-mote: and if he be innocent, let him seek
whatever lord he will, in virtue of that testimony;
because I grant that each of them who is innocent
may follow such lord as he will. And such reeve as
shall neglect this, and will not care about it, let him
pay to the king his " oferhyrnes," if any one truly
charge it to him, and he cannot exculpate himself.
And such reeve as shall take meed-money, and thereby suppress another's right; let him pay the king's

"oferhyrnes," and also bear the disgrace, so as we have ordained. And if it be a thane who shall so do, be it the like.

And let there be named, in every reeve's "man-ung," as many men as are known to be unlying, that they may be for witness in every suit. And be the oaths of these unlying men, according to the worth of the property, without election.

OF HIM WHO TRACES CATTLE.

2. And he who traces cattle into another's land; let him trace it out who owns that land, if he can; if he cannot, let the tracing stand for the fore-oath, if he accuse any one therein.

3. And let there be sung every Friday, at every monastery, by all God's servants, a fifty [psalms] for the king, and for all who will what he wills; and for the others, as they may merit.

And every man that will may make "bot" for every theft with the accuser, without any kind of "wite," until Rogation days; and be it after that as it was before.

4. And we ordained at Thunresfeld in the "gemot": if any thief or robber should flee to the king, or to any church and to the bishop; that he have a term of nine days. And if he flee to an "ealdorman," or an abbot, or a thane, let him have a term of three days. And if any slay him within that term; then let him make "bot" the "mund-byrd" of him whom he before had fled to; or let him clear himself with some twelve that he knew not of the "socn." And flee he to such "socn" as he may flee to, that he be not worthy of his life but as many days as we here

9

above have declared; and he who after that harbors him, let him be worthy of the same that the thief may be, unless he can clear himself, that he knew no guile nor any theft in him.

5. Thus far shall be the king's " grith " from his " burh "-gate where he is dwelling, on its four sides; that is, III. miles, and III. furlongs, and III. acres breadth, and IX. feet and IX. palms and IX. barleycorns.

OF INCENDIARIES AND "MORTH"-SLAYERS.

6. We have ordained concerning incendiaries and concerning "morth"-slayers; that the oath be augmented by threefold, and the ordeal-iron be increased so that it weigh three pounds; and that the man himself who is accused should go thereto, and let the accuser have the choice whether of water-ordeal or of iron-ordeal, whichsoever to him be the more desirable. If he cannot bring forth the oath, and he then be guilty, let it stand within the doom of the chief men belonging to the "burh," whether he shall have or not have his life.

OF FORFANG.

Let "forfang" everywhere, be it in one shire, be it in more, be fifteen pence, and for every one of small cattle always for each shilling a penny.

Concerning "forfang" the "witan" have counseled, that like judgment be held all over England; that is, for a man fifteen pence, and for a horse as much; whether it be in one shire, whether it be in more; lest that a powerless man toil far for his own, and also pay too much. Formerly it stood, that for all stolen cattle . . . and on its "forfang," payment be made ; that is, for every shilling a penny, be the cattle of whatever kind it may, if it be rescued from the hand of a thief: but if otherwise it be found in a hiding place, then the "forfang"-money may be less, because it was gotten with less danger.

DOOM CONCERNING HOT IRON AND WATER.

7. And concerning the ordeal we enjoin by command of God, and of the archbishop, and of all bishops : that no man come within the church after the fire is borne in with which the ordeal shall be heated, except the mass-priest, and him who shall go thereto : and let there be measured nine feet from the stake to the mark, by the man's feet who goes thereto. But if it be water, let it be heated till it low to boiling. And be the kettle of iron, or of brass, of lead or of clay. And if it be a single accusation, let the hand dive after the stone up to the wrist; and if it be threefold, up to the elbow. And when the ordeal is ready, then let two men go in of either side ; and be they agreed that it is so hot as we. before have said. And let go in an equal number of men of either side, and stand on both sides of the ordeal, along the church ; and let these all be fasting, and abstinent from their wives on that night; and let the mass-priest sprinkle holy water over them all, and let each of them taste of the holy water, and give them all the book and the image of Christ's rood to kiss : and let no man mend the fire any longer when the hallowing is begun ; but let the iron lie upon the hot embers till the last collect: after that, let it be laid upon the "stapela" ; and let there be no other speaking within, except that they earnestly pray to Almighty God that

he make manifest what is soothest. And let him go thereto; and let his hand be enveloped, and be it postponed till after the third day, whether it be foul or clean within the envelope. And he who shall break this law, be the ordeal with respect to him void, and let him pay to the king cxx. shillings as "wite."

"Wal-reaf" is a "nithing's" deed: if any one desire to deny it, let him do so with eight and forty full-born thanes.

V.

JUDICIA CIVITATIS LUNDONIÆ.

This is the ordinance which the bishops and the reeves belonging to London have ordained, and with "weds" confirmed, among our "frith-gegildas," as well "eorlish" as "ceorlish," in addition to the dooms which were fixed at "Greatanlea" and at Exeter and at "Thunresfeld."

THIS IS THEN FIRST:

1. That no thief be spared over XII. pence, and no person over XII. years, whom we learn according to folk-right that he is guilty, and can make no denial; that we slay him, and take all that he has; and first, take the "ceap-gild" from the property; and after that let the surplus be divided into II.; one part to the wife, if she be innocent, and were not privy to the crime; and the other into II.; let the king take half, half the fellowship. If it be "boc-land," or bishops' land, then has the land-lord the half part in common with the fellowship.

2. And he who secretly harbors a thief, and is privy to the crime and to the guilt, to him let the like be done.

3. And he who stands with a thief, and fights with him, let him be slain with the thief.

4. And he who oft before has been convicted openly of theft, and shall go to the ordeal, and is there found guilty; that he be slain, unless the kindred or the lord be willing to release him by his " wer " and by the full " ceap-gild," and also have him in "borh" that he thenceforth desist from every kind of evil. If after that he again steal, then let his kinsmen give him up to the reeve to whom it may appertain, in such custody as they before took him out of from the ordeal, and let him be slain in retribution of the theft. But if any one defend him, and will take him, although he was convicted at the ordeal, so that he might not be slain; that he should be liable in his life, unless he should flee to the king and he should give him his life; all as it was before ordained at " Greatanlea " and at Exeter and at " Thunresfeld."

5. And whoever will avenge a thief, and commits an assault, or makes an attack on the highway; let him be liable in cxx. shillings to the king. But if he slay any one in his revenge, let him be liable in his life, and in all that he has, unless the king is willing to be merciful to him.

SECOND:

That we have ordained: that each of us should contribute IV. pence for our common use within XII. months, and pay for the property which should be taken after we had contributed the money; and that we all should have the search in common; and that every man should contribute his shilling who had

property to the value of xxx. pence, except the poor
widow who has no "for-wyrhta" nor any land.

THIRD:

That we count always x. men together, and the
chief should direct the nine in each of those duties
which we have all ordained; and [count] afterwards
their "hyndens" together, and one "hynden"-man
who shall admonish the x. for our common benefit;
and let these xi. hold the money of the "hynden,"
and decide what they shall disburse when aught is to
pay, and what they shall receive, if money should
arise to us at our common suit; and let them also
know that every contribution be forthcoming which
we have all ordained for our common benefit, after
the rate of xxx. pence or one ox; so that all be fulfilled which we have ordained in our ordinances, and
which stands in our agreement.

FOURTH:

That every man of them who has heard the orders
should be aidful to others, as well in tracing as in pursuit, so long as the track is known; and after the
track has failed him, that one man be found where
there is a large population, as well as from one tithing where a less population is, either to ride or to go
(unless there be need of more), thither when most
need is, and as they all have ordained.

FIFTH:

That no search be abandoned, either to the north
of the march or to the south, before every man who
has a horse has ridden one riding; and that he who
has not a horse work for the lord who rides or goes

for him, until he come home ; unless right shall have
been previously obtained.

SIXTH :

1. Respecting our "ceap-gild ": a horse at half a
pound if it be so good; and if it be inferior, let it be
paid for by the worth of its appearance, and by that
which the man values it at who owns it, unless he
have evidence that it be as good as he says, and then
let [us] have the surplus which we there require.

2. An ox at a "mancus," and a cow at xx., and a
swine at x., and a sheep at a shilling.

3. And we have ordained respecting our "theow-
men," whom men might have; if any one should
steal him, that he should be paid for with half a
pound ; but if we should raise the "gild," that it
should be increased above that, by the worth of his
appearance, and that we should have for ourselves
the surplus that we there should require. But if he
should have stolen himself away, that he should be
led to the stoning, as it was formerly ordained; and
that every man who had a man should contribute
either a penny or a halfpenny, according to the number of the fellowship, so that we might be able to
raise the worth. But if he should make his escape,
that he should be paid for by the worth of his appearance, and we all should make search for him. If we
then should be able to come at him, that the same
should be done to him that would be done to a
"Wylisc " thief, or that he be hanged.

4. And let the "ceap-gild" always advance from
xxx. pence to half a pound, after we make search ;
further, if we raise the "ceap-gild" to the full "an-

gylde"; and let the search still continue, as it was before ordained, though it be less. ·

SEVENTH: '

That we have ordained: let do the deed whoever may that shall avenge the injuries of us all, that we should be all so in one friendship as in one foeship, whichever it then may be: and that he who should kill a thief before other men, that he be XII. pence the better for the deed, and for the enterprise, from our common money. And he who should own the property for which we pay, let him not forsake the search, on peril of our "oferhyrnes," and the notice therewith, until we come to payment; and then also we would reward him for his labor, out of our common money, according to the worth of the journey, lest the giving notice should be neglected.

EIGHTH:

1. That we gather to us once in every month, if we can and have leisure, the "hynden-men" and those who direct the tithings, as well with "bytt-fylling" as else it may concern us, and know what of our agreement has been executed; and let these XII. men have their refection together, and feed themselves according as they may deem themselves worthy, and deal the remains of the meat for love of God.

2. And if it then should happen that any kin be so strong and so great, within land or without land, whether XII.-"hynde" or "twy-hynde," that they refuse us our right, and stand up in defense of a thief; that we all of us ride thereto with the reeve within whose "manung" it may be.

3. And also send on both sides to the reeves, and desire from them aid of so many men as may seem to us adequate for so great a suit, that there may be the more fear in those culpable men for our assemblage, and that we all ride thereto, and avenge our wrong, and slay the thief, and those who fight and stand with him, unless they be willing to depart from him.

4. And if any one trace a track from one shire to another, let the men who there are next take to it, and pursue the track till it be made known to the reeve; let him then with his "manung" take to it, and pursue the track out of his shire if he can; but if he cannot, let him pay the "angylde" of the property: and let both reeveships have the full suit in common, be it wherever it may, as well to the north of the march as to the south, always from one shire to another; so that every reeve may assist another, for the common "frith" of us all by the king's "ofer-hyrnes."

5. And also that every one shall help another, as it is ordained and by "weds" confirmed; and such man as shall neglect this beyond the march, let him be liable in xxx. pence, or an ox, if he aught of this neglect which stands in our writings, and we with our "weds" have confirmed.

6. And we have also ordained respecting every man who has given his "wed" in our gildships, if he should die, that each gild-brother shall give a "gesufel" loaf for his soul, and sing a fifty, or get it sung within xxx. days.

7. And we also command our "hire-men" that each man shall know when he has his cattle, or when he has not, on his neighbors' witness, and that he point out

to us the track, if he cannot find it within three days ;
for we believe that many heedless men reck not how
their cattle go, for over-confidence in the " frith."

8. Then we command that within III. days he
make it known to his neighbors, if he will ask for the
" ceap-gild " ; and let the search nevertheless go on as
it was before ordained, for we will not pay for any
unguarded property, unless it be stolen. Many men
speak fraudulent speech. If he cannot point out to
us the track, let him shew on oath with III. of his
neighbors that it has been stolen within III. days, and
after that let him ask for his " ceap-gild."

9. And let it not be denied nor concealed, if our
lord or any of our reeves should suggest to us any .
addition to our " frith-gilds," that we will joyfully
accept the same, as it becomes us all, and may be ad-
vantageous to us. But let us trust in God, and our
kingly lord, if we fulfill all things thus, that the affairs
of all folk will be better with respect to theft than
they before were. If, however, we slacken in the
" frith " and the " wed " which we have given, and
the king has commanded of us, then may we expect,
or well know, that these thieves will prevail yet more
than they did before. But let us keep our " weds "
and the " frith " as is pleasing to our lord : it greatly
behoves us that we devise that which he wills ; and if
he order and instruct us more, we shall be humbly
ready.

NINTH:

That we have ordained: respecting those thieves
whom one cannot immediately discover to be guilty,
and one afterwards learns that they are guilty and

liable; that the lord or the kinsmen should release him in the same manner as those men are released who are found guilty at the ordeal.

TENTH:

That all the "witan" gave their "weds" all together to the archbishop at "Thunresfeld," when Ælfeah Stybb and Brihtnoth Odda's son came to meet the "gemot" by the king's command; that each reeve should take the "wed" in his own shire: that they would all hold the "frith" as king Æthelstan and his "witan" had counseled it, first at "Greatanlea," and again at Exeter, and afterwards at Feversham, and a fourth time at "Thunresfeld," before the archbishop, and all the bishops, and his "witan," whom the king himself named, who were thereat: that those dooms should be observed which were fixed at this "gemot," except those which were there before done away with; which was Sunday marketing, and that with full and true witness any one might buy out of port.

ELEVENTH:

That Æthelstan commands his bishops and his "ealdormen," and all his reeves over all my realm, that ye so hold the "frith" as I and my "witan" have ordained. And if any of you neglect it, and will not obey me, and will not take the "wed" of his "hiremen," and he allow of secret compositions, and will not attend to these regulations as I have commanded and it stands in our writs; then be the reeve without his "folgoth," and without my friendship, and pay me cxx. shillings; and each of my thanes who has land, and will not keep the regulations as I have commanded, [let him pay] half that.

TWELFTH:

1. That the king now again has ordained to his "witan" at "Witlanburh," and has commanded it to be made known to the archbishop by bishop Theodred, that it seemed to him too cruel that so young a man should be killed, and besides for so little, as he has learned has somewhere been done. He then said, that it seemed to him, and to those who counseled with him, that no younger person should be slain than xv. years, except he should make resistance or flee, and would not surrender himself; that then he should be slain, as well for more as for less, whichever it might be. But if he be willing to surrender himself, let him be put into prison, as it was ordained at "Greatanlea," and by the same let him be redeemed.

2. Or, if he come not into prison, and they have none, that they take him in "borh" by his full "wer," that he will evermore desist from every kind of evil. If the kindred will not take him out, nor enter into "borh" for him, then let him swear as the bishop may instruct him, that he will desist from every kind of evil, and stand in servitude by his "wer." But if he after that again steal, let him be slain or hanged, as was before done to the older ones.

3. And the king has also ordained, that no one should be slain for less property than xii. pence worth, unless he will flee or defend himself; and that then no one should hesitate, though it were for less. If we thus hold, then trust I in God that our "frith" will be better than it has before been.

THE LAWS OF KING EDMUND.

KING EDMUND'S INSTITUTES.

King Edmund assembled a great synod at London, during the holy Easter tide, as well of ecclesiastical as of secular degree. There was Oda archbishop, and Wulfstan archbishop, and many other bishops, meditating concerning the condition of their souls, and of those who were subject to them.

OF THE CHASTITY OF ECCLESIASTICS.

1. This is the first: that those holy orders who have to teach God's people by their life's example, hold their chastity according to their degree, as well of man's degree as of woman's degree, whichsoever it may be. If they do not so, then are they worthy of that which in the canon is ordained; that is, that they forfeit their worldly possessions and a consecrated burial-place, unless they make " bot."

OF TITHES AND CHURCH-SCOTS.

2. A tithe we enjoin to every Christian man by his Christendom, and church-scot, and "Rome-feoh," and plough-alms. And if any one will not so do, let him be excommunicated.

OF HOMICIDE.

3. If any one shed a Christian man's blood, let him not come into the king's presence, ere he go to penance, as the bishop may teach him, and his confessor direct him.

OF NUNS' FORNICATION AND OF ADULTERY.

4. He who commits fornication with a nun, let him not be worthy of a consecrated burial-place (unless he make "bot"), any more than a man-slayer. We have ordained the same respecting adultery.

OF THE REPAIRING OF CHURCHES.

5. We have also ordained: that every bishop repair the houses of God in his own [district], and also remind the king that all God's churches be well conditioned as is very needful for us.

OF PERJURERS AND "LYBLACS."

6. Those who swear falsely and work "lyblac," let them be for ever cast out from all communion with God, unless they turn to right repentance.

SECULAR.

Edmund king makes known to all people, both old and young, that are in his dominion, that which I have deliberated with the council of my "witan," both ecclesiastic and secular. First, how I might most promote Christianity. Then seemed it to us, first, most needful that we should most firmly preserve our peacefulness and harmony among ourselves, throughout all my dominion. To me and to us all are exceedingly offensive the unrighteous and manifold fightings that are among ourselves: we have therefore ordained:

OF HOMICIDE.

1. If any one henceforth slay any man, that he himself bear the "fæhthe"; unless, with the aid of his friends, and within twelve months, he compensate

it with the full "wer," be he born as he may be. But if the kindred forsake him, and will not pay for him, then I will that all the kindred be "unfah," except the perpetrator; if afterwards they do not give him either food or "mund." But if afterwards any one of his kindred harbor him, then be he liable in all that he possesses to the king, and bear the "fælithe" with the kindred, because they had previously forsaken him. But if any one of the other kindred take vengeance upon any other man, except on the real perpetrator, let him be foe to the king and to all his friends, and forfeit all that he owns.

IF A MAN SEEK ANOTHER IN A CHURCH, OR IN A KING'S "BURH."

2. If any one take refuge in a church, or my "burh," and one there seek him, or do him evil: be those who do that liable in the same that is heretofore ordained.

OF FIGHT–"WITE" AND "MAN–BOT."

3. And I will not that any fight-"wite" or "man-bot" be forgiven.

OF BLOOD–SHEDDING.

4. Also I make known that I will not have to "socn" in my household that man who sheds man's blood, before he has undertaken ecclesiastical "bot," and made "bot" to the kindred, . . . and submitted to every law, as the bishop shall teach him in whose shire it may be.

THANKS TO THOSE WHO ASSIST AGAINST THEFT.

5. Also I thank God, and you all who have well assisted me, and for the "frith" which we now have

with regard to theft: then I trust to you that ye will assist in this so much the better as there is the greater need for us all that it be observed.

OF "MUND-BRICE" AND "HAM-SOCN."

6. Also we have ordained, respecting "mund-brice" and "ham-socns"; that he who shall do it after this forfeit all that he owns, and be it in the king's doom whether he shall have his life.

OF "FÆHTHE."

7. The "witan" shall appease "fæhthe." First, according to "folk-right," the slayer shall give pledge to his "forespeca," and the "forespeca," to the kinsmen, that the slayer will make "bot" to the kin. Then after that it is requisite, that security be given to the slayer's "forespeca," that the slayer may, in peace, near, and himself give "wed" for the "wer." When he has given "wed" for this, then let him find thereto a "wer-borh": when that is done, let the king's "mund" be levied: within XXI. days from that day, let the "hals-fang" be paid: XXI. days from that, the "man-bot": XXI. days from that, the "frum-geld" of the "wer."

OF BETROTHING A WOMAN.

1. If a man desire to betroth a maiden or a woman, and it so be agreeable to her and her friends, then is it right that the bridegroom, according to the law of God, and according to the customs of the world, first promise, and give a "wed" to those who are her "foresprecas," that he desire her in such wise that he

will keep her, according to God's law, as a husband shall his wife : and let his friends guarantee that.

2. After that, it is to be known to whom the "foster-lean" belongs : let the bridegroom again give a "wed" for this; and let his friends guarantee it.

3. Then, after that, let the bridegroom declare what he will grant her, in case she choose his will, and what he will grant her, if she live longer than he.

4. If it be so agreed, then is it right that she be entitled to half the property, and to all, if they have children in common, except she again choose a husband.

5. Let him confirm all that which he has promised with a " wed "; and let his friends guarantee that.

6. If they then are agreed in every thing, then let the kinsmen take it in hand, and betroth their kinswoman to wife, and to a righteous life, to him who desired her, and let him take possession of the " borh" who has control of the " wed."

7. But if a man desire to lead her out of the land, into another thane's land, then it will be advisable for her that her friends have an agreement that no wrong shall be done to her; and if she commit a fault, that they may be nearest in the "bot," if she have not whereof she can make " bot."

8. At the nuptials, there shall be a mass-priest by law; who shall with God's blessing bind their union to all prosperity.

9. Well is it also to be looked to, that it be known, that they, through kinship, be not too nearly allied; lest that be afterwards divided, which before was wrongly joined.

10

THE LAWS OF KING EDGAR.

THIS IS THE ORDINANCE HOW THE HUNDRED SHALL BE HELD.

First, that they meet always within four weeks: and that every man do justice to another.

2. That a thief shall be pursued. . . .

If there be present need, let it be made known to the hundred-man, and let him [make it known] to the tithing-men; and let all go forth to where God may direct them to go: let them do justice on the thief, as it was formerly the enactment of Edmund. And let the "ceap-gild" be paid to him who owns the cattle, and the rest be divided into two; half to the hundred, half to the lord, excepting men; and let the lord take possession of the men.

3. And the man who neglects this, and denies the doom of the hundred, and the same be afterwards proved against him; let him pay to the hundred xxx. pence, and for the second time sixty pence; half to the hundred, half to the lord. If he do so a third time, let him pay half a pound: for the fourth time, let him forfeit all that he owns, and be an outlaw, unless the king allow him to remain in the country.

4. And we have ordained concerning unknown cattle; that no one should possess it without the testimonies of the men of the hundred, or of the tithing-man; and that he be a well trusty man: and, unless he have either of these, let no vouching to warranty be allowed him.

5. We have also ordained : if the hundred pursue a track into another hundred, that notice be given to the hundred-man, and that he then go with them. If he neglect this, let him pay thirty shillings to the king.

6. If any one flinch from justice and escape, let him who held him to answer for the offense pay the "angylde." And if any one accuse him of having sent him away, let him clear himself, as it is established in the country.

7. In the hundred, as in any other "gemot," we ordain : that folk-right be pronounced in every suit, and that a term be fixed when it shall be fulfilled. And he who shall break that term, unless it be by his lord's decree, let him make "bot" with xxx. shillings, and, on the day fixed, fulfill that which he ought to have done before.

8. An oxes bell, and a dog's collar, and a blast-horn ; either of these three shall be worth a shilling, and each is reckoned an informer.

9. Let the iron that is for the threefold ordeal weigh III. pounds ; and for the single, one pound.

I.

HERE IS THE ORDINANCE OF KING EDGAR.

This is the ordinance that king Edgar, with the counsel of his "witan," ordained, in praise of God, and in honor to himself, and for the behoof of all his people.

1. These then are first: that God's churches be entitled to every right ; and that every tithe be rendered to the old minster. to which the district belongs ; and

that be then so paid, both from a thane's "in-land,'"
and from "geneat-land," so as the plough traverses it.

OF CHURCH–SCOTS.

2. But if there be any thane who on his "boc-land"
has a church, at which there is a burial-place; let him
give the third part of his own tithe to his church. If
any one have a church at which there is not a burial-
place, then, of the nine parts, let him give to his
priest what he will; and let every church-scot go to
the old minster, according to every free hearth: and
let plough-alms be paid, when it shall be fifteen days
over Easter.

OF TITHES.

3. And let a tithe of every young be paid by Pentecost; and of the fruits of the earth by the equinox;
and every church-scot by Martinmass, on peril of the
full "wite" which the doom-book specifies: and if
any one will not then pay the tithe, as we have ordained, let the king's reeve go thereto, and the
bishop's, and the mass-priest of the minster, and take
by force a tenth part for the minster to which it is
due; and assign to him the ninth part; and let the
eight parts be divided into two, and let the land-lord
take possession of half, half the bishop; be it a king's
man, be it a thane's.

OF THE HEARTH–PENNY.

4. And let every hearth-penny be rendered by St.
Peter's mass-day: and he who shall not have paid it
by that term, let him be led to Rome, and in addition
thereto [pay] xxx. pence, and bring then a certificate
thence, that he has there rendered so much; and
when he comes home, pay to the king a hundred and

twenty shillings. And if again he will not pay it, let him be led again to Rome, and with another such "bot"; and when he comes home, pay to the king two hundred shillings. At the third time, if he then yet will not, let him forfeit all that he owns.

OF FESTIVALS AND FASTS.

5. And let the festivals of every Sunday be kept, from noontide of the Saturday, till the dawn of Monday, on peril of the "wite" which the doom-book specifies; and every other mass-day, as it may be commanded: and let every ordained fast be kept with every earnestness; and every Friday's fast, unless it be a festival: and let soul-scot be paid for every Christian man to the minster to which it is due; and let every church-"grith" stand as it has best stood.

II.

SECULAR ORDINANCE.

1. Now this is the secular ordinance which I will that it be held. This then is first what I will: that every man be worthy of "folk-right," as well poor as rich: and that righteous dooms be judged to him; and let there be such remission in the "bot" as may be becoming before God and tolerable before the world.

IN CASE ANY ONE APPLY TO THE KING: AND OF THE "WER."

2. And let no man apply to the king, in any suit, unless he at home may not be worthy of law, or cannot obtain law. If the law be too heavy, let him seek

a mitigation of it from the king: and, for any "bot"-worthy crime, let no man forfeit more than his "wer."

OF UNRIGHTEOUS JUDGMENT.

3. And let the judge who judges wrong to another pay to the king one hundred and twenty shillings as "bot"; unless he dare to prove on oath, that he knew it not more rightly: and let him forfeit for ever his thaneship; unless he will buy it of the king, so as he is willing to allow him: and let the bishop of the shire exact the "bot" into the king's hands.

IN CASE ANY ONE ACCUSE ANOTHER.

4. And he who shall accuse another wrongfully, so that he, either in money or prosperity, be the worse; if then the other can disprove that which any one would charge to him; be he liable in his tongue; unless he make him compensation with his "wer."

OF "GEMOTS."

5. And let the hundred-"gemot" be attended as it was before fixed; and thrice in the year let a "burh-gemot" be held; and twice, a shire-"gemot"; and let there be present the bishop of the shire and the "ealdorman," and there both expound as well the law of God as the secular law.

OF "BORHS."

6. And let every man so order that he have a "borh"; and let the "borh" then bring and hold him to every justice; and if any one then do wrong and run away, let the "borh" bear that which he ought

to bear. But if it be a thief, and if he can get hold of him within twelve months; let him deliver him up to justice, and let be rendered to him what he before had paid.

OF "TIHT–BYSIG" PERSONS.

7. And he who is "tyht-bysig," and is untrue to the people, and has shunned these "gemots" thrice; then let there be chosen from the "gemot" those who shall ride to him, and then let him yet find a "borh" if he can: but if he cannot, let them seize him as they can, whether alive or dead; and take all that he owns; and let the accuser be paid an "an-gylde" for his "ceap-gild": and let the lord more-over take half, half the hundred; and if either a kins-man or a stranger refuse the riding, let him pay to the king a hundred and twenty shillings: and let a noto-rious thief seek whatever he may seek, or he who is found in plotting against his lord, so that they never seek life; unless the king will grant them salvation of life.

OF MONEY AND MEASURES.

8. And let one money pass throughout the king's dominion; and that let no man refuse: and let one measure and one weight pass; such as is observed at London and at Winchester; and let the wey of wool go for cxx. p.; and let no man sell it cheaper; and if any one sell it cheaper, either publicly or privately, let each pay xl. shillings to the king, both him who sells it, and him who buys it.

SUPPLEMENT TO EDGAR'S LAWS.

1. Here is manifested in this writing how Edgar the king was deliberating what might be for "bot" in the pestilence, which much afflicted and decreased his people, widely throughout his dominion.—That then is first: that it seemed to him and his "witan" that a misfortune of such kind had been merited by sins, and by contempt of God's commandments, and most of all by the diminution of the need-"gafol," that Christian men ought to render to God in their tithing-scots. He thought on and considered the divine according to worldly usage. If any "geneat-man" neglect his lord's tribute, and do not render it to him at the right term, it may be expected, if the lord be merciful, that he will grant forgiveness of the neglect, and accept his tribute without a penalty. But if he, by his messengers, frequently remind him of his tribute, and he then be obdurate and think to resist it, it is to be expected that the lord's anger will so greatly increase, that he will neither grant him property nor life. Thus it is to be expected that our Lord will do, through the audacity with which people have resisted the frequent admonition that our teachers have made, respecting the need-"gafol" of our Lord; that is, our tithes and church-scots. Then I and the archbishop command, that ye anger not God, nor merit either the sudden death of this present life, nor, still more, the future one of eternal hell, by any diminution of God's dues: but that both rich and poor, who have any tilth, render to God his tithes with all joyfulness and without all grudge, as the ordinance teaches that my "witan" ordained at Andover, and now again con-

firmed with their "weds" at "Wihtbordesstan." Then
I command my reeves, by my friendship, and by all
which they possess, that they punish every of those
who will not render this, and shall break the "wed"
of my "witan" by any remissness, according as the
aforesaid ordinance teaches: and of the punishment be
there no forgiveness. If he be so poor that he do the
one or the other; either that he diminish the things
of God, to the perdition of his soul, or with anger of
mind more remissly treat them, than that which he
counteth to himself as his own; then is that much
more his own which ever lasts him to eternity, if he
would do it without grudge and with perfect gladness.
Then will I, that these God's dues stand everywhere
alike in my dominion, and that the servants of God,
who receive the moneys which we give to God, live a
pure life; that, through their purity, they may intercede for us with God; and that I and my thanes direct our priests to that which the pastors of our souls
teach us, that is our bishops, whom we ought never to
disobey in any of those things which they teach us on
the part of God, so that, through the obedience with
which we obey them on account of God, we may merit
that eternal life to which they fit us by doctrine, and
with example of good works.

2. I will that secular rights stand among every people as good as they can be best devised, to the pleasure of God, and to my perfect royalty, and to the need
and peace of rich and poor: and in every "burh," and
in every shire, that I may have my rights of royalty as
my father had; and that my thanes have their dignity,
in my time, as they had in my father's. And I will,
that secular rights stand among the Danes with as

good laws as they best may choose. But with the English, let that stand which I and my "witan" have added to the dooms of my forefathers, for the behoof of all the people. Let this ordinance, nevertheless, be common to all the people, whether English, Danes, or Britons, on every side of my dominion; to the end that poor and rich may possess what they lawfully acquire, and a thief not know where he shall deposit his theft, though he steal anything; and that, in their despite, they be so guarded against, that too many of them escape not.

3. This then is what I will: that every man be under "borh," both within the "burhs," and without the "burhs"; and let witness be appointed to every "burh" and to every hundred.

4. To every "burh," let there be chosen XXXIII. as witness.

5. To small "burhs," and in every hundred, XII.; unless ye desire more.

6. And let every man, with their witness, buy and sell every of the chattels that he may buy or sell, either in a "burh" or in a wapentake; and let every of them, when he is first chosen as witness, give the oath that he never, neither for money, nor for love, nor for fear, will deny any of those things of which he was witness, nor declare any other thing in witness, save that alone which he saw or heard: and of such sworn men, let there be at every bargain two or three as witness.

7. And he who rides in quest of any cattle, let him declare to his neighbors about what he rides; and when he comes home, let him also declare with whose witness he bought the cattle.

8. But if he, being out on any journey, unintentionally make a bargain, without having declared it when

he rode out, let him declare it when he comes home; and if it be live stock, let him, with witness of his township, bring it to the common pasture. If he do not so before five days, let the townsmen declare it to the "ealdor" of the hundred; and let them be exempt from "wite,". both themselves and their herdsmen, and let him forfeit the cattle who brought it thither; because he would not declare it to his neighbors; and let the "land-rica" take possession of half, and half the hundred.

9. But if it remain above v. days undeclared in the common pasture, let him forfeit the cattle, as we before ordained, and let every of the herdsmen suffer in his hide: and of this let there be no forgiveness, let them seek what they may seek: and, nevertheless, let him declare in whose witness he bought the cattle.

10. If he then declare, that he bought it with the witness of those men who are named as witness, either in "burh" or in hundred; and the "ealdor" of the hundred is informed that it is true, let him nevertheless forfeit the cattle; because he would not declare it to his neighbors, nor to the "ealdor" of his hundred, and let him have no greater harm from it.

11. But if he declare, that he bought it with witness, and that be false; be he the thief, and forfeit his head, and all that he owns: and let the land-lord hold the stolen cattle, and the "ceap-gild" of the cattle, till that the proprietor is informed of it, and with witness claims the cattle for his own.

12. Then will I, that, with the Danes, such good laws stand as they may best choose, and as I have ever permitted to them, and will permit, so long as life shall last me, for your fidelity which ye have ever

shewn me; and this I desire, that this one doom, concerning such inquiry, be common to us all, for security and peace to all the people.

13. And I will, that townsmen and their herdsmen have the same inquiry concerning my life cattle, and that of my thanes, as they have concerning their own. But if my reeve, or any other man, more or less powerful, shun this, and command things unseemly, either to townsmen or their herdsmen, let the Danes chuse, according to their laws, what punishment they will adopt respecting him.

14. With the English, I and my "witan" have chosen what the punishment shall be, if any man make resistance, or outright slay any one of those who are engaged in this inquiry, and give notice of secreted cattle; or any of those who bear true witness, and with his sooth save the guiltless, and lawfully foredo the guilty. Then will I, that ever be observed among you what you had chosen as "frith-bot," with great wisdom, and very agreeably to me. And be this supplement common to us all, who dwell in these lands.

15. Then let Oslac "eorl," and all the army dwelling in this "ealdordom," further this, that it stand to the glory of God, and to the benefit of the souls of us all; and to the "frith" of all the people. And let many writings be written concerning these things, and sent both to Ælfere "ealdorman," and to Æthelwine "ealdorman," and let them [send] in every direction; that this ordinance be known both to poor and rich.

16. I will be to you a very kind lord, the while that my life lasts, and I am exceedingly well disposed towards you all, because ye are so earnest about the "frith."

THE LAWS OF KING ETHELRED.*

I.

KING ETHELRED'S ORDINANCE.

This is the ordinance which King Ethelred and his
" witan " ordained as " frith-bot " for the whole
nation, at Woodstock, in the land of the Mercians,
according to the law of the English.

OF " BORHS."

1. That is, that every freeman have a true " borh,"
that the " borh " may present him to every justice, if
he should be accused. But if he be " tyht-bysig," let
him go to the threefold ordeal. If his lord say that
he has failed neither in oath nor ordeal since the
" gemot " was at " Bromdun "; let the lord take with
him two true thanes within the hundred, and swear
that never had oath failed him, nor had he paid " theof-
gyld "; unless he have the reeve who is competent to
do that. If then the oath succeed, let the man then
who is there accused choose whichever he will; either
single ordeal, or a pound-worth oath, within the three
hundreds, for above thirty pence. If they dare not
take the oath, let him go to the triple ordeal. If he
then be guilty; at the first time, let him make " bot "
to the accuser twofold; and to the lord, his " wer ";
and let him give true " borhs " that he will hereafter

---

*Ethelred, son of Edgar, succeeded to the throne, on the murder
of his brother Edward, in the year 978, and died in 1016.—*T.*

OF MERCHANT-SHIPS.

2. And let every merchant-ship have " frith " that comes withiu port, though it be a hostile ship, if it be not driven. And though it be driven, and it flee to any " frith-burh," and the men escape into the "burh," then let the men, and what they bring with them, have " frith."

OF THE KING'S " FRITH "-MEN.

3 And let every of our own " frith "-men have "frith," both by land and by water, both within port and without. If king Ethelred's " frith "-man come into "unfrith " land, and the army come thereto, let his ship and all his property have " frith." If he have drawn up his ship, or made a hut, or pitched a tent, let him and all his property have "frith." If he bear his property into a house, in common with the property of " unfrith "-men, let him forfeit his property, but himself have " frith " and life, if he make himself known. If the "frith "-man flee or fight, and will not make himself known; if he be slain, let him lie uncompensated.

IN CASE ANY ONE BE ROBBED IN A SHIP.

4. If any man be robbed of his property, and he knows by what ship, let the steersman give up the property; or let him go, with four others, and be the fifth himself, and make denial, and [declare] that he took it lawfully, as it was before agreed.

OF HOMICIDE.

5. If an Englishman slay a Dane, a freeman a freeman, let him pay for him with xxx. pounds, or let

the perpetrator be delivered up; and let the Dane do the same by an Englishman, if he slay him. If an Englishman slay a Danish thrall, let him pay for him with a pound; and so a Dane, in like manner, by an Englishman, if he slay him. If eight men be slain, that then is "frith"-breach, within a "burh" or without. Under eight men, let "bot" be made with the full "wer."

OF "FRITH"-BREACH WITHIN A "BURH."

6. If the "frith"-breach be committed within a "burh," let the inhabitants of the "burh" themselves go, and get the murderers, living or dead [or] their nearest kindred, head for head. If they will not, let the "ealdorman" go; if he will not, let the king go; if he will not, let the "ealdordom" lie in "unfrith."

Let every slaying, and every harrying, and every injury, that was committed before the "frith" was established, be disregarded; and let no man avenge them or ask for "bot." And that neither they nor we harbor the other's "Wealh," nor the other's thief, nor the other's foe.

OF ACCUSING A LANDSMAN.

7. And if it be said of a landsman that he has stolen cattle, or slain a man; and one shipman and one landsman say it; then let him not be entitled to any denial. And if their men slay our property, then shall they be outlaws, both to them and to us; and let them not be entitled to make any "bot." Twenty-two thousand pounds of gold and silver were given to the army in England for the "frith."

11

IN CASE ANY ONE ATTACH THAT WHICH HE HAD LOST.

8. If any one attach that which he had lost, let him with whom he attaches it declare whence it came to him; let him deliver it back, and appoint a "borh" that he will produce his warrantor at the place where it is claimed. If he vouch to warranty a living person, and he whom he vouches be in another shire; let him have as long a term as is requisite thereto. Let him deliver it up to the party who sold it to him, and desire that he clear, if he can. If he accept, he then clears him with whom it was first attached. Let him afterwards declare whence it came to him. If he declare over I. shire, let him have a term of I. week: if he declare over II. shires, let him have a term of II. weeks: if he declare over III. shires, let him have a term of III. weeks. Over as many shires as he declares, let him have a term of as many weeks. And let the parties always come to the place where it was first attached.

OF VOUCHINGS TO WARRANTY.

9. Formerly it stood, that everybody should vouch to warranty thrice where it was first attached, and afterwards should follow the warranty wherever it might be vouched. The "witan" then decreed, that it were better the warranty should always be made where it was first attached, until it could be known where it would stop; lest any one should cause a man of feeble means to toil too far and too long for his own. Let him toil the more, in whose hands lay the unjust gain, and less him who lawfully claims it. Let him also be cautious who attaches his own, that, at

every avowry, he have a true "borh," and let him
take care that he attach not wrongfully ; lest any one
annoy him as he thought to annoy another man.   If
any one vouch his warranty to a dead man (unless
he have heirs who will clear it), let him who vouches
it show by witness, if he can, that he justly makes
declaration ; and thereby let him clear himself. Then
will the dead be stigmatized, unless he have friends
who will legally clear him, as he himself should, if he
might, or were alive.   If then he have those friends,
who dare do so, then will the warranty fail, as well as
if he were alive, and made legal denial himself.   Then
will he be held guilty of theft, who had it in his possession ; for denial is always stronger than affirmation.
Likewise during the vouching to warranty ; if any
one accept, and make no further avowry, but will
possess it, this may not be refused, if true witness
make way for him to possession ; because possession
is always nearer to him who has than to him who
claims.

III.

These are the laws which king Ethelred and his
"witan" have decreed at Wantage, as "frith-bot."

1. That is : that his "grith" stand henceforth as it
originally stood in the days of his forefathers: that
that be "bot"-less which he shall give with his own
hand ; and for the "grith" which the "ealdorman"
and king's reeve, in the assembly of the five-burgs,
give, let "bot" be made with XII. hundred ; and for
the "grith" which is given in a "burh"-assembly, let

" bot " be made with VI. hundred; and for that which is given in a wapentake, let " bot " be made with a hundred, if it be broken; and for that which is given in an alehouse, let " bot " be made, for a dead man, with VI. half marks, and for a living one with XII. ores.

2. And that that which is declared with witness, no man pervert, either respecting the living or the dead. And let every one go to the witness of that which he dare swear, on the relic that is given into his hand.

3. And that "land-cop," and "hlaford's gifu," which he has rightfully to give, and " lah-cop," and " wit-word " and witness, stand so that no man pervert them: and that a " gemot " be held in every wapentake; and the XII. senior thanes go out, and the reeve with them, and swear on the relic that is given to them in hand, that they will accuse no innocent man, nor conceal any guilty one: and let them then take the " tiht-bysig " men who have to do with the reeve, and let each of them give a " wed " of VI. half marks, half to the " land-rica," and half to the wapentake; and let every one buy himself law with XII. ores, half to the " land-rica," half to the wapentake; and let every " tiht-bysig " man go to the threefold ordeal, or pay fourfold.

4. But if the lord be willing to clear him with two good thanes, that he had never paid " theof-gild " since the " gemot " was at " Bromdun," nor had he been accused; let him go to the single ordeal, or pay three-fold. If he then be foul, let him be smitten, so that his neck break; and if he avoid the ordeal, let him pay an "angylde" to the proprietor, and to the " land-rica " xx. ores, and go afterwards to the ordeal. And

if the proprietor will not attend the ordeal, let him pay xx. ores, and let his suit be lost; and let him, nevertheless, go to the ordeal, before the "land-rica," or pay twofold.

5. And if any one have cattle for which no " borh " has been given, and the "land-ricas" attach it; let him surrender the cattle, and pay xx. ores.

6. And let every accuser have power of whichever he will, whether water or iron; and let every vouching to warranty, and every ordeal, be in the king's " burh "; and if he flee from the ordeal, let the " borh " pay for him according to his " wer."

7. And if any one will clear a thief, let him deposit one c. as " wed," half to the " land-rica," and half to the king's reeve within port; and let him go to the threefold ordeal. If he be clean at the ordeal, let him take up his kinsman; but if he be foul, let him lie where he lay, and pay one c.

8. And let every moneyer, who is accused of striking false money since it was forbidden, go to the threefold ordeal; and if he be foul, let him be slain. And let no man have a moneyer, except the king. And let every moneyer who is accused buy him law with xii. ores.

9. And let no one slay an ox, except he have the witness of two true men, and that he keep for three nights the hide and the head; and the same with a sheep. And if he dispose of the hide before that, let him pay xx. ores.

10. And let every "flyma" be a "flyma" in every land, who is so in one.

11. And let no man have any " socn " over a king's thane, except the king himself.

12. And in a king's suit, let every man deposit a "wed" of VI. half marks; and in an "eorl's," and a bishop's, a "wed" of XII. ores; and in every thane's, a "wed" of VI. ores.

13. And if any man be accused of feeding the man who has broken our lord's "grith," let him clear himself with thrice XII.; and let the reeve name the "lad." And if any man take him about with him, let them both be worthy of one justice. And let doom stand where thanes are of one voice: if they disagree, let that stand which VIII. of them say. And let those who are there out-voted pay, each of them, VI. half marks. And where a thane has the choice of two things, love or law, and he then choose love, let that stand as firmly as the doom. And whoever after that permits a "lad," or whoever gives it, let him pay VI. half marks.

14. And he who sits, without contest or claim on his property, during life; that no one have an action against his heir after his day.

15. And he who robs a man by light day, and he declare it in three "tuns"; that he be not entitled to any "frith."

16. And the moneyers who work within a wood, or elsewhere; that they be liable in their lives, unless the king will be merciful to them.

IV.—*Not translated.*

V.

IN NOMINE DOMINI,
ANNO DOMINICÆ INCARNATIONIS M. VIII.

This is the ordinance that the king of the English, and both the ecclesiastical and lay "witan," have chosen and advised :

1. This then is first: that we all love and worship one God, and zealously hold one Christianity, and every heathenship totally cast out : and this we all have, both with word and with "wed," confirmed; that, under one kingship, we will observe one Christianity. And the ordinance of our lord and of his "witan " is; that just law be set up, and every unlawfulness carefully abolished ; and that every man be regarded as entitled to right; and that peace and friendship be lawfully observed, within this land, before God and before the world.

2. And the ordinance of our lord and of his " witan " is ; that Christian men, and uncondemned, be not sold out of the country, especially into a heathen nation: and be it zealously guarded against, that those souls perish not that Christ bought with his own life.

3. And the ordinance of our lord and of his " witan " is ; that Christian men, for all too little, be not condemned to death: but in general let mild punishments be decreed, for the people's need ; and let not for a little God's handywork and his own purchase be destroyed, which he dearly bought.

4. And the ordinance of our lord and of his " witan" is ; that men of every order readily submit, before God and before the world, each to that law which is

appropriate to him : and above all, let the servants of
God, bishops and abbots, monks and mynchens, priests
and nuns, submit to the law, and live according to
their rule, and fervently intercede for all Christian
people.

5. And the ordinance of our lord and of his "witan "
is ; that every monk who is out of minster, and
heeds no rule, do as it behoves him : let him willingly
retire into a minster, with all humility, and abstain
from misdeeds, and make " bot " very strictly for that
which he may have broken : let him be mindful of the
word and " wed " which he gave to God.

6. And let the monk who has no minster come to
the bishop of the diocese, and engage himself to God
and to men, that he three things especially thenceforth will observe ; that is, his chastity, and monkish
raiment, and to serve his Lord, as well as he best can :
and if he that perform, then is he worthy of being the
better respected, let him dwell where he may.

7. And let canons, where their benefice is, so that
they may have a refectory and a dormitory, keep
their minster rightly, and with purity, as their rule
may teach : or it is right that he forfeit the benefice
who will not do so.

8. And we pray and instruct all mass-priests, that
they secure themselves against the ire of God.

9. Full well they know, that they have not rightfully, through concubinage, intercourse with woman :
and let him who will abstain from this, and preserve
his chastity, have God's mercy ; and, in addition
thereto, for worldly honor, that he be worthy of
thane-" wer " and thane-right, both in life and in
the grave : and he who will not that which is befit-

ting his order, let his honor wane before God and before the world.

10. And also let every Christian man carefully eschew unlawful concubinage, and rightly observe the divine law. And let every church be in the "grith" of God, and of the king, and of all Christian people: and let no man henceforth reduce a church to servitude; nor unlawfully make church-mongering; nor turn out a church minister, without the bishop's counsel.

11. And let God's dues be willingly paid every year: that is, plough-alms, xv. days after Easter, and a tithe of young by Pentecost, and of earth-fruits by Allhallows' mass, and Rome-"feoh" by St. Peter's mass, and light-scot thrice in the year.

12. And it is most proper that soul-scot be always paid at the open grave: and if any corpse be laid out of its proper shrift-district elsewhere, let soul-scot be, nevertheless, paid to the minster to which it belonged; and let all God's dues be diligently furthered, as is needful, and let festivals and fasts be rightly held.

13. Let Sunday's festival be rightly kept, as is thereto becoming: and let marketings and folk-motes be carefully abstained from on that holy day.

14. And let all St. Mary's feast-tides be strictly honored; first with fasting, and afterwards with feasting: and at the celebration of every apostle, let there be fasting and feasting; except that on the festival of St. Philip and St. James we enjoin no fast, on account of the Easter festival.

15. Else, let other festivals and fasts be strictly observed, so as those observed them who best observed them.

16. And the "witan" have chosen, that St. Edward's mass-day shall be celebrated over all England on the xv. kal. April.

17. And to fast every Friday, unless it be a festival.

18. And ordeals and oaths are forbidden on festival-days, and on the regular Ember-days, and from Adventum Domini till the octaves of the Epiphany; and from Septuagesima till xv. days after Easter.

19. And at those holy tides, let there be, as is right, to all Christian men general peace and concord; and let every strife be appeased.

20. And if any one owe another "borh" or "bot," on account of secular matters, let him fulfill it willingly, before or after.

21. And let every widow, who conducts herself lawfully, be in God's "grith" and the king's: and let every one continue XII. months husbandless: afterwards let her choose what she herself will.

22. And let every Christian man do as is needful to him; let him strictly keep his Christianity, and accustom himself frequently to shrift; and fearlessly declare his sins, and earnestly pray as he may be instructed; and let every one prepare himself to go to housel oft and frequently: let every one direct himself and his words and works justly, and carefully keep his oath and "wed."

23. And let every injustice be carefully cast out from this country, as far as it can be done.

24. And let fraudulent deeds, and hateful illegalities, be earnestly shunned; that is, false weights, and wrongful measures, and lying witnesses, and shameful fightings.

25. And horrid perjuries and diabolic deeds, in

"morth "-works and in homicides, in thefts and in
plunderings, in avarice and covetousness, in gluttony
and drunkenness, in árts of fraud and in various
breaches of law, and in breaches of holy orders, and
in adulteries, and misdeeds of many kinds.

26. But let God's law be henceforth zealously
loved, by word and deed; then will God soon be merciful to this nation. And let "frithes-bot," and
"feos-bot," every-where in the country, and "burh-
bot" on every side, and "bric-bot," and the armaments also, be diligently attended to; according to
what is always prescribed, when there is need.

27. And with respect to naval armaments, as may
be most diligently; so that every one be stationed
immediately after Easter, every year.

28. And if any one without leave return from the
"fyrd" in which the king himself is, let it be at peril
of himself and all his estate; and he who else returns
from "fyrd" let him be liable in cxx. shillings.

29. And if any excommunicated man, unless it be
a "frith "-suppliant, dwell anywhere in the king's
proximity, before he has earnestly submitted to
divine "bot"; then be it at peril of himself, and of
all his property.

30. And if any one plot against the king's life, let
him be liable in his life; and if he desire to clear himself, let him do so according to the king's "wer-gild,"
or with threefold ordeal, by the law of the English.

31. And if any one anywhere commit "forsteal,"
or open opposition to the law of Christ or of the king;
let him pay either "wer" or "wite" or "lah-slit,"
always according as the deed may be: and if he resist
against right, by any violation of the law, and so act

that he be slain, let him lie uncompensated to all his friends.

32. And ever henceforth, let the illegalities be suppressed, which before this were commonly too widespread.

33. And let every illegality be carefully abolished; because through that it shall turn to some good in the country, that injustice be abolished, and righteousness loved, before God and before the world.

34. It is the duty of us all to love and worship one God, and strictly hold one Christianity, and totally cast out every kind of heathenism.

35. And let us faithfully support one royal lord, and all defend life and land together, as well as we best may; and to God Almighty pray for aid with inward heart.

VI.

COUNCIL OF ENHAM.
OF THE ORDINANCES OF THE "WITAN."

1. These are the ordinances which the councilors of the English selected and decreed, and strictly enjoined that they should be observed. And this then is first,—The primary ordinance of the bishops—that we all diligently turn from sins, as far as we can do so, and diligently confess our misdeeds, and strictly make "bot," and rightly love and worship one God, and unanimously hold one Christianity, and diligently eschew every heathenism, and diligently promote prayer among us, and diligently love peace and

concord, and faithfully obey one royal lord, and diligently support him, with right fidelity.

2. And it is the ordinance of the "witan," that
abbots and abbesses rightly order their own life, and
also wisely keep their flocks; and that men of every
order willingly submit, before God and before the
world, each to that law that is appropriate to him:
and especially, that God's servants, bishops and abbots, monks and mynchens, canons and nuns, turn to
right, and live according to rule, and intercede fervently for all Christian people.

3. And it is the ordinance of the "witan," that
every monk who is out of minster, and heeds no rule,
do as it behoves him; let him willingly retire into a
minster, with all humility, and abstain from misdeeds, and make "bot" very strictly for that which
he may have committed: and let him be mindful of
the word and "wed" which he gave to God. And let
the monk who has no minster come to the bishop of
the diocese, and engage himself to God and to men,
that he three things especially thenceforth will observe; that is, his chastity, and monkish raiment, and
to serve his Lord, as well as he best can: and if he
that perform, then is he worthy of being the better
respected, let him dwell where he may.

4. And that canons, where their benefice is, so that
they may have a refectory and a dormitory, keep
their minster with purity, as their rule may teach, or
as is right: and let him who will not so do forfeit the
benefice.

5. And all God's servants, and priests above all,
we beseech and enjoin, that they obey God, and love
chastity, and secure themselves against God's ire.

Full well they'know, that they have not rightfully, through any concubinage, intercourse with woman : but it is the worse, that some have two or more ; and one, though he had forsaken her whom he had previously, he, she being living, often takes another, as is not allowable for any Christian man to do: and let him who will refrain from this, and preserve his chastity, have God's mercy ; and, in addition thereto, for worldly honor, that he be worthy of thane-" wer," and thane-right, both in life and in the grave : and he who will not that which is fitting to his order, let his honor wane both before God and before the world.

6. And moreover we will beseech every friend, and all people also diligently teach, that they, with inward heart, love one God, and carefully shun every heathenism.

7. And if witches or soothsayers, magicians or whores, " morth "-workers or perjurers, be anywhere found in the country, let them diligently be driven out of this country, and this people be purified : or let them totally perish in the country, unless they desist, and the more deeply make " bot."

8. And it is the ordinance of the " witan," that just laws be established before God and before the world, and every illegality carefully abolished, and that every man henceforth, whether poor or rich, be considered worthy of " folk-right " ; and that peace and friendship be duly held, within this country, before God and before the world.

9. And it is the ordinance of the " witan," that Christian men, and uncondemned persons, be not sold out of the country, at least not into a heathen nation ;

but let it be carefully guarded against, that those
souls be not made to perish that Christ has bought
with his own blood.

10. And it is the ordinance of the "witan," that
Christian men be not, for altogether too little cause,
condemned to death; but in general let mild punishments be decreed, for the people's need; and let not
for a little God's own handywork, and his own purchase, be destroyed, which he dearly bought: but let
every deed be heedfully distinguished, and doom, according to the deed, be moderated in degree; so that
before God it be fitting, and before the world bear-
able. And let him who judges others bear in mind
very seriously what he himself desires, when he thus
speaks: " Et dimitte nobis debita nostra," et reliq.

11. And we direct very earnestly, that every Christian man carefully avoid unlawful concubinage, and
rightly observe Christian law.

12. And let it never be, that a Christian man marry
within the relationship of VI. persons, in his own kin,
that is within the fourth degree; nor with the relict
of him who was so near in worldly relationship; nor
with the wife's relation, whom he before had had.
Nor with any hallowed nun, nor with his god-mother,
nor with one divorced, let any Christian man ever
marry; nor have more wives than one, but be with
that one, as long as she may live; whoever will
rightly observe God's law, and secure his soul from
the burning of hell.

13. And let every church be in God's "grith," and
in the king's, and in all Christian people's.

14. And let every church-"grith" within walls,
and the king's "hand-grith," be equally inviolate.

15. And let no man henceforth reduce a church to servitude, nor unlawfully make church-mongering, nor turn out a church minister, without the bishop's counsel.

16. And let God's dues be lawfully and willingly paid every year; that is, plough-alms, at least, xv. days after Easter.

17. And a tithe of young by Pentecost, and of earth-fruits by Allhallows' mass.

18. And Rome-"feoh" by St. Peter's mass, and church-scot by Martinmass.

19. And light-scot thrice in the year.

20. And it is most proper that soul-scot be always paid at the open grave.

21. And if any corpse be laid out of its proper district elsewhere, then let the soul-scot be, nevertheless, paid to the minster to which it belonged : and let all God's dues be willingly furthered, as is needful.

22. And let festivals and fasts be rightly kept. Let Sunday's festival be rightly kept, as is thereto becoming : and let marketings, and folk-motes, and huntings, and worldly works, be strictly abstained from on that holy day. And let all St. Mary's solemn feast-tides be strictly honored, first with fasting, and afterwards with festival: and at the celebration of every apostle let strict fast be held, except that on the festival of St. Philip and St. James we enjoin no fast, on account of the Easter festival, unless any one will : else let other festivals and fasts be strictly observed, so as those observed them who best observed them.

23. And ember-days and fasts, so as St. Gregory himself prescribed to the English nation.

24. And let fast be kept every Friday, unless it be a festival.

25. And ordeals, and oaths, and marriages, are always forbidden on high festival days and on the regular ember-days ; and from Adventum Domini till the octaves of the Epiphany; and from Septuagesima till xv. days after Easter. And at those holy tides, let there be, as it is right, to all Christian men, general peace and concord, and let every strife be appeased : and if any one owe another "borh" or "bōt" on account of secular matters, let him willingly fulfill it to him, before or after.

26. And let every widow, who conducts herself lawfully, be in God's "grith," and the king's, and let every one continue xii. months husbandless ; afterwards let her choose what she herself will.

27. And let every Christian man do as is needful to him ; let him strictly keep his Christianity, and accustom himself frequently to shrift, and fearlessly declare his sins, and earnestly pray, as he may be instructed ; and let every one who will understand his own need also prepare himself to go to housel, at least thrice in the year, so as it is requisite for him.

28. And let every friend direct his words and works aright, and heedfully keep his oath and " wed "; and let every injustice be carefully cast out from this country, as far as it can be done. And let fraudulent deeds, and hateful illegalities, be earnestly shunned ; that is, false weights, and wrongful measures, and lying witnesses, and shameful fightings, and foul fornications, and horrid perjuries, and diabolic deeds, in " morth "-works and in homicides, in thefts and in plunderings, in cravings and in rapaciousness,

12

in gluttony and in drunkenness, in arts of fraud
and in various breaches of law, in adulteries and
in breaches of holy orders, in breaches of festivals and
in breaches of fasts, in sacrileges, and in misdeeds of
many kinds.

29. And let it be well understood, that all such are
to be censured, and never to be loved.

30. But let God's law be henceforth zealously
loved, by word and deed; then will God soon be
merciful to this nation.

31. Let us also all very earnestly deliberate concerning " frithes-bot," and concerning " feos-bot."

32. So concerning " frithes-bot," as may be best to
the proprietor and most hostile to the thief. And so
concerning " feos-bot," that one money go over all the
nation, without any counterfeit. And let weights
and measures be carefully rectified; and every illegality be henceforth avoided. And let " burh-bots "
and " bric-bots " be commenced on every side, and the
armaments also, and naval armaments, in like manner,
always when there may be necessity; so that the
common need be provided for.

33. And it will be prudent, that, every year, immediately after Easter, ships of war be made ready.

34. And if any one of the people injure a ship of
war, let him strictly make " bot " for it, and to the
king the " mund ": and if any one so injure it that it
be useless, let him pay for it fully, and to the king
the " mund-bryce."

35. And if any one return from the " fyrd," in which
the king himself is, without leave, let him peril his
estate.

36. And if " morth "-workers, or perjurers, or no-

torious homicides, are so daring, that they dwell in the king's proximity, before they shall have undertaken "bot," before God and before the world, then let them peril their estate and all their possessions; unless they are "frith"-suppliants.

37. And if any one plot against the king's life, let him be liable in his life, and in all that he owns, if it be proved against him : and if he desire to clear himself, and may, let him do so with the most solemn oath, or with threefold ordeal, by the law of the English; and by the law of the Danes, according as their law may be.

38. And if any one, against the law of Christ or of the king, commit "forsteal" anywhere, let him pay "wer" or "wite," as the deed may be: and if he resist, and himself so do that any one slay him, let him lie uncompensated.

39. And if any one defile a nun, or force a widow, let him make "bot" for that deeply, before God and before the world.

40. And let it ever be considered, in every way, how methods may chiefly be devised for the behoof of the nation, and true Christianity best exalted, and every illegality most effectually suppressed : because through that it shall turn to some good in the country, that injustice be abolished, and righteousness loved, before God and before the world.

41. Now we will also earnestly instruct God's ministers, that at least they carefully consider themselves, and, with the succor of God, love chastity, and strictly attend to their books and prayers, and daily and nightly, oft and frequently, call to Christ, and earnestly pray for all Christian people.

42. We will also yet earnestly admonish every friend, as it is our duty frequently to do, that every one earnestly consider himself, and that he earnestly turn from sins, and that he correct other men for injustice, and that above all other things he love his Lord, and that he oft and frequently have in mind that of which it is most needful oftenest to remind men; that is, that they unanimously have orthodox belief in the true God, who is ruler and maker of all creatures; and that they rightly hold orthodox Christianity, and that they willingly obey the divine instructors, and willingly follow God's doctrines and laws; and that they everywhere willingly maintain the " grith " and " frith " of God's churches, and frequently greet them with light and with offerings, and that they there earnestly pray to Christ.

43. And that they lawfully render God's dues every year, and rightly hold festivals and fasts.

44. And that they strictly abstain from Sunday marketings and popular meetings.

45. And that they always defend and honor God's ministers.

46. And that they comfort and feed God's poor.

47. And that they do not too often oppress widows and step-children, but willingly gladden them.

48. And that they do not vex or provoke foreigners or comers from afar.

49. And that they do not altogether too much command injustice to other men; but that every man enjoin to others that justice which he desires shall be enjoined to him, according as it is reasonable; and that is very just law.

50. And he who anywhere henceforth shall corrupt

just laws, either of God or of men, let him strictly make " bot " for it, in whatever manner is fitting, as well with divine " bot " as with secular correction.

51. And if for a " god-bot " a pecuniary " bot " shall arise, so as wise secular " witan " may have established as a penalty, that belongs lawfully, by the direction of the bishops, to the buying of prayers, to the behoof of the poor, and to the reparation of churches, and to the instruction and to the clothing and to the feeding of those who minister to God, and for books, and for bells, and for church-garments; and never for worldly idle pomp, but as a secular correction for divine purposes, sometimes as " wite," sometimes as " wer-gyld," sometimes as " hals-fang," sometimes as " lah-slit "; sometimes in estate, sometimes in goods; and sometimes in more, sometimes in less.

52. And ever, as any one shall be more powerful here in the eyes of the world, or, through dignities, higher in degree, so shall he the more deeply make " bot " for sins, and pay for every misdeed the more dearly; because the strong and the weak are not alike, and cannot raise a like burthen; no more than the unhale is like to the hale: moderation is therefore to be used; and discreetly are to be distinguished, both in divine shrifts and in secular corrections, age and youth, rich and poor, hale and unhale, and every order. And if it be, that any one unwillingly or unintentionally do anything amiss, he shall not be like to him who misdoes intentionally and of his own will: and also he who is an involuntary doer of that which he misdoes, he is ever worthy of protection and of the better doom, because he was an involuntary doer of that which he did.

53. Let every deed be carefully distinguished, and doom ever be guided justly, according to the deed, and be modified according to its degree, before God and before the world; and let mercy be shown, for dread of God, and kindness be willingly shown, and those be somewhat protected who need it; because we all need that our Lord oft and frequently grant his mercy to us. Amen.

VII.

OF "GRITH" AND OF "MUND."

1. God's "grith" is of all "griths" the most excellent to deserve, and most earnestly to be preserved; and next thereto, the king's.

2. Then it is right that God's church-"grith," within walls, and a Christian king's hand-"grith," stand equally inviolate.

3. And formerly the chief places and exalted degrees were entitled to great dignity and "mund," and could give "griith" to those who needed it, and sought it, always according to the dignity which appertained thereto: and thus it stood in those days among the English,

4. That if a man who had forfeited his life sought the king, the archbishop, or the "ætheling"; then had he nine days "grith," for the saving of his life; unless the king would grant him a longer period.

5. And if he sought a suffragan bishop, or an "ealdorman," or an exalted chief place; then had he VII. days "grith"; unless a longer should be granted him.

6. And in the law of the Kentish people, the king

and the archbishop possess a like and equally dear "mund-bryce."

7. And in those laws, the archbishop's property is to be compensated elevenfold, and the king's, ninefold.

8. And the "mund-byrd" of Christ's church is the same as the king's.

9. And in the South-Angles' law, "grith"-law stands thus: that if any one fight in a church, or in the king's house; then let all he possesses be condemned, and let it be in the king's power whether he have life or not.

10. And if any one fight in a minster without a church, let him make "bot" for all, with full "bot," which thereto appertains, according to the rank of the minster.

11. And if any one, in any other way, commit the king's "mund-bryce," let him make "bot" for it with v. pounds, by the law of the English; an archbishop's and an "ætheling's" "mund-bryce,' with three pounds; another bishop's and an "ealdorman's," with II. pounds.

12. And if any one engage in a fight in the presence of an "ætheling" or an archbishop, let him make "bot" with CL. shillings: if in presence of another bishop or an "ealdorman" this happen, let him make "bot" with C. shillings.

13. And in the North-Angles' law it stands, that he who slays any one within church walls shall be liable in his life; and he who wounds shall be liable in his hand; and let him who slays any one within church doors give to the church CXX. shillings, according to the North-Angles' law.

14. And let a freeman who harms a living person in his "mund-byrd" pay xxx. shillings.

15. And he who fights or steals in the king's "burh," or in his proximity, shall be liable in his life; unless the king will allow him to be redeemed by his "wergild."

16. And if a man who has forfeited his life seek a sanctuary, and thereby gain refuge for his life; let there then be one of three for his life, unless he obtain remission more favorably; "wer-gild," perpetual thralldom, imprisonment.

17. And be it of these three whichever it may; whether he pay, whether he serve, or whether he suffer; let him find "borh," if he can; and if he cannot, then let him swear, that he will never neither steal, nor bear away cattle, nor avenge his punishment.

18. And if he belie any of these, let him proceed nowhere again for his life, nor gain refuge.

19. Let "hælnes-grith" and "had-grith" be lawfully observed, always very strictly; and God's laws followed, and teachers listened to, as is becoming thereto. Bishops are heralds, and teachers of God's law; and they shall fervently, oft and frequently, call to Christ, and mediate diligently for all Christian people; and they shall preach and diligently set example, for the religious behoof of a Christian nation.

20. For him who scorns to listen to them, let that be only between him and God himself.

21. But there are some men who on account of their pride, and also on account of birth, scorn to obey divine superiors, as they ought to do, if they desired right; and often apply themselves to blame what they ought to praise, and account the worse, for

their humble birth, those whose forefathers were not
in the world either wealthy or proud, through worldly
splendor, nor, in this transient space of life, flourish-
ing or powerful: but these are neither wise nor
wholly discreet, who will not obey God, nor better
understand, how often he has from little raised to
great, those who obeyed him and justly spake. We
know that through God's grace a thrall has become a
thane, and a "ceorl" has become an "eorl," a singer
a priest, and a scribe a bishop.

22. And formerly, so as God decreed, a shepherd
became a king, and he was very great: also, so as God
decreed, a fisher became a bishop, and he was very
dear and acceptable to Christ.

23. Such are the gifts of God, who can easily from
little raise to great, all that he himself will, so as the
psalmist truly said, when he thus sang: Quis sicut
Dominus Deus noster, etc., suscitans a terra inopem,
et de stercore erigens pauperem, ut collocet eum cum
principibus, cum principibus populi sui: he under-
stands those that have fear of God, and heed wisdom.

24. And wise were also in former days those
secular "witan" who first added secular laws to the
just divine laws, for bishops and consecrated bodies;
and reverenced, for love of God, sanctity, and the
sacred orders; and God's houses and God's servants
firmly protected.

25. And in what, indeed, can ever any man in the
world worship God more zealously than in churches
and in sanctuaries, and besides, in the sacred high
orders.

26. And, oh! with what thought can any man, indeed, so do, that he fervently pray in church, and zeal-

ously bow to God's altars, and before or after, within or without, plunder the church, and corrupt or impair that which to the church belongs.

27. Or with what thought can any man ever think in his mind, that he inclines his head to the priests, and desires blessing, and attends their masses in church, and kisses their hand at the passing of the bread, and then straightway thereafter should injure or revile them by word or deed.

28. But sanctity and sacred orders, and the hallowed houses of God, shall always be zealously venerated, for dread of God, and God, with inward heart, be ever loved.

29. And it is also much needful to every man, that he enjoin to others that justice which he desires shall be enjoined to him, according as his condition may be.

30. We have all one Heavenly Father, and one spiritual mother, which is called "Ecclesia"; that is God's church; and, therefore, are we brothers.

31. And then it is also just, that each of us observe justice towards another; and that every church be always in the "grith" of God Almighty, and of all Christian people; because every church-"grith" is Christ's own "grith," and every Christian has great need that he hold in great respect that "grith."

VIII.—*Not translated.*

IX.

ANNO M.XIIII. AB INCARNATIONE DOMINI NOSTRI JESU CHRISTI.

OF CHURCH–" GRITH."

1. This is one of the ordinances which the king of the English composed with the counsel of his " witan. " That is first: that he will that all God's churches be entitled to full " grith " ; and if ever any man henceforth so violate God's church-" grith," that he be a homicide within church walls, then be that " botless " ; and let every one of those who are friends to God pursue him ; unless it happen that he escape thence, and seek so awful a sanctuary, that the king through that grant him life, against full " bot," both to God and to men.

2. And that then is first, that he pay his own " wer " to the king and to Christ, and thereby inlaw himself to " bot " : because a Christian king is accounted Christ's vicegerent among Christian people, and his duty is to avenge offense to Christ very severely.

3. And if it then come to " bot," and the king allow it, then let " bot " be made for the church-" grith " to that church, according to the king's full " mund-bryce " ; and let purification of the minster be gotten, as is thereto befitting ; and especially let intercession be fervently made with God.

4. And if else, no man being slain, church-" grith " be broken, let " bot " be strictly made, as the deed may be : be it through fighting, be it through robbery, be it through fornication, be it through what it may ; first, let " bot " be made for the " grith-bryce " to the

church, as the deed may be, and as the rank of the church may be.

5. All churches are not secularly entitled to equal rank, although divinely they have like consecration. For the "grith-bryce" of a chief minster, in cases entitled to "bot," let "bot" be made according to the king's "mund," that is, with v. pounds by English law; and of a minster of the middle class, with a hundred and twenty shillings, that is, according to the king's "wite": but of a yet less, with sixty shillings; and for a field church, with xxx. shillings. Judgment shall ever be with justice, according to the deed, and mitigation according to its degree.

6. And respecting tithe; the king and his "witan" have chosen and decreed, as is just, that one third part of the tithe which belongs to the church go to the reparation of the church, and a second part to the servants of God; the third to God's poor, and to needy ones in thralldom.

7. And be it known to every Christian man, that he pay to his Lord his tithe justly, always as the plough traverses the tenth field, on peril of God's mercy, and of the full "wite," which king Edgar decreed; that is:

8. If any one will not justly pay the tithe, then let the king's reeve go, and the mass-priest of the minster, or of the "land-rica," and the bishop's reeve, and take forcibly the tenth part for the minster to which it is due, and assign to him the ninth part; and let the eight parts be divided into two, and let the landlord take possession of half, half the bishop; be it a king's man, be it a thane's.

9. And let every tithe of young be paid by Pente-

cost, on pain of the " wite " ; and of earth-fruits by the equinox, or, at all events, by Allhallows' mass.

10. And let Rome-"feoh" be paid every year by St. Peter's mass; and let him who will not pay it give in addition xxx. pence, and to the king pay cxx. shillings.

11. And let church-scot be paid by Martinmass; and let him who does not pay it indemnify it with twelvefold, and cxx. shillings to the king.

12. Plough-alms, it is fitting that they be paid, on pain of the "wite," every year, when xv. days are passed after Easter-tide; and let light-scot be paid at Candlemass; let him do it oftener who will.

13. And it is most proper that soul-scot be always paid at the open grave.

14. And let all God's dues be furthered diligently, as is needful.

15. And if any one refuse that, let him be compelled to what is right by secular correction ; and let that be in common to Christ, and to the king, as it formerly was.

16. And let festivals and fasts be rightly held, on peril of the " wite."

17. And let Sunday marketings be strictly forbidden, on peril of full secular " wite."

18. And let the rank of the servants of the altar be respected for fear of God.

19. If a mass-priest, living according to rule, be accused in a simple suit, let him celebrate mass, if he dare, and clear himself on the housel, himself alone : and in a triple suit, let him clear himself, if he dare, likewise on the housel, with two of his fellow ecclesiastics.

20. If a deacon, living according to rule, be accused in a simple suit, let him take two of his fellow ecclesiastics, and clear himself with them : and if he be accused in a triple suit, let him take six of his fellow ecclesiastics, and clear himself with them, and be himself the seventh.

21. And if a secular mass-priest be charged with an accusation, who follows no life of rule, let him clear himself so as a deacon, who lives a life of rule.

22. If a friendless servant of the altar be charged with an accusation, who has no supporters to his oath ; let him go to the "corsnæd," and then thereat fare as God will, unless he may clear himself on the housel.

23. And if any one charge one in holy orders with "fæhthe," and say that he was a perpetrator or adviser of homicide, let him clear himself with his kinsmen, who must bear the "fæhthe" with him, or make "bot" for it.

24. And if he be kinless, let him clear himself with his associates, or fast for "corsnæd"; and thereat fare as God may ordain.

25. And no minster-monk may anywhere lawfully demand "fæhthe-bot," nor pay "fæhthe-bot": he forsakes his law of kin when he submits to monastic law.

26. If a mass-priest become a homicide, or otherwise flagrantly commit crime, let him then forfeit both his order and his country, and be an exile as far as the pope may prescribe to him, and strictly do penance.

27. If a mass-priest stand anywhere in false witness, or in perjury ; or be cognizant and perpetrator

of thefts; let him then be cast out from the community of ecclesiastics, and forfeit both their society and friendship and every dignity; unless he the more deeply make " bot " to God and men, entirely as the bishop may direct him; and find himself " borh, " that thenceforth he will ever abstain from the like: and if he desire to clear himself, let him clear himself according to the degree of the deed, either with a threefold or with a simple " lad, " according as the deed may be.

28. If a servant of the altar, by the instruction of books, his own life rightly order, then let him be entitled to the full " wer " and dignity of a thane, both in life and in the grave.

29. And if he misorder his life, let his honor wane, according as the deed may be.

30. Let him know, if he will, that it befits him not to have any concern either with woman or with temporal war; if he desire uprightly to obey God, and observe God's laws, as is properly becoming to his order.

31. And we earnestly instruct, and affectionately beseech, that men of every order live that life which is becoming to them: and we will that henceforth abbots and monks live more according to rule than before this they had in custom.

32. And the king commands all his reeves, in every place, that ye protect the abbots on all secular occasions, as ye best may; and as ye desire to have God's or my friendship, that ye aid their stewards everywhere to right; that they themselves may the more uninterruptedly dwell closely in their minsters, and live according to rule.

33. And if any one wrong an ecclesiastic or a foreigner, through any means, as to money or as to life; or bind, or beat, or insult him in any way; then shall the king be unto him in the place of a kinsman and of a protector, unless he else have another.

34. And let "bot" be made both to him and to the king, as is fitting, according as the deed may be; or let him avenge the deed very deeply.

35. It is very justly incumbent on Christian men, that they very diligently avenge any offense against God.

36. And wise were those secular "witan" who to the divine laws of right added secular laws, for the people's government; and directed the "bot" to Christ and the king, that many should thus of necessity be compelled to right.

37. But in those "gemots," though deliberately held in places of note, after Edgar's lifetime, the laws of Christ waned, and the king's laws were impaired.

38. And then was separated what was before in common to Christ and the king in secular government; and it has ever been the worse before God and before the world: let it now come to an amendment, if God will it.

39. And an amendment, however, may yet come, if it be diligently and earnestly undertaken.

40. And if any one will properly cleanse the land, then must he inquire and diligently trace where the criminals have their dwelling, who will not desist, nor make "bot" before God; but wherever they may be found, let them be compelled to right, willingly or unwillingly; or let them altogether withdraw from the country, unless they submit and turn to right.

41. If a monk or a mass-priest become altogether an apostate, let him be for ever excommunicated, unless he the more readily submit to his duty.

42. And he who holds an outlaw of God in his power over the term that the king may have appointed, he acts, at peril of himself and all his property, against Christ's vicegerent, who preserves and sways over Christianity and kingdom as long as God grants it.

43. But let us do as is needful to us; let us take to us for an example that which former secular " witan " deliberately instituted; Æthelstan, and Edmund, and Edgar who was last: how they worshiped God, and observed God's law, and rendered God's tribute, the while that they lived. And let us love God with inward heart, and heed God's laws, as well as we best can.

44. And let us zealously venerate right Christianity, and totally despise every heathenism; and let us faithfully cherish one royal lord, and let every friend love his fellow with right fidelity, and cherish him with justice.

There is something of liberality in the spirit of Ethelred's laws. Yet the brutal superstition of trials by ordeal prevailed in their highest pretensions during this reign. There seems to be some conceptions of justice between man and man expressed in these laws, yet the clearance from charges of crime, through compurgators, was continued as in the earlier ages. The method of trial seems to have been this: The accused went into court and swore to his innocence of the offenses charged against him; if he could then bring the number of compurgators prescribed, which varied as their rank varied, who would swear to his good character and that they believed his oath, he so cleared himself of the charge. There were cases in which facts were inquired into, as in cases of vouching to warranty in the title to cattle and other personal property, but the judgment in such cases was limited to the retention or surrender of the property. Unless theft was developed by the inquiry, no personal punishment followed. The detailed method of vouching to warranty shows the very limited extent of commerce. The compounding of felonies for " bot " or fines must have had a corrupting influence on a government with an empty treasury. Especially the compounding for ordeals must have converted this method of trial into a squeezing process to replenish the national finances.

It is a difficult problem, in considering the laws of this reign, whether the Christianity of the times mitigated the severity of the laws or increased it. When the public imposts, secular and religious, were all regularly and faithfully paid, the government seemed to have a fatherly interest in the welfare of its subjects. It sought to enforce what it esteemed a high morality and purity of life ; especially on the part of the clergy. And yet from the offenses described and the penalties enacted the lower orders of the clergy were a degenerate, vile crowd. The higher clergy had become ministers of state, and as such seemed to appreciate character in morals and the real public interests of the country. The ecclesiastical laws of this reign have the features of decretals of the ecclesiastical authority.

ORDINANCE
RESPECTING THE "DUN-SETAS."

This is the ordinance which the "witan" of the English race and the counselors of the "Wealh" nation established among the "Dun-setas"; that is:

OF THE TRACING OF STOLEN CATTLE.

1. If any one pursue the track of stolen cattle from one "stæth" to another, then let him commit the tracing to the men of the country, or show by some mark that it is rightfully pursued. Let him then take to it who owns the land, and have the inquiry to himself, and IX. days afterwards compensate for the cattle, or deposit an " under-wed " on that day, which shall be worth half as much again as the cattle; and in IX. days from that time let him redeem the " wed" by lawful payment. If it be said that the track is wrongfully pursued, then must he who traces the cattle lead to the " stæth," and there himself one of six unchosen men, who are true, make oath that he according to folk-right makes lawful claim on the land, as his cattle went thereup.

OF DOING JUSTICE BETWEEN "WEALHS" AND ENGLISH.

2. It is meet always after IX. days, between the " stæths," that one man do justice to another, both with respect to " lad " and in every suit that may be between them. There stands no other " lad " in an ac-

cusation, save the ordeal, between "Wealas" and Englishmen, unless it be allowed. From either "stæth" to the other a pledge must be given, unless justice may be got in any other way.

OF PLEDGES.

3. If a pledge be taken on a man's cattle for another man's account, then let him for whose account it is taken get the pledge home, or let him satisfy from his own property him who owns the cattle. Then he must needs do right who before would not. XII. "lahmen" shall explain the law to the "Wealas" and English, VI. English and VI. "Wealas." Let them forfeit all they possess, if they explain it wrongly; or clear themselves that they knew no better.

OF HIM WHO FAILS IN A "LAD."

4. Though, in an accusation of theft, a "lad" fail to an Englishman or to a "Wealh," let him pay the "angylde" [only] of that with which he was charged. Of the other "gild" nothing, no more than of the "wite."

OF HOMICIDE.

5. If a "Wealh" slay an Englishman, he need not pay for him on this side except with half his "wer"; no more than an Englishman for a "Wealh" on that side; be he thane-born, be he "ceorl"-born: one half of the "wer" in that case falls away.

IN CASE AN ENGLISHMAN JOURNEY INTO "WYLISC" LAND.

6. Neither is to travel, neither a "Wealh" in the English land any more than an Englishman in the

"Wylisc," without the appointed man of the country, who shall receive him at the "stæth," and bring him thither again without guile. If the man of the country be cognizant of any guile, then let him be liable in the "wite," unless he clear himself of that cognizance. So also let every one who is cognizant or perpetrator, where an outlandish man injures an inlandish one, clear himself of that privity, according to the value of the property ; and let that be a "cyre-ath " : and he who charges him, let him begin his suit with a " for-ath." If the " lad " fail, let him pay two-fold, and to the lord his " wite."

OF THE WORTH OF ALL CATTLE, IF IT BE LOST.

7. A horse shall be paid for with xxx. shillings, or an expurgation after that rate ; a mare with xx. shillings, or after that rate ; and a " winter-steal " the same : a "wilde-weorf " with xii. shillings, or after that rate ; and an ox with xxx. pence ; a cow with xxiv. pence ; a swine with viii. pence ; a man with a pound; a sheep with i. shilling ; a goat with ii. pence. Other unseen things may be estimated on oath, and then paid for accordingly.

OF CATTLE ATTACHED OVER THE STREAM.

8. If cattle be attached, and the party will vouch to warranty over the stream ; then let him place an " in-borh " or deposit an " under-wed," that the suit may have an end. Let him who claims it make an oath, himself one of six, that as he claims it so it was stolen from him ; and let him who vouches to warranty make an oath alone, that he vouches to warranty the person who sold it to him. If one beyond

the stream will lay claim to it, then must that be with ordeal. Like to that shall an Englishman do justice to a " Wealh."

OF "WENT–SÆTAS " AND " DUN–SÆTAS."

9. Formerly the " Went-sætas " belonged to the " Dun-sætas," but more properly they belong to the West Saxons: there they shall give tribute and hostages. The " Dun-sætas " also need, if the king grant it to them, that at least " frith "-hostages be allowed them.

THE LAWS OF KING CNUT.*

ECCLESIASTICAL.

This is the ordinance that king Cnut, king of all England, and king of the Danes and Norwegians, decreed, with counsel of his " witan," to the praise of God, and to the honor and behoof of himself: and that was at the holy tide of Midwinter, at Winchester.

1. That then is first, that, above all other things, they should ever love and worship one God, and unanimously observe one Christianity, and love king Cnut with strict fidelity.

2. And to hold in "grith" and in "frith," and fre-

---

* CNUT, or CANUTE, THE DANE.—Cnut, the King of Denmark, became monarch of all England in the year 1017, and died, after a reign of about eighteen years, in 1035. He seems to have been interested in the externals of Christianity, and was an intelligent king and, for his day, an able statesman. He assembled a parliament or witan before whom he proclaimed laws in the interests of the church and affecting the secular interests of the kingdom. The latter, being a part of the civil laws of the times, are in the order of our discussions. Cnut governed England as a conqueror, but there are very few of the features of despotism in his laws. Many of them had been of force in the kingdom for centuries. As I embody them at length in the text it will be seen that they contrast favorably with the brutal barbarisms brought into the country by William the Conqueror half a century later. Cnut was better than many of the Saxon kings, still he governed England chiefly under Anglo-Saxon laws. Yet there were perpetuated in his reign the three barbarisms of trial by compurgators, trial by ordeal, and trial by battle.

quently to seek God's churches, for the salvation of
souls and the behoof of ourselves. Every church is
by right in Christ's own "grith," and every Christian man has great need that he show great reverence for that " grith " ; because God's " grith " is of
all " griths " the most excellent to merit, and the
best to preserve, and next thereto, the king's. Then
is it very right, that God's church-" grith " within
walls, and a Christian king's hand-" grith " stand
equally inviolate ; and let him who infringes either
forfeit land and life, unless the king will be merciful
to him. And if ever any man henceforth so break
God's church-" grith," that he be a homicide within
church-walls, then be that " botless " ; and let every
one of them who is a friend to God pursue him ; unless it happen that he escape thence, and seek so awful a sanctuary, that the king through that grant him
life against full " bot," both to God and to men. And
that is then first : that he pay his own " wer " to
Christ and to the king, and thereby inlaw himself to
" bot " : and if it then come to " bot," and the king
allow it, then let " bot " be made for the church-
" grith " to that church, according to the king's full
" mund-bryce," and the purification of the minster be
gotten, as is thereto befitting ; and let " bot " be
fully made, both with " mæg-bot," and man-" bot,"
and especially let intercession be fervently made
with God.

3. And if else, no man being slain, church-" grith "
be broken, let " bot " be strictly made, according as
the deed may be : be it through fighting, be it through
robbery, be it through what it may be. First, let
" bot " be made for the " grith-bryce " to the church,

according as the deed may be, and as the rank of the church may be. All churches are not secularly entitled to a like degree of reverence, although divinely they have like consecration. The "grith-bryce" of a chief minster, in cases entitled to "bot," is according to the king's "mund," that is, v. pounds by English law ; and in Kent, for the "mund-bryce," v. pounds to the king, and three to the archbishop : and of a minster of the middle class, cxx. shillings, that is, according to the king's "wite": and of one yet less, where there is little service, provided there be a burial place, lx. shillings : and of a field church, where there is no burial place, thirty shillings.

4. It is very justly incumbent on all Christian men, that they very strictly observe "grith" and "frith" toward holy things, and holy orders, and the hallowed houses of God ; and that they reverence every holy order, according to its rank : because (understand who is willing or able) much and great is that which the priest has to do, for the behoof of the people, if he justly please his Lord. Much is the supplication, and great is the hallowing which sendeth away devils and putteth them to flight, as often as baptism is performed or housel hallowed: and holy angels hover there around and protect the deeds, and, through God's powers, support the priests, as often as they rightly minister to Christ ; and so they always do, as often as they earnestly, with inward heart, call to Christ, and fervently intercede for behoof of the people ; and therefore, for fear of God, rank is discreetly to be acknowledged in holy orders.

5. And if it happen that a priest who lives according to rule be charged with an accusation and with

evil practices, and he know himself innocent thereof;
let him celebrate mass if he dare, and himself clear
himself on the housel, in a simple suit: and in a threefold suit, let him also, if he dare, clear himself on the
housel with two of his fellow ecclesiastics. If a deacon, living according to rule, be accused in a simple
suit, let him take two of his fellow ecclesiastics, and
with them clear himself: and if he be accused in a
threefold suit, let him take VI. of his fellow ecclesiastics, and with them clear himself, and be himself the
seventh. If a secular mass-priest be charged with an
accusation, who has no regular life, let him clear himself as a deacon who lives a life of rule: and if a
friendless servant of the altar be charged with an accusation, who has no support to his oath, let him go
to the " corsnæd," and then thereat fare as God will,
unless he may clear himself on the housel. And if a
man in orders be charged with " fæhthe," and it be
said, that he was perpetrator or adviser of homicide,
let him clear himself with his kinsmen, who must bear
the " fæhthe " with him, or make " bot " for it: and
if he be kinless, let him clear himself with his associates, or betake himself to fasting, if that be necessary, and go to the " corsnæd," and thereat fare so as
God may ordain : and no minster-monk may lawfully
anywhere demand " fæhth-bot," nor pay " fæhth-bot."
He forsakes his law of kin when he submits to monastic law. And if ever a mass-priest stand anywhere
in false witness or in perjury, or be cognizant and
perpetrator of thefts, then let him be cast from the
community of ecclesiastics, and forfeit both their society and friendship and every dignity; unless he the
more deeply make " bot " to God and men, as the

bishop may direct him, and find himself " borh," that
henceforth he will ever abstain from the like. And
if he desire to clear himself, then let him clear himself according to the degree of the deed, either with a
threefold or with a simple " lad," according as the
deed may be.

6. And we will, that men of every order readily
submit, each to that law which is becoming to him;
and above all, let the servants of God, bishops and
abbots, monks and mynchens, canons and nuns, submit to law, and live according to rule, and by day
and by night, oft and frequently, call to Christ, and
fervently intercede for all Christian people. And we
beseech and instruct all God's servants, and especially priests, that they obey God and love chastity,
and secure themselves against God's ire, and against
the fierce burning which rageth in hell. Full well
they know, that they have not lawfully through concubinage intercourse with woman; and let him who
will abstain from this, and preserve his chastity, have
God's mercy, and, for worldly honor, be he worthy of
thane-law. And let every Christian man also, for
dread of his Lord, strictly eschew unlawful concubinage, and rightly observe the divine law.

7. And we instruct and beseech and, in God's
name, command, that no Christian man ever marry
in his own family within the relationship of VI. persons: nor with the relict of his kinsman who was so
near of kin ; nor with the relative of the wife whom
he had previously had ; nor with his godmother, nor
with a hallowed nun, nor with one divorced, let any
Christian man ever marry, nor any fornication anywhere commit; nor have more wives than one, and

let that be his wedded wife; but let him be with her alone, as long as she may live, whoever will rightly keep God's law, and secure his soul against the burning of hell.

8. And let God's dues be lawfully and willingly paid every year: that is, plough-alms at least by fifteen days after Easter, and a tithe of young by Pentecost, and of earth-fruits by Allhallows' mass: and if then any one will not pay the tithe as we have decreed; that is the tenth acre, so as the plough traverses it; then let the king's reeve go, and the bishop's, and the " land-riça's," and the mass-priest of the minster, and take forcibly the tenth part for the minster to which it is due, and assign to him the ninth part; and let the eight parts be divided into two, and let the land-lord take possession of half, half the bishop, be it a king's man, be it a thane's.

9. And Rome-" feoh " by St. Peter's mass; and whoever withholds it over that day, let him pay the penny to the bishop, and xxx. pence thereto, and to the king cxx. shillings.

10. And church-scot at Martinmas; and whoever withholds it over that day, let him pay it to the bishop, and indemnify him xi. fold, and to the king cxx. shillings.

11. But if there be any thane who has a church on his " boc-land," at which there is a burial-place, let him give the third part of his own tithe to his church. And if any one have a church at which there is no burial-place, let him do for his priest what he will from the nine parts. And let every church-scot go to the old minster, according to every free hearth.

12. And light-scot thrice in the year: first, on Easter-eve, a half-penny worth of wax for every hide; and again on Allhallows' mass, as much, and again on the purification of St. Mary, the like.

13. And it is most proper that soul-scot be always paid at the open grave: and if any corpse be laid out of its proper shrift-district elsewhere, let soul-scot be, nevertheless, paid to the minster to which it belonged.

14. And let all God's dues be diligently furthered, as it is needful. And let festivals and fasts be rightly held; and let every Sunday's festival be held from the noon of Saturday till the dawn of Monday, and every other mass-day as it is commanded.

15. And Sunday marketing we also strictly forbid, and every folk-mote, unless it be for great necessity: and let huntings and all other worldly works be strictly abstained from on that holy day.

16. And let every appointed fast be held, be it Ember fast, be it Lent fast, be it any other fast, with all earnestness; and on every St. Mary's mass, and on every apostle's mass, let fast be kept, except that on St. Philip and St. James's mass we enjoin no fast, because of the Easter festival: and every Friday's fast, unless it be a festival. And no one has need to fast from Easter to Pentecost, unless it be prescribed to any one, or he otherwise will. And from mid-winter to the octaves of the Epiphany, that is seven days after the twelfth mass-day.

17. And we forbid ordeals and oaths on festival-days, and ember-days, and lenten-days, and regular fast-days, and from Adventum Domini until the eighth day be passed after the twelfth mass-day; and

from Septuagesima till **xv.** days after Easter. And
St. Edward's mass-day, the " witan " have chosen
that it shall be celebrated over all England on the
xv. kl. April. And St. Dunstan's mass-day on the
xiv. kl. Junii. And, at those holy tides, let there be,
as it is right, to all Christian men, general peace and
concord, and let every dispute be settled. And if
any one owe to another " borh " or " bot " for secular
matters, let him willingly fulfill it to him, before or
after.

18. And we beseech, for God's love, every Christian
man, that he well understand his own need : because
we all have to await a time, when it will be better for
us than all that is on middle earth, that we had always
earnestly performed God's will, while it was in our
power : but when we shall have the simple reward of
that which we had before done in life, woe then to
those who had before merited hell torment. But let
us very earnestly turn from sins, and every one of us
willingly confess his misdeeds to our confessors, and
ever abstain, and willingly make " bot " : and let
every one of us enjoin to others that which we desire
should be enjoined to us : that is just doom, and very
acceptable to God, and he shall be very happy who
keeps that doom ; for God Almighty made us all, and
afterwards bought us at a high price, that is, with his
own life, which he gave for us all.

19. And let every Christian man do as is needful
to him ; let him strictly keep his Christianity, and
also prepare himself to go to housel at least thrice in
the year ; every one himself, who will understand his
own need, so as is needful to him. And let every
friend guide his words and works aright, and care-

fully keep oath and " wed " ; and let every injustice
be strictly cast out of this country, as far as it can be
done ; and let God's law be henceforth earnestly
loved by word and by work ; then will God's mercy
be the more ready for us all.

20. Let us also earnestly do, as we will yet teach,
let us all be always faithful and true to our lord, and
ever exalt his dignity with all our powers, and execute his will ; because all that we ever do as just fidelity to our lord, we do it all to our own great behoof ;
because God verily is faithful to him who is rightly
faithful to his lord : and also, every lord has very
great need that he treat his men justly.

21. And we very earnestly instruct all Christian
men, that they ever love God with inward heart, and
diligently hold orthodox Christianity, and diligently
obey the divine teachers, and meditate on and inquire
into God's doctrines and laws, oft and frequently, for
their own behoof.

22. And we instruct, that every Christian man
learn so that he may at least be able to understand
aright orthodox faith, and to learn the Paternoster
and Creed : because with the one every Christian
man shall pray to God, and with the other, manifest
orthodox faith.   Christ himself first sang Paternoster,
and taught that prayer to his disciples ; and in that divine prayer there are VII. prayers.   Therewith, who
inwardly sings it, he ever sends to God himself a mes-
sage regarding every need a man may have, either for
this life or for that to come.   But how then can any
man ever inwardly pray to God, unless he have
inward true love for and right belief in God? for
after his departure hence, he may not, in community

with Christian men, rest in a hallowed burial-place, or here in life be worthy of housel. Nor is he well a Christian who will not learn it ; nor may he lawfully receive another man at baptism, nor at the bishop's hand, before he so learns it that he well knows it.

23. And we instruct, that every one shield himself very carefully against deep sins and diabolical deeds at every time ; and that he very carefully make " bot," by counsel of his confessor, who, through impulse of the devil, has fallen into sins.

24. And we instruct, that every one ever guard himself against foul lasciviousness, and against fornication, and against every kind of adultery.

25. And we also earnestly instruct every man, that he constantly have the dread of God in his mind, and, by day and by night, that he fear for sins, dread dooms-day, and shudder for hell, and ever suppose the end of his day near to him.

26. Bishops are heralds, and teachers of God's laws, and it is for them earnestly to preach and set example for spiritual behoof; heed it who will : because weak is the shepherd found for the flock who will not defend with his cry the flock that he has to feed, (unless he can do otherwise,) if there any spoiler begins to spoil. There is none so evil a spoiler as is the devil himself; he is ever busy about that alone, how he can most injure the souls of men. Therefore must the shepherds be very watchful and diligently crying out, who have to shield the people against the spoiler ; such are bishops and mass-priests, who are to preserve and defend their spiritual flocks with wise instructions, that the madly audacious were-wolf do not too widely devastate, nor bite too many of the

spiritual flock: and he who scorns to listen to God's preachers, let that be between him and God himself. Ever be the name of God eternally blessed, and to him praise and glory and honor for ever and ever. Amen.

SECULAR.

This then is the secular ordinance which, by the counsel of my "witan," I will that it be observed over all England.

1. That is then the first that I will: that just laws .be established, and every unjust law carefully suppressed, and that every injustice be weeded out and rooted up, with all possible diligence, from this country. And let God's justice be exalted; and henceforth let every man, both poor and rich, be esteemed worthy of folk-right, and let just dooms be doomed to him.

2. And we instruct, that though any one sin and deeply foredo himself, let the correction be regulated so that it be becoming before God and tolerable before the world. And let him who has power of judgment very earnestly bear in mind what he himself desires, when he thus says: "Et dimitte nobis debita nostra, sicut et nos dimittimus." And we command that Christian men be not, on any account, for altogether too little, condemned to death: but rather let gentle punishments be decreed, for the benefit of the people; and let not be destroyed for little God's handy-work, and his own purchase which he dearly bought.

3. And we command, that Christian men be not too readily sold out of the land; and especially be

to
on-
rie-
ern-
l the
n that
lse, let
ht that
. neither
cuse the
e, let him
nd if the
doom as he

carefully rec-
enceforth ab-

ricg-bots," and
out; and "fyr-
. for our common

ed, in every wise,
be devised for the
ox Christianity most
diligently abolished :
turn to some good in
ut down, and justice
he world.   Amen.
ich the king enjoys over
is, "mund-bryce" and
"flymena-fyrmth," and

not brought into heathendom; but let it be carefully guarded against, that those souls be not made to perish which Christ bought with his own life.

4. And we command, that ye undertake diligently to cleanse the country on every side, and everywhere to desist from evil deeds: and if witches or diviners, " morth "-workers or adulteresses, be anywhere found in the land, let them be diligently driven out of this country; or let them totally perish in the country, except they desist and the more thoroughly amend.

And we command, that adversaries and outlaws of God and men retire from the country, unless they submit and the more earnestly amend: and let thieves and public robbers forthwith perish, unless they desist.

OF HEATHENISM.

5. And we earnestly forbid every heathenism : heathenism is, that men worship idols; that is, that they worship heathen gods, and the sun or the moon, fire or rivers, water-wells or stones, or forest trees of any kind; or love witchcraft, or promote " morth "-work in any wise; or by " blot," or by " fyrht "; or perform any thing pertaining to such illusions.

6. Let manslayers and perjurers, violators of holy orders and adulterers, submit and make " bot "; or with their sins retire from the country.

7. Let cheats and liars, robbers and reavers, have God's anger, unless they desist, and the more thoroughly amend: and whoever will lawfully cleanse the country, and suppress injustice, and love righteousness, then must he diligently correct such things, and shun the like.

8. Let all of us likewise very earnestly take into consideration "frith-bot" and "feos-bot": so concerning "frith-bot," as may be best for the proprietor, and most hostile to the thieves: and so concerning "feos-bot," that one money pass over all the nation, without any counterfeit, and let no man that refuse; and he who after this shall make false, let him forfeit the hands with which he wrought that false, and not redeem them with any thing, neither with gold nor with silver: and if any one accuse the reeve, that he wrought that false by his leave, let him clear himself with a threefold "lad": and if the "lad" then fail, let him have the same doom as he who wrought the false.

9. And let weights and measures be carefully rectified, and every species of injustice henceforth abstained from.

10. And let "burh-bots," and "bricg-bots," and " scip-forthungs," be diligently set about; and "fyrdungs" also, whenever it is requisite, for our common need.

11. And be it constantly inquired, in every wise, how counsel may most especially be devised for the benefit of the nation; and orthodox Christianity most exalted, and unjust laws most diligently abolished: because through that it shall turn to some good in the country, that injustice be put down, and justice loved, before God and before the world. Amen.

12. These are the rights which the king enjoys over all men in Wessex: that is, "mund-bryce" and "ham-socn," "forstal," and "flymena-fyrmth," and

"fyrd-wite," unless he will more amply honor any one, and concede to him this worship.

OUTLAWRIES.

13. And whoever does a deed of outlawry, let the king have power of the "frith." And if he have "boc-land," let that be forfeited into the king's hand; be he man of whatever man he may. And take notice, whoever may feed or harbor the "flyma" shall pay five pounds to the king, except he shall clear himself that he knew not of his being a "flyma."

14. And in Mercia he enjoys all as is here before written, over all men.

15. And by Danish law he enjoys "fight-wites," and "fyrd-wites," and "grith-bryce," and "ham-socn," unless he will honor any one more amply: and if any one keep or harbor a "frithless" man, let him make "bot" for it, as the law formerly was. And he who shall henceforth set up unjust law, or doom unjust doom, for hatred or bribery, let him be liable to the king in a hundred and twenty shillings, by English law, unless he dare to prove on oath that he knew not aught more just; and let him ever forfeit his thaneship, unless he repurchase it of the king, and as he will allow him. And by Danish law, let him be guilty of "lah-slit," unless he clear himself, that he knew no better. And he who denies just law and just doom, let him be liable unto him who is entitled to it: either to the king in cxx. shillings, or to an "eorl" in lx. shillings, or to the hundred in xxx. shillings; so with every of them, if it so happen, by English law: and he who by Danish law shall corrupt just law, let him pay "lah-slit."

16. And he who shall accuse another wrongfully, so that he be the worse either in substance or advancement, if then the other can show to be false that which one would charge upon him ; let him be liable in his tongue, unless he redeem himself with his " wer."

17. And let no one apply to the king, unless he may not be entitled to any justice within his hundred; and let the hundred-" gemot " be applied to, under penalty of the " wite," so as it right is to apply to it.

18. And thrice a year let there be a " burh-gemot," and twice, a shire-" gemot," under penalty of the " wite,". as is right; unless there be need oftener. And let there be present the bishop of the shire and the " ealdorman," and there let both expound as well the law of God as the secular law.

OF DISTRESS.

19. And let no man take any distress, either in the shire or out of the shire, before he has thrice demanded his right in the hundred. If at the third time he have no justice, then let him go at the fourth time to the shire-" gemot "; and let the shire appoint him a fourth term. If that then fail, let him take leave, either from hence or thence, that he may seize his own.

THAT EVERY MAN SHALL BE IN A TITHING.

20. And we will, that every freeman be brought into a hundred, and into a tithing, who wishes to be entitled to " lad " or to " wer," in case any one shall slay him after he is XII. years of age ; or let him not afterwards be entitled to any free rights, be he

" heorth-fæst," be he follower. And that every one be brought into a hundred and in " borh "; and let the " borh " hold and lead him to every plea. Many a powerful man will, if he can and may, defend his man in whatever way it seems to him that he may the more easily defend him; whether as a freeman or a " theow." But we will not allow that injustice.

OF THIEVES.

21. And we will, that every man above twelve years make oath that he will neither be a thief nor cognizant of theft.

22. And let every true man who has not been " tiht-bysig " and has failed neither in oath nor ordeal within his hundred, be entitled to a single "lad." And for an untrue man, let a single oath be chosen in three hundreds, and a threefold oath as far as it belongs to the " burh "; or let him go to the ordeal, and let a single "lad" be preceded by a single "for-ath," and a threefold " lad " by a triple "for-ath." And if a thane have a true man to take the "for-ath" for him, be it so. If he have not, let him begin his suit himself: and let no " for-ath " ever be remitted.

23. And let no man be entitled to any vouching to warranty, unless he have true witness whence that came to him which is attached with him; and let the witness declare, by the favor of God and his lord, that he is a true witness for him, as he saw with his eyes and heard with his ears that he rightfully obtained it.

24. And let no one buy any thing above the value of four pence, either living or lying, unless he have the true witness of four men, be it within a " burh,"

be it up in the country. For if it then be attached, and he have no such witness, let there be no vouching to warranty; but let his own be rendered to the proprietor; and the "æfter-gild," and the "wite," to him who is entitled thereto. And if he have witness, as we have here before ordained, then let it be thrice vouched to warranty: at the fourth time, let him keep possession of it, or render it to him who owns it. And it seems right to us, that no man should hold possession where there is witness, and it can be known that it had been abstracted: [and] that no man ought to claim possession, at the earliest, before six months after it had been stolen.

25. And he who is "tiht-bysig," and untrue to the people, and avoids the "gemot" thrice; then let there be selected, from the fourth "gemot," those who shall ride to him; and let him still find a "borh," if he can: but if he cannot, let them seize him as they can, whether alive or dead, and take all that he owns. And let the accuser be paid his "ceap-gild"; and let the lord take possession of half, half the hundred. And if one or other, either a kinsman or a stranger, refuse the riding, let him pay to the king one hundred and twenty shillings.

OF THIEVES.

26. And let the notorious thief seek whatever he may seek, or he that is discovered in treason against his lord, so that they never seek life; and he who after this steals, let him seek what he may, so that he never seek life in [case of] open theft.

27. And let him who in the "gemot" shall defend himself or his man by "wither-tihtle" have wholly

sued in vain ; and answer to the other as shall seem right to the hundred.

28. And that no one receive any man longer than three nights, unless he shall recommend him whom he before followed : and let no one dismiss his man before he be clear of every suit to which he had been previously cited.

29. And if any one find a thief, and voluntarily let him escape, without hue and cry, let him make " bot " with the thief's " wer," or clear himself with a full oath, that he knew of no guile in him. And if any one hear the hue and cry, and disregard it, let him pay the king's " ofer-hyrnes," or fully clear himself.

30. And if any man be so untrue to the hundred, and so " tiht-bysig,"and three men together then accuse him, let there be no other [course] but that he go to the threefold ordeal. But if the lord say that neither oath nor ordeal had failed him since the " gemot " was at Winchester, let the lord take to him two true men within the hundred, and swear that never oath or ordeal had failed him, nor had he paid " theof-gyld " ; unless he have the reeve who is competent to do that. If then the oath succeed, let the man who is accused choose whichever he will ; either a single ordeal, or a pound-worth oath, within the three hundreds, for above xxx. pence. And if they dare not take the oath,.let him go to the triple ordeal ; and let the triple ordeal be commenced thus : let him take five, and be himself the sixth ; and if he then be foul, at the first time, let him make " bot " to the accuser twofold ; and to the lord who is entitled to his " wite," with his " wer " ; and let him appoint

true "borhs," that he will hereafter abstain from every evil. And at the second time, let there be no other "bot," if he be foul, than that his hands be cut off, or his feet, or both, according as the deed may be. And if he then have wrought yet greater wrong, then let his eyes be put out, and his nose and his ears, and the upper lip be cut off; or let him be scalped: whatever of these then, those shall counsel whose duty it is to counsel thereupon; so that punishment be inflicted, and also the soul preserved. But if he run away, and avoid the ordeal, let the "borh" pay to the accuser his "ceap-gyld," and to the king his "wer"; or to him who is entitled to his "wite." And if any one accuse the lord, that he ran away by his counsel, and had previously acted unlawfully; let him take to him five true men, and be himself the sixth, and clear himself thereof. If the purgation succeed, let him be entitled to the "wer": and if it do not succeed, let the king take the "wer," and let the thief be an outlaw to all people.

OF "HIRED-MEN."

31. And let every lord have his household in his own "borh"; and if any one accuse his man of any thing, let him answer within the hundred wherein he is cited, as just law is. And if he be accused, and he run away, let the lord pay the man's "wer" to the king. And if any one accuse the lord, that he ran away by his counsel, let him clear himself with five thanes, and be himself the sixth. If the purgation fail him, let him pay to the king his "wer," and let the man be an outlaw.

32. And if a "theowman" be foul at the ordeal,

let him be branded the first time; and at the second time, let there be no other "bot" except the head.

OF UNTRUE MEN.

33. And if there be any man who is untrue to all the people, let the king's reeve go, and bring him under "borh," that he may be led to justice to those who accuse him. But if he have no "borh," let him be slain, and be laid in the "ful." And if any one stand up for him, let them both be worthy of one law. And whoever neglects this, and will not further it, as is the decree of us all, let him pay to the king one hundred and twenty shillings.

34. And at a "ladung," let one law stand between "burhs."

OF FRIENDLESS MEN.

35. And if a friendless man or a comer from afar be so distressed, through want of friends, that he has no "borh" at the "frum-tihtle"; let him then submit to prison, and there abide, until he go to God's ordeal, and there let him fare as he may. Verily he who dooms a worse doom to the friendless and the comer from afar than to his fellow, injures himself.

OF A FALSE OATH.

36. And if any one swear a false oath on a relic, and he be convicted, let him forfeit his hands, or half his "wer"; and let that be common to lord and bishop. And let him not be thenceforth oath-worthy; unless he the more thoroughly before God make "bot," and find him "borh" that he will ever after abstain from the like.

OF FALSE WITNESS.

37. And if any one stand openly in false witness, and he be convicted ; let not his witness afterwards stand for aught, but let him pay to the king, or to the " landrica," according to his " heals-fang."

38. At no time is injustice allowed ; and yet at festival-tides, and fast-tides, and in festival-places, one ought most earnestly to take care.   And always as a man is mightier or of greater degree, so ought he the more thoroughly to make " bot " for injustice, before God and before the world.   And let divine " bot " be earnestly and constantly sought, according as the books prescribe ; and let secular " bot " be sought according to secular law.

39. If any one kill a servant of the altar, let him be an outlaw to God and to men, unless he the more thoroughly make " bot " through exile, and also to the kindred, or clear himself by a " wer-lad " ; and within thirty days let him set about the " bot," both to God and to men, on peril of all he possesses.

40. And if any one wrong a man in holy orders, or a foreigner, through any means, as to money or as to life, then shall the king be unto him in the place of a kinsman and of a protector, unless he have another lord besides.   And let " bot " be made to the king as it may be fitting ; or let him avenge the deed very deeply.   It belongs very rightly to a Christian king that he avenge God's anger very deeply, according as the deed may be.

OF MEN IN HOLY ORDERS.

41. If a servant of the altar be a homicide, or else work iniquity very enormously ; let him then forfeit

both degree and country, and go in exile as far as the pope shall prescribe to him, and earnestly do penance. And if he will clear himself, let him clear himself with a threefold ["lad"]; and unless he begin the "bot" within xxx. days, to God and to men, let him be an outlaw.

THAT NO ONE BIND OR BEAT A MAN IN HOLY ORDERS.

42. If any one bind or beat or grossly insult a man in holy orders, let him make "bot" to him as it may be right, and to the bishop, with an altar-"bot," according to the degree of his order; and to the lord or the king, according to the full "mund-bryce"; or clear himself with a full "lad."

43. If a man in holy orders defile himself with a crime worthy of death, let him be seized, and held to the bishop's doom, according as the deed may be.

44. If a man who has committed a crime worthy of death desire confession, let it never be denied him: and if any one deny it him, let him make "bot" for that to the king with a hundred and twenty shillings, or clear himself; let him take five, and be the sixth himself.

OF THE HOLY DAY FESTIVAL.

45. If it can be helped, no condemned man should ever be put to death on a Sunday festival, unless he flee or fight: but let him be secured, and held till the festival-day be past. If a freeman work on a festival-day, then let him make " bot " with his "heals-fang," and, above all, earnestly make "bot" to God, so as he may be instructed. If a "theowman" work, let him pay with his hide, or "hide-gild," according as

the deed may be. If a lord compel his "theow" to work upon a festival-day, let him forfeit the "theow," and be he afterward folk-free; and let the lord pay "lah-slit" among the Danes, and "wite" among the English, as the deed may be; or clear himself.

OF FASTING.

47. If a freeman break a lawful fast, let him pay "lah-slit" among the Danes, and "wite" among the English, as the deed may be. It is sinful, that any one, at a lawful fast-tide, eat before the time, and yet worse that any one defile himself with flesh-meat. If a "theowman" do so, let him pay with his hide, or "hide-gild" as the deed may be.

48. If any one openly commit lent-breach, through fighting, or through fornication, or through robbery, or through any heinous misdeeds, let the "bot" be twofold, as on a high festival, as the deed may be; and if any one deny it, let him clear himself with a threefold "lad."

IF ANY ONE REFUSE DIVINE DUES.

49. If any one with violence refuse divine dues, let him pay "lah-slit" among the Danes, and full "wite" among the English, or let him clear himself: let him take XI., and be himself the twelfth. If he wound any one, let him make "bot" for it, and pay full "wite" to the lord, and redeem his hand of the bishop, or lose it. If he kill any one, let him be an outlaw, and let every one of those pursue him with hue and cry who desire right. If he act so that he be killed through striving against right, if that can be proved, let him lie uncompensated.

50. If any one commit "had-bryce," let him make "bot" according to the degree of the order, as well with "wer," as with "wite," and with "lah-slit," and with all his possession.

OF ADULTERY.

51. If any one commit adultery, let him make "bot" for it as the deed may be. It is a wicked adultery when a married man lies with a single woman, and much worse, with another's wife, or with one in holy orders.

OF INCEST.

52. If any one commit incest, let him make "bot" for it according to the degree of kin; as well with "wer," as with "wite," and with all his possessions. It is by no means alike whether a man lie with a sister, or if it were a distant relative.

OF WIDOWS AND MAIDS.

53. If any one ravish a widow, let him make "bot" for it with his "wer." If any one ravish a maid, let him make "bot" for it with his "wer."

THAT NO WOMAN COMMIT ADULTERY.

54. If, during her husband's life, a woman lie with another man, and it become public, let her afterwards be for a worldly shame as regards herself, and let her lawful husband have all that she possessed; and let her then forfeit both nose and ears: and if it be a prosecution, and the "lad" fail, let the bishop use his power, and doom severely.

55. If a married man lie with his own maid servant, let him forfeit her, and make "bot" for himself to

God and to men: and he who has a lawful wife, and also a concubine, let no priest administer to him any of those rites which ought to be administered to a Christian man; ere he desist, and so deeply make "bot" as the bishop may teach him; and let him ever desist from the like.

56. If foreigners will not correct their fornications, let them retire from the land, with their possessions and sins.

57. If there be open "morth," so that a man be murdered, let the slayer be delivered up to the kinsmen; and if there be a prosecution, and he fail at the "lad," let the bishop doom.

OF PLOTTING AGAINST A LORD.

58. If any one plot against the king, or his lord, let him be liable in his life, and in all that he owns, except he go to the threefold ordeal.

OF "BORH-BRYCE."

59. If any one break the king's "borh," let him make "bot" for it with v. pounds. If any one break an archbishop's or an atheling's "borh," let him make "bot" for it with three pounds. If any one break a suffragan bishop's or an "ealdorman's" "borh" let him make "bot" for it with two pounds.

OF HIM WHO FIGHTS IN THE KING'S HOUSEHOLD.

60. If any one fight in the king's household, let him forfeit his life, unless the king will be merciful to him.

IN CASE ANY ONE DISARM ANOTHER.

61. If any one unlawfully disarm a man, let him

compensate with his "heals-fang"; and if he bind him let him compensate with half his "wer."

"GRITH-BRYCE."

62. If any one in the "fyrd" commit "grith-bryce," let him forfeit his life, or his "wer-gild." If he co-operate, let him make "bot" according as the deed may be.

"HAM-SOCEN."

63. If any one commit "ham-socen," let him make "bot" for it with five pounds to the king by English law, and by Danish law as it formerly stood; and if he there be killed, let him lie uncompensated.

"REAF-LAC."

64. If any one commit "reaf-lac," let him give it up, and compensate, and be liable in his "wer" to the king.

HOUSE-BREAKING.

65. House-breaking, and arson, and open theft, and open "morth," and treason against a lord, are, by the secular law, "botless."

"BURH-BOT."

66. If any one neglect "burh-bot," or "bricg-bot," or "fyrd-fare," let him make "bot" with one hundred and twenty shillings to the king by English law, and by Danish law as it formerly stood; or let him clear himself: let XIV. be named to him, and let him choose XI. To church-"bot" all men must lawfully give assistance.

OF A GOD-"FLYMA."

67. If any one unlawfully have a God-"flyma," let him give him up to justice, and compensate to him to

whom it is due, and pay to the king according to his
"wer-gild." If any one have and hold an excommunicated person or an outlaw, let him peril himself and
all his property.

68. And if any one will earnestly turn from wrong
again to right, let him have mercy shown him, or fear
of God, as best may be, very earnestly.

69. And let us do as is requisite for us: let us ever
help those the speediest who stand most in need of
help; then shall we obtain the reward of it, where it
will be most agreeable to us. For we ought always,
for love and fear of God, to doom and prescribe more
lightly to the feeble man than to the strong; because
we know full well that the powerless cannot raise a
like burthen with the powerful, nor the unhale a like
with the hale; and therefore we ought to moderate,
and discreetly distinguish between age and youth,
wealth and poverty, freedom and slavery, hale and
unhale. And both in religious shrifts and secular
dooms these things ought to be discriminated. Moreover, in many a deed, when any one is an involuntary
agent, then is he the better deserving of protection,
because he did what he did from necessity: and if any
one do a thing unwillingly, it is not at all like that
which he does willfully.

70. This then is the alleviation which it is my will to
secure to all the people of that which they before this
were too much oppressed with. That then is first: that
I command all my reeves that they justly provide on my
own, and maintain me therewith; and that no man need
give them any thing as "feorm-fultum," unless he himself be willing. And if any one after that demand a
" wite," let him be liable in his " wer " to the king.

15

OF THE HERIOT.

71. And if any one depart this life intestate, be it through his neglect, be it through sudden death; then let not the lord draw more from his property than his lawful heriot. And, according to his direction, let the property be distributed very justly to the wife, and children, and relations; to every one, according to the degree that belongs to him.

72. And let the heriots be as it is fitting to the degree. An "eorl's" such as thereto belongs, that is: eight horses, four saddled and four unsaddled, and four helmets, and four coats of mail, and eight spears, and as many shields, and four swords, and two hundred mancuses of gold. And after that, a king's thane's, of those who are nearest to him: four horses, two saddled and two unsaddled, and two swords, and four spears, and as many shields, and a helmet, and a coat of mail, and fifty mancuses of gold. And of the medial thanes: a horse and his trappings, and his arms; or his "heal's-fang" in Wessex; and in Mercia, two pounds, and in East-Anglia, two pounds. And the heriot of a king's thane among the Danes, who has his "socen," four pounds. And if he have further relation to the king: two horses, one saddled and the other unsaddled, and one sword, and two spears, and two shields, and fifty mancuses of gold: and he who is of less means, two pounds.

73. And where the husband dwelt without claim or contest, let the wife and the children dwell in the same, unassailed by litigation. And if the husband, before he was dead, had been cited; then let the heirs answer, as himself should have done if he had lived.

OF A WIDOW: THAT SHE CONTINUE XII. MONTHS HUSBANDLESS.

74. And let every widow continue husbandless a twelvemonth: let her then choose what she herself will; and if she, within the space of a year, choose a husband, then let her forfeit her " morgen-gyfu," and all the possessions which she had through the first husband; and let the nearest kinsmen take the land and the possessions that she had before. And let him [the husband] be liable in his " wer " to the king, or to him to whom he may have granted it. And though she be taken forcibly, let her forfeit the possessions, unless she bé willing to go home again from the man, and never again be his. And let not a widow take the veil too precipitately. And let every widow pay the heriots, " wite-less," within twelve months; except it be convenient to her earlier.

75. And let no one compel either woman or maiden to him whom she herself mislikes, nor for money sell her; unless he is willing to give any thing voluntarily.

IN CASE A MAN SET HIS SPEAR AT ANOTHER MAN'S DOOR.

76. And I hold it right, though any one set his own spear at the door of another man's house, and he have an errand therein; or if any one quietly lay any other weapon, where they would be still if they might; and any man then seize the weapon, and do any harm therewith; then it is right that he who wrought that harm, also make " bot " for the harm. And he who owns the weapon, let him clear himself, if he dare, that it never was either by his will, or in his control, or by his counsel, or with his cognizance: then is it

God's law, that he be innocent; and let the other, who wrought the deed, see that he make "bot" as the law may teach.

OF STOLEN PROPERTY.

77. And if any man bring a stolen thing home to his cot, and he be detected [by the owner]; it is just that he [the owner] have what he went after. And unless it has been brought under his wife's key-lockers, let her be clear; for it is her duty to keep the keys of them; namely, her "hord-ern," and her chest, and her "tege." If it be brought under any of these, then is she guilty. And no wife may forbid her husband that he may not put into his cot what he will. It was ere this, that the child which lay in the cradle, though it had never tasted meat, was held by the covetous to be equally guilty as if it had discretion. But henceforth I most strenuously forbid it, and also very many things that are very hateful to God.

OF HIM WHO FLEES FROM HIS LORD.

78. And the man who shall flee from his lord, or from his comrade, by reason of his cowardice, be it in the ship-"fyrd," be it in the land-"fyrd"; let him forfeit all that he owns, and his own life, and let the lord seize his possessions, and his land, which he previously gave him: and if he have boc-land, let that go into the king's hands.

OF HIM WHO FALLS BEFORE HIS LORD.

79. And if a man fall before his lord in the "fyrd-ung," be it within the land, be it without the land, let the heriots be forgiven; and let the heirs succeed to the land and the property, and divide it very justly.

80. And he who has defended land, with the witness of the shire; let him have it undisputed, during his day and after his day, to sell and to give to him who is dearest to him.

OF HUNTING.

81. And I will that every man be entitled to his hunting, in wood and in field, on his own possession. And let every one forego my hunting: take notice where I will have it untrespassed on, under penalty of the full "wite."

82. And let "drinc-lean" and a lord's "riht gifu" ever stand unchanged.

83. And I will that every man be entitled to "grith," to the "gemot" and from the "gemot"; except he be a notorious thief.

84. And he who violates these laws, which the king has now given to all men, be he Danish or be he English, let him be liable in his "wer" to the king: and if he again violate them, let him pay twice his "wer": and if he be then so daring that he violate them a third time, let him forfeit all that he possesses.

85. Now I earnestly beseech and in God's name command every man, that he with inward heart bow to his Lord, and many times and oft meditate very earnestly what is for him to do and what to forego. It is very needful to us all, that we love God, and follow God's law, and diligently attend to our divine teachers; because they shall lead us forth at the doom, when God will deem to every man according to his former works. And happy will be the pastor who then can joyfully lead his flock into God's kingdom, and to heavenly bliss, for their former deeds. And

well for that flock which followeth the pastor, who weaneth them from devils and gaineth them to God. Let us all then, with unity of heart, diligently please our Lord, as is right, and ever henceforth diligently shield ourselves against the hot burning which seetheth in hell. And let our instructors and divine preachers now also do as it is right and needful for all men, by announcing frequently the divine benefits; and let every one who has discretion diligently listen to them; and let every one hold the divine doctrine very fast in his thought, for his own advantage: and let every man, in honor of his Lord, ever gladly do what good he may, both by word and deed; then shall God's mercy be the readier to us. Ever let God's name be eternally blessed, and praise be to him, and glory and honor for ever and ever. May God Almighty have mercy on us all, as his will may be, and preserve us ever to all eternity. So be it. Amen.

THE LAWS OF KING EDWARD THE CON-
FESSOR.

Here begins the law of Edward, the glorious king of the English.

Four years after the gaining of this land, namely England, by King William, by the advice of his barons he caused to be summoned throughout all the counties of the land the English nobles, wise men, and those learned in their own law, that he might hear from themselves their customs. Twelve men having, therefore, been elected from the assemblies of the whole land, they swore, first of all, by an oath, that in so far as they were able, proceeding in the right path, they would show forth the things ordained in their laws and customs, passing over nothing, adding nothing, changing nothing by prevarication.

OF THE PEACE AND LIBERTY OF THE HOLY CHURCH.

1. Accordingly taking a beginning from the holy church, through which king and people have the power of remaining surely, its peace and the liberty of coming together must be affirmed. Let all the clergy, scholars, and all their possessions, wherever they may be, have the peace of God and the holy church.

AT WHAT TIMES PEACE MUST BE OBSERVED.

2. From the advent of our Lord until the octave of Epiphany, the peace of God and the holy church shall

be throughout the kingdom. In like manner, from
Septuagesima until the octave of Easter. So from
the Ascension of our Lord until Trinity Sunday. So
on all the days of these three periods. So on all the
Saturdays of the whole year from three o'clock in the
afternoon, and all the following day. So on the day
before the Feast of Saint Mary, of Saint Michael, of
Saint John the Baptist, of all the Holy Apostles and
of those saints whose feasts shall be set forth by the
priests in church on Sundays, and on the day before
the feast of All Saints on the first day of November,
always from three o'clock in the afternoon and the
whole of the following day. So on the celebrations of
the feasts of the saints whoever lived in the parishes
where their churches are. And if any one out of piety
shall come to honor a saint, let him remain and depart
in peace. In like manner let there be peace in going
and returning to all Christians going to the house of
God on account of a sermon; in like manner to those
going to dedications, to synods, and to conventions,
whether they be summoned or have something there
to do on their own account. And if any excommunicated person shall come to the bishop, for the purpose
of making amends, let him, as if having received abso-
lution, in going and returning have the peace of God
and the holy church. But if any one shall wrong him
let the bishop exercise his right of justice. But if the
offender be unwilling to amend for the bishop's justice
let the bishop show the matter to the king, and the
king shall compel the wrong-doer to make amends
to them he wronged and to the bishop and to the
king himself. And so justly shall the sword aid the
sword.

3. Whenever a justiciary of the king, or any other justiciary of whomsoever he may be, shall hold pleadings or a court, if there shall be a minister of the bishop present, and shall show the cause of the holy church, let it, first, be brought to the end, whichever seems the more reasonable, on that same day. For it is right that everywhere God should be honored by his servants.

OF THE LIBERTY OF THOSE THAT HOLD FIEFS OF THE CHURCH.

4. Whosoever holds of the church, or remains in a fief of the church, shall not plead outside the ecclesiastical court, if he have a wrong in the case of any one, until, but may it not happen,* he shall fail of justice in the ecclesiastical court.

OF THOSE THAT FLY TO THE CHURCH FOR REFUGE.

5. Whatever accused person or malefactor flies to the church for refuge, let him be safe from the time that he has gone into the entrance, and let him be seized in no way by any person following upon him, except by the priest of that place or by his servant. And if in flying he turn aside to the house of the priest or to his court, let him find there the same security and liberty as at the church, so long as the priest's house, however, or the court remain the fief of the church. If he be a thief or a robber, let him give back what he has in his possession in regard to which he has done wrong, and if he has used it up and shall have of his own private property in good

---

* Latin, *quod absit.*

condition that which he can give back, let him restore
it to the man from whom he stole.   But if he shall
have stolen frequently and by chance has thus frequently fled for shelter, having given up what he took
away, let him leave the country and not return.   And
if he return let not any one dare to receive him unless
by the consent of the justiciaries of our lord the king.

OF THOSE THAT BREAK THE PEACE OF THE CHURCH.

6. If any one shall have broken the peace of the
church, then is the right of judgment of the bishops.
And if by fleeing or by proudly scorning it he make
light of their sentence, let complaint in regard to this
man be brought to the king after forty days and let
the justiciary of the king put him under bail and
surety, if he can seize him, until in the first place to
God, and then to the king, he shall give satisfaction.
And if within thirty-one days he cannot be found by
his friends or by the justiciary of the king, let the
king with his own mouth outlaw him.   And if afterward he shall be found and can be held, let him be
given up alive to the king; or if he defend himself let
his head be sent, for from the day of his outlawing
he wears the head of a wolf, which by the English is
called wluesheued.   And this is the common judgment
in regard to outlaws.

OF TITHES.

7. Of all crops the tenth sheaf must be given to the
holy church.   If any one has a herd of mares, let him
give up the tenth colt, if he has only two or three, a
denarius for each colt.   He that has many cows, the
tenth calf, he that has one or two, an obolus for each

calf. And if he makes cheese from the cows, the tenth cheese, or else the milk of the tenth day.

8. The tenth lamb, the tenth fleece, the tenth cheese, the tenth piece of butter, the tenth pig. In regard to bees, according to what is produced by them in a year. Nay, even in regard to woods, meadows, waters, mills, parks, preserves, fish-ponds, shrubberies, gardens, business dealings and of all things similar that the Lord has given, let the tenth be given back, and he that shall retain it shall be compelled by the court of the holy church and by the court of the king, if necessary, to give it up. This Saint Augustine preached and these things have been yielded by the king and ratified by the barons and the people, but afterward, by the instigation of the devil, many persons kept back these things, and the priests that were rich were not very careful in seeking out those tenths, but because in many places there are now three or four churches, where at that time there was but one, the tenths have accordingly begun to decrease.

OF THOSE THAT MAKE A TRIAL BY WATER OR HOT IRON.

9. At the trial, let the minister of the bishop with his clerks sit with the justiciary of the king and with the lawyers of that county, so that they may see and hear that all things are done properly, and that those whom God through his mercy and their judgment has saved may be at peace and depart in freedom, and in regard to those whom their own iniquity and injustice have condemned, the justiciary of the king shall see that justice is done. But the barons that have courts of their own shall see to it that they act in these cases

so that they shall not come into the condition of criminals in the sight of God and shall not offend the king. And if a case in regard to the men of other barons comes into his court, there shall be present the justiciary of the king, since without him it ought not to take place. And if there shall be barons that have not courts of justice, in the hundred, where the pleadings are held at the nearest church where a court of the king has been, it shall be decided, the rights of the barons being preserved.

OF PETER'S PENCE WHICH IS CALLED ROMESCOT.

10. Every one that has 30 pennyworth [annual value] of live property of his own, in his house, shall pay by the law of the English Peter's penny, and by the law of the Danes half a mark. This moreover is to be called for on the feast of Saint Peter and Saint Paul, and it shall not be withheld beyond the feast of Saint Peter ad vincula [1st of August]. If any one, however, withholds it, let complaint be brought to the justiciary of the king, since this penny is the alms of the king, and let the king's justiciary make him give up the money and a penalty beside, to the king and to the bishop. And if any one has several houses, from the one of which he is a resident on Saint Peter and Saint Paul's Day, let him give the penny.

OF DANEGELD.

11. The paying of Danegeld was first decreed on account of pirates. For, harassing the land, they were threatening its destruction so far as they were able. But for the sake of repressing their power it was decreed to pay annually twelve denarii, as Danegeld,

from each hide of all the land, to hire those that would
go to resist the attack of the pirates.   From this
Danegeld, however, all the land that was the property
of the church and was the Lord's, and also the property of the parish churches, was quit and free, and they
paid nothing in its redemption, because they had greater
trust in the words of the holy church than in the defense of arms.   And this liberty the holy church enjoyed up to the time of William the Younger, who
sought from the barons of the whole land aid for retaining Normandy from his brother Robert, who was
going to Jerusalem.   And they granted him four
solidarii from each hide, not excepting the holy
church.   While the collection of this money was
going on, the church cried out, seeking its freedom
from taxation again, but it availed it nothing.

OF THE VARIOUS PEACE OF THE KING AND OF THE
    FOUR HIGHWAYS OR KING'S ROADS, AND OF THE
    RIVERS HEREIN MENTIONED, BY THE NAVIGATION
    OF WHICH FOOD IS BROUGHT FROM DIFFERENT
    PLACES TO THE CITIES OR BOROUGHS.

12. The peace of the king is various.   One given
by his own hand, which the English call kinges hand-
sealde grith.   Another of the day on which first he
was crowned.   This lasts eight days.   At the birth of
our Lord, eight days, and eight at Easter, and eight
at Whitsunday.   Another is given by its special writ.
Another which the four highways have; namely,
Watlingstrete, Fosse, Hikenildstrete, Ermingstrete, of
which two stretch out in the length of the kingdom
and two in the breadth.   Another which the waters
have, by the navigation on which, from various places

food is brought to the cities and boroughs. This peace, however, of his own hand, of the days of his coronation, and of the writ, is under the law of one penalty. In like manner the four highways and the great waters in regard to attack. But if any work be built let it be destroyed and a half be given as a recompense. Whoever has broken the peace in the eighteen hundreds of the Danelag,* his body also is at the mercy of the king, by the law of England his wer, that is his price, and the recompense for the slaying of those slain he shall pay to the lords of those slain. The recompense for slaying a serf or bondman in the Danelag is twelve ora; in the case of freemen, three marks. By the English law to the king or archbishop, three marks for their men; to a bishop of the shire, to a nobleman of the shire, or to the steward of the king, twenty solidarii; to the other barons, ten solidarii. Let him make restitution to the parents or prepare for war. Whence the English had a saying: *Bicge spere of side other bere*, which means, either buy from them that the spear be covered up, or bear it. But let the peace of the four highways and of the great waters, placed in the greater judgment of penalties which we have above mentioned, be held from assault. And if mills, fisheries or any other things whatever be prepared for destroying the freedom of them, let these things be destroyed, the roads and the water-ways repaired and a recompense to the king shall not be forgotten. Other roads from city to city, from borough to borough, by which men travel for selling their wares or other business of their own, are under the

---

*X et VIII Hundreda in Danelage.

law of the shire. And if anything be built for their disturbance, let it be pulled down to the ground and the ways repaired, and according to the law of the shire, to the governor and lieutenant governor let restitution be made. In like manner in regard to smaller navigable streams with those things that are necessary to cities and boroughs, namely, woods and the rest. They shall be under the law of the smaller roads in regard to penalties.

DIVISIONS OF THE SHIRES AND HUNDREDS.

13. The divisions of the shires of the king are properly under the law of the king's four highways. The divisions of the hundreds and wapentakes are under the governors and lieutenant governors with the law of the county.

OF TREASURETROVE.

14. Treasures in the earth are the king's unless they be found in a church or a cemetery. And if they be found there, the gold is the king's; and if there be silver, half is the king's and half the church's where it has been found, whether the church may be rich or poor.

OF MURDER.

15. When any one was reported murdered by any one, unless his murderer was found, he was sought throughout the town, and if he could be found he was given up to the justiciary of the king for death within eight days. But if he could not be found, they had a month and a day for seeking him in his refuge. And if he was not found, forty-six marks were collected in the town, and if the town was not

able to pay so large a sum, what could not be collected in the town was collected in the hundred. But since it was all put together by the town, the barons have provided that what was collected throughout the hundred should be sealed with the seal of some baron of the shire and carried to the treasury of the king and that they should keep it there for a whole year; and if within a year the murderer could be found, justice should be done in his case and they should get back their marks. But if he should not be found within a year, the parents of the dead man should have six marks. But if he had no parents, his lord or his companion in arms, if he had one bound by good faith to him. But if he had neither of these, the king of the realm under whose peace and rule all the English live shall have the six marks along with his forty.

OF THE FIRST USE OF THE TERM MURDER.

16. Murders were first so called in the time of King Canute, who after gaining the land and pacifying it for himself sent his army back home, at the prayer of the barons of his land, and they were bound by an oath to the king that those whom he kept in the land should have a firm peace. But if any one of the English should slay any of them, if he could not defend himself by the judgment of God, by fire or water, justice should be done in his case. But if he should flee away, the crime should be punished as aforesaid.

OF THE DIVERSE POWERS OF THE KING.

17. Now the king, who is the lieutenant of the Highest King, was appointed to this end, that he

should rule and defend from injuries the kingdom and the people of God and above all the holy church, but should pluck out and destroy evil doers. But if he does otherwise, he loses the name of king, as witness Pope John, to whom Pepin, and Charles his son, not yet kings, but princes under a bad king of the Franks, wrote asking if thus the kings of the Franks ought to remain contented with only the name of kings. To them he answered: "It is right to call kings those that watchfully defend and rule the church of God, imitating the Psalmist king who said, 'He that worketh evil shall not dwell within my house.'" [Ps. ci. 7.]

WHAT THEY WHOM THE KING HAS PLEASED TO FREE FROM DEATH OUGHT TO DO.

18. However, if any one having done wrong, being in peril of life or limb for his evil deed, has sought the king's pity, the king can pardon him if he chooses, by the power of his dignity. And let the man do restitution to him to whom he did wrong, whom he formerly injured, in so far as he is able, and let him find sureties of peace and lawful behavior. But if he cannot, he shall be an exile from his native land. The king has another power also of mercy over captives, in that whenever he comes into a city, borough, or town, or even in the way, if there be a captive there, he can free him from captivity. Let however the freedman do right to him he injured to his utmost ability. But murderers or traitors to whom the king has given life or limb shall, keeping by the law, in no wise remain in the country, but shall swear to go to the sea, to whichever shore the justiciary shall deter-

mine and there to sail as soon as they can get a ship
and a breeze. If, however, having perjured themselves, they remain in the land, should any one be able
to find them justice shall be done in their cases. And
if any one knowingly keep them for a single night, by
the former law of the English and Danes he shall pay
a penalty. If for a second night, double, and if for
a third night, he is a companion and in an equal degree
in their evil deeds.

OF THE WIVES OF CRIMINALS.

19. If criminals have wives and the women shall
remain in the land, and any one of the relatives of the
murdered person shall say that these women were
counselors or accessories of them that did the murder
or act of treason, the women shall clear themselves,
if they can, by the judgment of God, and if God's
mercy and their own right shall save them, they shall
lawfully remain with their private properties and
dowries. And infants that were born before the
crime shall not be counted as outlaws on account of
the crimes that their fathers did after their birth, nor
shall they lose their inheritance.

OF FRITHBORG AND WHAT THE YORK PEOPLE ALONE CALL TEN MENNE TALE, THAT IS, THE OATH OF TEN MEN.

20. There is another very great means of peace,
through which all are held in a firmer position, namely
by the firmness of suretyship, which the English call
Frithborg, except the York people, who call it Ten
Menne Tale, which is the reckoning of ten men. And
that is that all men, of all the towns of the whole king-

dom ought to be bound by the oath of ten that if one of the ten do wrong, nine may hold him to the right. But if he flee away, if they shall say that they cannot hold him to the right, then shall be given to them by the king's justiciary at least three months and a day. If they can find him let them lead him to justice. Let him, then, of his own property restore the damage he has done, and let justice be done on his body, if he has done wrong to this extent. But if within the above mentioned limit, he cannot be found, since in every frithborg there is a chief whom they call frithborghened, the chief man himself shall take two of the better men* in his frithborg, and from the three frithborgs his nearest neighbors, the chief man of each one and in like manner two of the better men if he can get them, and they being twelve let him free himself and his frithborg if he can from the evil deed and the flight of the above mentioned evil doer. And, if he cannot do it, he shall restore the damage which the man has done from the property of the evil doer, as far as it goes, and from his own, and let them pay to justice what has lawfully been judged in their case. And moreover the oath that they could not establish before their neighbors let them swear by themselves that they are free from guilt. And if they can find an evil doer again, let them lead him to the justiciary if they can, or tell to the justiciary where he is.

DESCRIPTION OF VARIOUS LIBERTIES.

21. Archbishops, bishops, noblemen, and barons had both their soldiers and their personal attendants: namely, butlers, cup-bearers, chamberlains, cooks, and

---

*Meliores.

pastry cooks, under their own frithborgs, and they in turn their armor bearers and other servants of their own under their frithborg, but if these last do wrong and a complaint go up from their neighbors about them, the lords shall bring them to justice in their own court if they have sac, and soc, tol and theam, and infangenetheof.

WHAT ARE SAC AND SOC, TOL AND THEAM AND INFANGENETHEOF?

22. It is *soc* that if any one seeks anything on the lord's land, even a theft, it is the lord's right of judgment whether it be found or not. It is *sac* that if any one shall accuse falsely* any one by name in regard to anything, and he shall deny it, awarding the penalty of the proof or denial, whichever it shall turn out, shall be the lord's. *Tol*, which the Romans call Theloneum, is the liberty of buying and selling on his land. *Theam*, that if any one raise a complaint† against any one and himself cannot show cause for it, the awarding the penalty and justice shall be as in the case of accusation above, in the hands of the lord. In regard to *infangenetheof*. His is the right of examining a thief of his own men if he be taken on his own property. And those that have not the customs which have been mentioned above before the justiciary shall make the matter right, either in the hundred or in the wapentake or in the shires.

OF GUESTS.

23. If any óne entertains any one known or unknown for two nights, he can consider him as his

---

*Calumpnor.   †Interciebat.

guest. But if the guest do wrong, he shall not incur damage for him. But if the man whom the guest wronged shall say before the justiciary that the wrong was done through the advice of the host, he shall free himself by an oath along with two of his legal neighbors, if he can, in regard to the advice and the deed. But if he cannot, he shall pay damages and a penalty. But if the guest shall have been entertained for the third night and shall do wrong to any one, let the host hold him to the right as if he were one of his family, as the English say, " Tuwa nicte geste, the thirde nicte agen hine " [Two nights a guest, the third night his own]. Yet if he cannot hold him to the right let him have a limit of a month and a day, and if he can find him let him, the guest, bring back the damage he has done and a penalty, if he is able, even with his body if the penalty be so far. If the malefactor, however, cannot restore the damage that he did, let the host that entertained him restore it and the penalty, and if the justiciary hold him in suspicion, let him clear himself in the court of the hundred or shire.

OF FINDS.

24. If any one shall bring anything into the city or an animal or any money, and shall say that he found it, before he shall bring it into his own house or the house of another, let him bring it to church, and make the priest of the church come, and the governor of the town and of the better men of the town as many as he can by summons of the mayor* and when they have come together he shall show to them the

---

*Prefecti.

whole thing found whatever it is, and the mayor shall
send to the four nearest towns and to their several
priests, and their mayors, and these mayors shall take
with them each one three or four of the better men
of the town and shall show to them the whole thing
that was found.   And after their testimony the chief
under whose rule the finder was, shall keep the find
until the next day, and then, with some neighbors of
his that saw the find, let him go to the governor of
the hundred in which the village is and show the
whole matter to him.   And if the lord in whose land
the thing was found have not his customs, namely, of
sac and soc he shall give it all to the governor of the
hundred if he wish to have it.   And if his lord have
his own customs let the man obtain his right in the
court of his lord.

OF THE JEWS.

25. Be it known that all the Jews, wherever in the
kingdom they are, should be lawfully under the
guardianship and defense of the king.   Nor let any
one of them, without the king's permission, put himself under any rich man, for the Jews themselves and
all their property is the king's.   But if any one shall
detain them or their money, the king if he wish and
can may demand it as his own property.

OF THE PEACE OF THE KING AND HOW THEY THAT HAVE PEACE BY HIS OWN HAND OR BY HIS WARRANT OUGHT TO BEHAVE THEMSELVES.

26. Of those that have the peace of the king be it
enacted: that, since it is in the highest degree necessary for them that they keep it toward all lawful persons, they may not on account of the peace keep back

service from their lords nor the rights to their neighbors if they owe any, for he is not worthy to have peace that does not love to observe peace. But if confiding in the peace which he has, through pride he shall wrong any one, let him restore damages and as much again, which the English call "astrikibthet" penalty.

ALSO HOW OR WHAT THEY THAT BROKE THE PEACE OF THE KING WERE WONT TO PAY, WHAT TO THE KING AND WHAT TO THE DECANUS.

27. Peace given by the hand of the king and in the eight days within which he was first crowned and the peace of the above-mentioned feasts and the peace by warrant of the king, have one measure of paying restitution, and in that court which is deemed greatest in the shire where the peace was broken, for example in the Danelag through the eighteen hundreds, the number fills up 144 libræ, for the Danes and Norwegians called eight libræ the restitution for a hundred. Nor is this without a reason, for of this the king has a hundred solidarii, and the governor of the shire, fifty, who has every third denarius of the penalty. But the decanus has the other ten except in the case of the peace of the king, namely, of the peace given by his own hand and at his first coronation, and at the above-mentioned feasts, Christmas, Easter, and Whitsunday.

WHY FRITHBORGS WERE MADE.

28. When, however, they saw that certain base persons were doing evil to their neighbors the wiser men took council among themselves how they could

repress them, and so they placed in each ten frithborgs justiciaries, whom we may call decani, but in
English they are called tyenthe heued, that is tenth
head.   These, then, between the villages, between the
neighbors, judged cases, and in regard to what penalties there were they made corrections and ordinances,
namely, in regard to pastures, meadows, crops, suits
between neighbors and of many things of this kind
which frequently arise.

29. But when greater cases arose they referred
these to the greater justiciaries whom the above-
mentioned wise men placed above them, namely over
the ten decani, whom we may call centurions, for they
judged over a hundred frithborgs.

OF THE HUNDREDS AND WAPENTAKES AND WHY THEY ARE CALLED WAPENTAKES.

30. Everichshire, Nicholeshire, Nottinghamshire,
Leicestershire, Northamptonshire, and as far as the
Watlingstrete and eight miles beyond the Watlingstrete are under the law of the English.   What others
call hundreds the above-mentioned shires call wapentakes, and that not without reason, for when any one
received the command of the wapentake, on the appointed day all the elders appeared before him, in the
place where they were wont to be assembled, and
when he dismounted from his horse, all stood over
against him and he held his spear upright while all
touched his spear with theirs. So they established
themselves for him. And the word is from arms,
because they call arms wappa, and taccare to establish.

OF THE TREHINGS AND WAPENTAKES AND HUNDREDS.

31. There were also other powers above the wapentakes, which they called trehings, namely, a third part of the shire, and those that rule over it they call trehingrefs, to whom were brought cases which they could not settle in the wapentakes. And what the English called a hundred these called a wapentake, and what the English called three hundreds, being three or more, they called trehings. And what could not be decided in the trehing was kept for the shire.

WHAT GOVERNOR AND RULE AND ALDERMAN (WHO IN LATIN IS CALLED SENIOR POPULI) ARE AND HOW GREATLY THE NAME GOVERNOR IS STRETCHED.

32. Moreover greve is a word meaning power. Nothing seems to give a better translation than prefectura (rule, government). For greve is said of the shire, wapentake, hundred, borough, and town, and seems to be compounded of the English grith, Latin pax (peace), and ve, Latin, meaning what ought to exact grith or peace from those that bring upon the earth *ve*, that is misery and woe, on the highest authority of our Lord Jesus Christ, who says "Woe (ve) to thee, Bethsaida, woe to thee, Chorazin." The Frisians and the Flandrians call their nobles meregraves, as if greater or good peace-makers; and just as now they that have rule over others are called greves, so then they were called aldermen, not on account of their age but on account of their wisdom.

LAWS OF THE DANES.

33. There was also a law of the Danes in Norfolk, Suffolk, and Canterburyshire, which held as the pen-

alty of an evil deed, where the above-mentioned counties had their eighteen hundreds, the ten and a half [mark?], and on the kindred analogy of the Saxons, because at that time the greatest recompense for an evil deed among the Saxons was eighty-four libræ. In all other cases and penalties they had the same customs as the above-mentioned Northmen.

WHY THE LAW OF KING EDWARD WAS AUTHORIZED BY WILLIAM KING OF THE ENGLISH.

34. When King William himself heard this and other laws of the kingdom he specially valued this and wished that it be observed through the whole kingdom, because the predecessors of himself and of all the Normans came from Norway and they ought rightly to follow its law when it was honorable, as being deeper and more honorable than all the others, namely, the laws of the Britons, Picts and Angles. But all the fellow countrymen who told the laws besought him exceedingly that he would grant to them to have the laws and customs under which their predecessors and his had lived and they themselves had been born, because it was hard for them to undergo laws and to give judgment in regard to those things of which they were ignorant. And this they begged by the soul of King Edward, who had granted to him the kingdom and of whom the laws were, and not of other persons. At length by the advice and prayer of his barons, he kept quiet and so the laws of King Edward were authorized, which were first invented and set forth in the time of King Edgar, his grandfather, but after Edgar's death were given up for sixty-eight years. Edward his son, born of his

wife, reigned four years less sixteen weeks. And he dying through a wile on the part of his stepmother, innocently, on account of his innocent life, chaste and full of alms-giving, they gave out his slaying as a martyrdom and called him a saint. Afterward Ælldred, his brother, took the throne and reigned, in many dangers, for thirty-eight years. After his death his son Edmund, whose surname was Ironside, reigned nearly nine months, in which he fought like a man against Canute, King of the Danes, five times. The last war being settled, they made peace with each other. The kingdom of England, indeed, they divided, half to Canute and half to Edmund, on this condition that if either of them survived he should possess all the property of the other and in the mean time neither of them should be crowned. But when this agreement was confirmed, all the first men of England consenting, at the end of the first month Edmund died and was taken from this life, alas! Canute indeed took the whole kingdom of England and reigned nearly eighteen years. At his death Harold, falsely deemed his son by almost all, succeeded and reigned five years. After whom Hardicanute, the son of Canute and Emma Alfuera, sister of Robert of Normandy and mother of King Edward, reigned for two years less twelve weeks. And so were completed the sixty-eight years when the laws were in disuse. But after King Edward came to the throne, by advice of the barons of the kingdom he made the law that was given up, to be revised and confirmed because it seemed honorable to them and his grandfather had ordained it, and so the law is called the law of King Edward, which was first disused at the death of Edgar, his grandfather, until his own time.

OF THE ARRIVAL OF SAINT MARGARET, MOTHER OF THE KING OF SCOTLAND, AND OF EDGAR ATHELING HIS BROTHER, IN ENGLAND, OF WHICH SAINT EDWARD THE KING WAS UNWILLING TO MAKE HIM HIS HEIR, AND AFTERWARD MADE DUKE WILLIAM HIS HEIR, WHICH HE WAS UNWILLING TO DO IN REGARD TO EDGAR.

35. The above mentioned Edmund had a son, who was called Edward, who at the death of his father fled in fear from this land to the land of the Rugi, which we call Russia, and the king of this land, Malesclodus by name, when he gave audience to him and knew who and whence he was, kept him honorably. And Edgar himself took there a wife of noble lineage, of whom was born to him Edgar Atheling and Margaret, Queen of Scotland, and Christiana her sister, to whom King Edward gave land, whom afterward Radolfus of Linisia married, on account of which King Edward, her uncle, sent and made him come to him. But he and his wife did not live long after their coming. Their son Edgar, Edward kept with him and brought up as his son. Because, indeed, he thought to make him his heir he called him Atheling, which we translate by Domicellus. Now we use this of more persons, for we call the sons of the barons Domicelli, but the English no one but the sons of kings. But if we wish to say it more exactly let us say that in the language of a certain part of Saxony an image is called ling, and Aethel is English for noble, which compounded, Aetheling is noble image,

from which the West Saxons, namely the men of Exeter have a saying of the greatest contempt, in that when moved by the highest wrath they call one another a hinderling, that is, one sunk down from all honor. But the king, Edward, because he knew the worthlessness of his race, and especially of the sons of Godwin, namely Harold, Tosti, Gurth and Leofwin, perceived that things could not be firm or stable under Edgar, and adopted William, Duke of' Normandy, son of Robert, Edward's uncle, and William afterward, by the grace of God, obtained his right in the battle against the above mentioned Harold.

OF THOSE SLAIN FOR THIEVING.

36. If after justice has been done, any one shall make complaint to the justiciary that he, the dead man, was slain unjustly, and that unjustly he lies among thieves, if he shall say that he wishes to contest* this let him give bail and sureties. And let there be given to him the limit of one month that he may obtain the relatives of the slain man on each side of his line, on his father's side twelve and on his mother's side six. And if these eighteen are willing to contest with him who first made the complaint and who gave bail, let each one of them give bail with a sword† and find such sureties as are able to pay back satisfaction, that is his price, if they cannot decide. And then the slayer shall give his bail and shall find sureties to the effect that the man was justly slain and justly lies among thieves, being a thief. And then in the first place let him say for what theft and

---

* Diracionare.   † Cum gladio.

for what reason he was slain. And if he shall know that he was taken alive let him name the justiciary and the judges, and the legal witnesses of the neighbors. And if they shall prove for him that justice was done justly, and that it was for theft in his case, the slayer shall be quit, and they that made the complaint shall pay the bail. But if the judges and witnesses shall fail him and the decision shall be that he was unjustly slain, the slayer shall pay his bail to the justiciary of the bishop and the sureties shall have the right of prosecuting him. And afterward the bishop's justiciary shall cause a procession to be made with the priest clad in an alb and maniple and stole, and the other clergy in surplices with holy water and a cross and candles and a censer with holy water and incense, and so shall they take the dead man from the earth and carry him to the church, laying him on a bier, and after singing a mass and the holy service they shall bury him as a Christian. And from that day within sixteen days let the slayer give to the bishop three recompenses; one because he slew a lawful person unjustly for a thief, a second because he buried his brother as a thief, this the English call his emcristen, the third because he gave bail for deciding the suit and could not win.

OF USURERS.

87. Usurers indeed Edward forbids to live in his kingdom. And if any one be proved such he shall lose all his possessions and be held an exile. Moreover he said this, that in the court of the king of the Franks, while he remained there, not without justice was usury called the root of all evils.

OF BUYING LIVE ANIMALS AND OLD CLOTHING.

38. It was also forbidden in the law for any one to buy a live animal or used clothing without sureties and good witnesses. And if there was any gold or silver, in regard to which the buyer might be in doubt, he should not buy it save in the presence of goldsmiths and money dealers. And if they see something that is the property of the church or the treasuries, let him not buy it without a pledge. And if the seller cannot get pledges, let it be kept along with the money until his lord come or some one else that can justly warrant him. But if any one buys on other terms let him lose what he has stupidly bought and a penalty, and afterward let the justiciary inquire among the lahmen and the better men of the borough or hundred or town where the buyer remains, of what town he was, and if any heard of him before as accused of illegal conduct. But if they bear witness against him of illegality let him free himself in the county court that he did not know the seller was guilty in this selling nor in any other illegality. If, moreover, he shall know the seller, who and where he is, let him tell it and let the justiciary seek him to do justice, and if he cannot be found, let him be outlawed.

OF THE SLAYING OF ANIMALS TOWARDS CHRISTMAS.

39. But when it was said that they should not buy animals without pledges, the butchers, whom the English call fleismangeres, made complaint from the cities and boroughs, because they had to buy, kill, and sell animals every day. The citizens and burgesses complained also on account of their customs, because on and about Saint Martin's day they used to buy

animals without a pledge, and make their killing toward Christmas, which customs we do not take away from them, for they are just and wisely arranged customs, but we make the law in regard to wares bought in the presence of witnesses and with the knowledge of the seller.

Here end the laws of King Edward, first set forth by Edgar his grandfather, and confirmed by William, Conqueror of England, having previously been approved by King Canute in his time.

THE LIBERTY OF CITIZENS.

1. Be it known that from the city out in every direction for three miles, a man must not let nor hinder another nor even do business with him, if he wishes to come to the city in its peace. But when he has come into the city then he may trade with any one, rich or poor.

OF THE LIBERTY OF THE CITIZENS OF LONDON.

2. Be it known also that a man that is of the court of the king or a baron ought not to be entertained three times in the house of a citizen of London, either by freedom or custom, except free of expense by his host. For if he bring force against his entertainer in his own house and shall be slain, the host may choose six of his relatives and himself the seventh shall swear that on account of the reason above given he slew him. And so shall he remain quit toward the king and the parents and lords of the slain man.

---

*Liberacione vel consuetudine.

ALSO OF LONDON.

3. It is to be known also that a citizen of London outside the walls of the city shall plead before the king not any one else. For if he has done a wrong which can be satisfied by money, he is not to be fined more than his wer, namely, a hundred solidarii.

4. The lieutenant governors shall not dare to take away the money of any one of the city nor to call in any one, remaining in their soc to the pleadings of the king, until the guardian of that soc in which he remains has been wanting to the lieutenant in holding to the right unless he shall find the man in the soc of the king openly and plainly doing wrong.

5. Also a citizen, if he comes to the assembly of the people or the council without any summons to plead, need not answer to any one in regard to a complaint unless he wishes to.

6. Again, if a citizen of London wishes to sell his land on account of its poorness, neither his son nor his parents can prevent him unless they wish to buy it on his giving it up.

7. If any citizen of London hold any land for a year and a day without an action, he need not answer to any one remaining in the city, unless he that afterward brought the action was then of such an age as not to know how to bring the action or unless illness prevented him or he was not in this country.

8. Therefore, a foreign merchant, after he has entered the city by whomsoever he pleases shall be entertained. But let him see to it that he does not sell his wares by cutting them and that if he bring things stained with yellow* he shall sell not less than

---

*Fulco.

17

twelve at once. And if he brings pepper, or cummin, or ginger, or alum, or basil, or lac, or incense, let him sell not less than twenty-five pounds at one time. But if he has brought bells, let him not sell at one time less than a thousand. And if he bring clothes of silk, or wool, or lineh, let him see to it not to cut them, but to sell them whole. But if he bring wax, let him see to it that he sell not less than twenty-five pounds. Also let the foreign merchant not sell any fresh bread, or tincture in the city, or any other ware that belongs to the citizens to do.

9. A foreign merchant with his associate may not make any ware within the city for the purpose of selling it again in the city, nor may he hire a citizen to make any ware nor longer in the city remain.

These laws, bearing the name of Edward the Confessor, were really set out or written down by a commission summoned by William the Conqueror, and have authority only as a compilation. But as a record made by William, or under his authority, they properly have a place here as showing what of Saxon law was recognized by William on his accession to the kingdom. These laws are antecedent to the new system introduced by the Conqueror from the continent out of which was developed the system known as The Common Law of England. I am not prepared to say how critical the translation of these laws may be. But this is immaterial, as my only object in including them at all in this volume is an historical showing of the scope and subjects of the prevailing laws at the period when the machinery which produced the common law was put in motion. But I have no doubt Mr. Gilman has given a fair translation of the Latin text contained in the publication of British Commission of Records. Edward the Confessor died in 1066, the same year of the conquest.

RETROSPECT OF SAXON LAWS.

In retrospect of the Saxon laws, we remark, they develop not only the conditions and progress of the country, but the growth and progress of a legal system. Laws are really the best criterions by which to judge of the character of a people, and to appreciate the changes transpiring in a state, for laws enacted against crimes presume a necessity in that respect. In general, we observe that the larger the nation and the more dense the population the more severe are the penalties for the breach of the laws. It would seem from some of these old Saxon laws, that the more profound the regard of the government to religion, or rather to superstition, the more inhuman and barbarous legal penalties became. But this view should be qualified by the consideration of the increased numbers to be restrained, and that growing wealth or property increases temptations to crime. The beggar may well say, "my poverty is my protection." If such realize any suffering not the result of want it is usually a mistake on the part of those criminally inclined, unless the purpose is to reduce such class to actual slavery. They have no gold or silver or jewels that are usually the robber's temptation. To give order to our remarks, we gather from these laws special topics, and trace the changes relating thereto through all the days of the Saxon and Danish kings. And, first, of

MARRIAGE.

In 77 Ethelbert: "If a man *buy* a maiden with

cattle, let the bargain stand, if it be without guile; but if there be guile, let him bring her home again, and let his property be restored to him."

In 78 *Ib.:* " If she bear a live child, let her have half the property, if the husband die first." [Natural law charges the husband with the duty of contributing to the support of his own children.]

In 79 *Ib.:* " If she wish to go away with her children, let her have half the property."

Edmund, A. D. 946: Betrothal of a woman (1, 2, 3, 4, 5, 6, 7, 8, 9). Marriage was to be celebrated by a mass priest; care should be taken that the parties were not too nearly related. Ecclesiastical law restricted marriage between kindred up to the seventh degree, two or three degrees more strict than the inhibition of the Mosaic law.

Ethelred vi. 12 limits marriage between kindred up to the fourth degree. In Canute 74, every widow was required to remain single twelve months. To violate this law forfeited all rights in the former husband's estate. By 75 Canute, no one should compel a widow or maiden to marry one she dislikes, nor be sold for money, unless the proposed husband might give anything voluntarily. This law was a restriction on tutors or guardians.

PROPERTY.

The scope in which these ancient laws operated with respect to the civil state is best gathered from the subjects to which they relate. As property was generally made a compensation for crime, so upon it was predicated the civil conditions of different classes of the people. Hence the nature, kind, and extent of

the property held by these Saxon communities becomes material in the exposition of the object and
intendments of their legal statutes.

, Titles to real property, whether in individuals or
the state, would be very precarious in a country subject to internecine wars, where the victor took, not
only the power and the right to govern the conquered, but claimed the absolute ownership of all that
they had, and thought it a mercy to allow them their
lives, on their accepting the condition of slavery.
Probably during the Saxon *régime*, continuing with
the reign of the Danes over six hundred years,
scarcely a fourth part of all those centuries was the
country free from foreign and domestic wars ; any interest in personal title to the lands in those who
cultivated it was scarcely to be thought of. If the
peasant could harvest his crop for this year, it was
too much an uncertainty as to who would own the
soil next year to make it expedient for him to seek
an uncertain ownership in the land so likely to be
wrested from him.

While to the king and his nobility was remitted the
duty of defending the land, they naturally claimed a
paramount title in that which they had protected ;
and titles in land, in the mere citizen, were only recognized after centuries of infinitesimal accretions
from royal power. But designations apply to land
both with respect to their condition and ownership.
In the first place there was the " *tun*," embracing doubtless a house and field or meadow with buildings. It
grew to represent a *town*. Then there was the *close*,
meaning land fenced in, out of *folc-land* or com-
mons. The close had analogies to a farmstead with

dwelling and other buildings. Then there was a *flet*, meaning a hut, cottage, or ale-house. There were hydes and yards of land, referring to quantity without regard to any one's holding or the nature of the title held.

REAL ESTATE.

Edor-breach—Burglary, breaking into a close and residence. Æthelbirht 27.

If a man burn or hew another's wood without leave. Alfred 12; Athelstan i. 6; Athelstan iv. 6.

Hynd-man designates a citizen or thane as to the quantity of land in his holding. *Bot* or fines vary, as he might be a two hynd-man or a twelve hynd-man. Alfred 40; Ine 43.

Boc-land seems to have been the oldest title subordinate to the eminent domain of the crown, of lands in England. The term signifies simply book-land, or land whose title and investment was recorded or in writing. It is distinguished from folc-land, which was common land used and occupied by the people in common, subject to many undefined duties to the lord or the king. Boc-land not only had its title vested by charter, but the nature and extent of the estate granted were defined, and the burdens or charges were limited and stated. The nobility, clergy, churches, and ordinary citizens might be grantors of boc-land, subject to the taxes or services specified in the charter granting them. Such grants might be for life or for years, or estates of inheritance. Such grants would generally in their early use be limited to the great lords, temporal or spiritual, of the kingdom; but at length become available to common men, when the economies of the government dictated it.   A king without subjects would be esteemed a crank; and if he would have subjects they must be subsisted from the soil.   To do this, the soil must be cultivated; and inducements for such cultivation must be offered to the industrial strength of the nation.

Reaf-lac, in Ine 10, is in the nature of what is known in modern law as *forcible entry and detainer*, in which robbery might be committed.   Canute Sec. 64.

A ceorl's (husbandman) or peasant's close ought to be fenced.   If it be unfenced and his neighbors' cattle stray in he must bear the damage.   Iue 40 and 42.

The taking of wood without leave incurred the fine of 60 shillings.   Ine 44.

If one found among his swine those belonging to his neighbor, the neighbor must pay one shilling if they had come there but once, but 6 shillings if oftener.

Those seized of lands must have one-half or over under cultivation.   Ine 64, 65, and 66.   A lord letting land for rent must put a dwelling on it.   Ine 67.

Statute of Limitations as to Land.   And he who sits without contest or claim on his property during life that no one have an action against his heir after his death.   Ethelred iii. 14; Canute Sec. 73.

DOWER.

Dower in lands is said to have been unknown to the Roman law, though traces of it were found among the northern nations; yet it may be doubted if it existed in England, or, if it did, that it applied to any class below the thanes or nobility, for these held the paramount titles, under the chiefs, to all the lands. Hence it is not singular that we find scarcely a shadow of evidence of such an estate in the old Saxon laws. Endowments at the door of the church, or otherwise, on the day of marriage, related simply to goods and chattels. From the best attainable evidence, estates in dower of lands in England had their origin under *Norman law*, after the Conquest. It is to be presumed that, to the extent of the estates in lands that became vested in the commonalty, their widows would seek by themselves, or their kindred, to extend their rights in personalty in like proportions to the realty. But the policy of the feudal law, then prevailing, to prevent the disintegration of landed estates, when dower came to be defined and settled, limited it to the *use* of one-third the realty during the life of the endowed. Dower has a natural basis in the necessities of the survivors of those dying seized of lands. The widow charged generally with the care and maintenance of children would have a natural claim on the estate of her deceased husband such as it might be ; and when such estate in lands increased in its extent and character the estate in dower would be enlarged from the lesser to be a charge on the greater estate, up to the life use of a fee simple absolute.

It is evident that the widow's rights in her deceased husband's property had respect to the care and support of children, as provided in Æthelbirht 78, 79, and 80. In case she cared for the children she took one-half, otherwise her share was as one child. " If the husband wish to have them, [let her portion be] as one child." In Æthelbirht 81 : If she bear no child, let her paternal kindred have what her father's family bestowed on her, at her marriage, and the gifts made to the wife by the husband the morning after marriage. The first of these was called the *fioh*, and the latter the *morgen gyfe*. (A. D. 616.)

This law operated in case of the husband's death, and she went to her paternal home, in her widowhood, for care and protection.

In 6 Hlothhære and Eadric (A. D. 673), it is provided: "If a husband die, wife and child yet living, it is right that the child follow the mother; and let there be sufficient '*borh*' [security] given to him [the child] from among his paternal kinsmen, to keep his property till he be ten years of age." Ine 31 provides: "If a man buy a wife, and the marriage take not place, let him give the money, and compensate and make '*bot*' to his surety as his breach of covenant may be." A. D. 688—725.

Ine 38: "If a *ceorl* and his wife have a child, and the *ceorl* die, let the mother have her child, and feed it. Let six shillings be given her for its fostering; a cow in summer, an ox in winter. Let the kindred take care of the frum-stol [or dwelling] until the child be of age."

A ceorl was of a degree above a theow, an esne, or slave; a freeman, probably a farmer who might be attached to the soil.

But in noting subsequent changes at the Conquest we remark the subject of dower is discussed at considerable length by Glanville. As a provision for a widow, as we have said, it was unknown among the Romans, and in the days of the earlier Saxon kings it was, doubtless, limited to chattels, as the citizen could hardly be presumed to have an absolute estate

in fee in lands; though the legal incidents affecting
agriculture and stock raising, contained in the Saxon
laws, show occupation of the soil, under some tenure
probably less than an actual estate in fee or in perpetuity. The king in theory was the owner, by title
paramount, of all the lands in the kingdom. Grants,
however, to the nobility did not revert to the king on
the death of the grantee, but descended to heirs according to the character of the estate. Then the
farmers held of the king, or of the great lords. If it
were *boc-lands* or book-lands,—held by writing or book,
—it would descend to heirs, and in this the wife might
be endowed. But *folc-land* was land common in its
title to all the people or the king. But under certain
qualified holdings and subject to certain taxes or burdens it became occupied separately by a tenantry
with scarcely a lien on their several possessions, with
scarcely the quality of an estate on which a descent
could be cast. The children of the deceased tenant
might have a sort of good will to continue the possession on assuming the burdens on the land, but the
rights of such succession were too intangible to predicate an estate in dower thereon.

The widows of the nobility might at length become
endowed in the castles and manors of which their
husbands died seized; and estates in dower so recognized might attach to the lands of freemen when their
holdings in fee or in perpetuity became fixed and
regular.

But in the earliest Saxon times the wife at the time
of her marriage was endowed by her husband with
dower, either in specified property or, if none were
specified, then generally in all he then possessed.

But it could not afterwards be enlarged to embrace after-acquired property of the husband, and as property in land became available in the domestic interests of life, the custom of dower followed such conversion of personalty into realty where the estate acquired was sufficient to sustain a right of dower so that dower, when admeasured, became an estate in land. Glanville's proposition, that a wife might be endowed in the personal estate of her husband, which was true in the early Saxon times, was only disputed after the law of dower was changed by the seventh chapter of *Magna Charta*, giving the wife dower "in all the lands of which the husband was seized at any time during coverture."

In the time of Glanville dower might be made by the husband less than one-third, but it could not be made more. If specific property was mentioned by the husband in his declaration at the door of the church, at the time of the marriage, and this was found to exceed one-third of what he then had, the admeasurement of the dower would reduce it to one-third, excluding all after-acquired property. Under the law of dower in Glanville's day, its admeasurement must have been complicated and uncertain. It must have been a question of fact, in most cases, to be proved years after the marriage, as to what the endowment at the church door was. Unless it were a custom to make a record in the church books, the change of a lifetime would have rendered the answer to this question very uncertain. The fixing of the dower by the Magna Charta on all the lands the husband had or acquired during the marriage, not only enlarged and made more certain the rights of the widow, but relieved the courts from a great inconvenience. Dower then became an estate or right vested by law, that could not be altered or changed by the acts of the husband alone.   The wife could make a jointure to bar her dower, or with her husband convey it to a purchaser, with the land, or the law might take it away for offenses on her part against the marriage relation.

ROYAL DIGNITY AND AUTHORITY.

In Æthelbirht 3: If the king drink at any one's home and any one there do him injury, or steal from his person, let such make twofold compensation. This nation of drunkards, according to Hume, protected the king when drunk, as well as the citizen. Perhaps the king suspected that the hospitality of his subjects might have a motive beyond mere social enjoyment.

Stealing from the king involved a penalty of ninefold. *Ib.* 4.

Burg brice, breaking into houses or gardens of the king, *bot* 120 shillings.   Ine 45.

Injuries to the king's servants, and to those under his protection, were punished by penalties to the king.   *Ib.* 2, 5, 7, 8, 10, 11, 12.

"If any one fight in the king's hall, or draw his weapon and be taken; be it in the king's judgment, either death or life, as he (the king) may be willing to grant him," etc. Alfred 7; Ine 6; Ethelred vii., 12, 15.

"Let the word of a bishop and of the king be, without an oath, incontrovertible."   Wihtræd 16.

If any one plot against the king's life let him be liable in his life; unless he clear himself. Ethelred v. 30; vi. 37.

SLAVERY.

Slavery did not have a beginning with the old Britons, the Romans, or the Saxon rule in England. It is one of the prehistoric incidents of human conditions. The world, from the very beginning of sin and crime, was cursed with human slavery. It was a refinement on the natural selfishness of depraved humanity, for it drew after it most cruel necessities of torture and murder, to maintain it. It was against the very instincts of humanity, against human consciousness of justice and right. Its victims were in rebellion, in antagonism to the power that ruled them. It only waited its opportunity, and its power, to revenge. Hence, in an age when every other class could condone their crimes by the payment of money, the slave, for any offense, was subject to scourging and mutilation, as these old laws put it, must suffer in his hide.

Yet slavery where master and slave are of the same race is probably less servile than where slaves are prisoners reduced to slavery as captives in foreign wars; and, especially, where color and race are made the basis of slavery. Then the condition or the state of society in that remote age imposed emergencies on the master and servant to mutually aid each other in the protection of the local estates from the incursion of foreign enemies, or the local strifes of contending nobles at home.

Military retainers had a rank above mere slaves or peasants on the soil. They were vassals subject to military conscriptions, as vassals of the lord or the crown. But otherwise they farmed their lands as independent citizens.

In every age the inexorable laws of slavery reduce man to the condition of a chattel. A slave can own nothing, and even his children must follow the condition of the mother, so any punishment can only be inflicted on his person.

But this law, without which slavery could hardly be perpetuated, had exceptions with the old Anglo-Saxons, on the principle, I presume, that a freeman who was permitted to marry a slave became her owner, for so much that the offspring were in his power, as their father. But this rule only applied to the children born to slave mothers in wedlock with a freeman.

CONSTITUTION OF THE COURTS.

Another subject for special inquiry, in considering the Anglo-Saxon *régime*, is the constitution of the courts, for laws have little significance when there is no power or agencies to enforce them.

In the days of Æthelbirht, we have no indications as to how the laws were enforced. As the kingdom of Kent was about the size of a county, the administration of justice was practicable in the king's hall by the king in person, or by those appointed to sit as judges in his place. There was, probably, something like a rude administration of justice in the towns or other divisions of the country. But these courts made no records, and have perished from the knowledge of history.

In Hlothhaire and Eadric 5, the *stermelda* is mentioned, as a judicial officer, with functions somewhat like those of the modern sheriff; also the *methel* and the *thing*. The former supposed to be the court of the hundred, the latter of the tithing. It seems the records were filed in those courts, and the parties afterwards sought an arbitrator to determine the cause.

In Ine 8 a *scir-man* is mentioned as one before whom justice might be demanded.

A *scir-man gemot* afterwards meant a county court.

Every hundred was under the control of an ealdorman. And the *hundred gemot* or county court was held monthly, while the *burgh gemot* was held thrice, and the *shire gemot* twice, in a year. And at this last court, the bishop of the shire and ealdorman were to be present and administer the laws, as well the law of God as the secular law. Laws of King Edgar ii. 5. A. D. 959 to 975.

Subsequent to the Conquest, earls sat as judges in the county courts.

The term justiciary was applied to the chief judge of the king's court in the days of Edward the Confessor, A. D. 1043–66.

So these Anglo-Saxon courts were constituted coming down to the reign of this last Saxon king. But it is of less account as to who administered the laws, in that remote age, than *how* they were administered. I should, however, note the office of the reeve, who, in addition to his judicial office in the lower courts known afterwards as the sheriff's tourn, was the active executor of the decrees of the higher courts; then he was bailiff, both to the crown and the clergy, in collecting and farming the revenues of the king and the church, within the shire or the limit of his jurisdiction. His office in this latter capacity resembled that of sheriff in the United States, being an executive rather than a judicial office. At a later period he, could hold all pleas as a magistrate, except pleas of the crown.

MANNER OF CONDUCTING TRIALS.

In Hlothhaire and Eadric 8, 9, 10, A. D. 673 : If one make plaint against another in a suit, after he has given him security, then after three days let them seek for themselves an *arbitrator*, unless a longer period be desired by him who carries on the suit. After the suit is settled [determined] let the man do justice to the other within seven days. Let him satisfy him either in money or with an oath, whichever be desired by him. But if he will not do this, then let him pay one hundred pence without an oath; within one day after let them settle.

We are not to presume but that in cases where direct testimony was available as to facts in issue in civil and criminal trials, such testimony was admitted and had force in determining the judgment. But the judicial burden imposed was the determination of cases where no such evidence was attainable, and where from the ignorance of the witnesses it failed of a proper statement to make the basis of any intelligent conclusions. Besides, every man being open to suspicion, and liable to charges of offenses, he would likely be biased in his statements, and justice would so be perverted. There appears to have been another idea, that justice was safer and law and order would be better preserved, when whole neighborhoods were made responsible for the results of judicial proceedings, than when such were the result of the prejudices and hostilities of suitors or their individual witnesses.

In the absence of direct proofs, on either side, the accused might produce a prescribed number of his neighbors, as *œwda men* or witnesses, or,' more properly, compurgators; and if they did not know the facts they were allowed to swear that from their knowledge of the accused they believed him to be innocent of the charge preferred against him. The number of such witnesses became important, as their testimony was equivalent to testimony in modern criminal trials of the previous good character of the accused.

But in such a case the accused had to swear to his innocence, and the compurgators, that they believed his oath. The number and rank of the compurgators was fixed by the rank of the accused; varying from five to eleven. The higher rank might swear for a lower, but those of lower rank could not swear for a higher. A thane must clear himself with the oath of twelve thanes, counting himself as one. In some cases a larger number of compurgators was required.

The oath of the lord was sometimes sufficient to clear a vassal or a slave. The oaths of the nobility counted in favor of inferior persons according to their *wer-gild* or legal value. And the single oath of a stranger accused, when taken on the relics at the church altar, was, in some cases, sufficient to clear him from the charge. This was allowed in the interest of Christian hospitality to a foreigner, who, away from home and all his friends, could find none who could swear for him on knowledge and a good conscience. There was a necessity in the case that

18

they should take the chance of punishing an innocent man or allowing him to go free, on his making a
most solemn asseveration of his innocence, though
we can hardly presume that such a defense would
prevail against positive proof of guilt.

Every person seems, in that age, to be liable to the
charge of crime, even when no witnesses were available to support the charge; and he must repel the
presumption of his guilt.by showing his standing with
his neighbors. This was the reverse of the rule of
law that presumes every man to be innocent until he
is proved guilty. Whether it was the policy of the
government to make every man's safety depend on
the friendship of his neighbors, or that this was the
best form of trial that could be devised in that rude
and ignorant age, does not appear. Such dependence
on one's neighbors would doubtless have a strong influence in preventing or diminishing crime. On the
whole, judgments so settled might have been safer to
the people than any other available method of arriving
at a conclusion; especially while the law presumed
every accused man guilty till he proved his innocence.

When we come to matters of property, every man
accused of the theft of property in his possession
might vouch to the warranty of his title to the property in the king's hall, or otherwise, in the king's
court. This was done by bringing the person from
whom he bought it, or the witnesses who stood by
at the time of its purchase.

This vouching to warranty, of goods—including
cattle—alleged to have been stolen by the person
in whose possession they were found, is provided for
in all the Saxon laws, was repeated and amplified by

Canúte the Dane, and adopted by William the Conqueror. The proceeding was something in this wise: the claimant of property found in the possession of another proceeded to attach the property, claimed either by legal process or, it seems more likely, by taking actual possession of it without process. But if the party with whom the property was found offered to vouch to the warranty of his title by showing from whom and where he purchased it, and gave bohr, or security, to do so, he was allowed a prescribed time to do so, before the property could be taken by the claimant. But proof of his honest purchase of the property was not always conclusive, for the last seller might have sold stolen goods. The vouching to warranty might be a duty imposed on not more than two prior owners. If the proofs failed then the claimant took the property; otherwise it was left with the party in whose possession it was found. This proceeding was really the process of a replevin suit as known at the present day.

Several of the Saxon laws contain injunctions that the purchasers of property have witnesses to their transactions available in any vouching to warranty that might be imposed on them. In Alfred and Guthrum 4, every man is required to know his warrantor.

That every man have his warrantor. Edward 1.

That he who vouches have unlying witnesses. Edward 1.

In Hlothhaire and Eadric 16, if any Kentish-man buy a chattel in Lunden-wic let him have two or three men to witness, or the king's wic-reeve. Then if he was afterwards compelled to vouch to warranty he could prove the transaction or establish his title to the goods in case the seller could not be found. (See Oaths 2, 3, 4, 5.)

TRIAL BY ORDEAL.

Trial by ordeal, in a superstitious age, was to the populace a sort of appeal to providence for the solving of legal conclusions where evidence had failed of satisfying the judicial mind as to the guilt or innocence of the accused. In the popular conception, there seems to have been a necessity that every accused person should be either convicted or exonerated from any charge made against him. The rule of law then was the reverse of what obtained under the administration of the common law; to wit, "That every person is to be esteemed *innocent* until proved guilty." But in these old Saxon courts every accused person must clear himself or herself by swearing to his or her innocence, and producing a prescribed number of neighbors as compurgators, who would swear that they believed the accused's oath of innocence. Failing in finding the necessary compurgators, the accused was condemned to pay *bot* and *wer*, or to suffer in life and limb, or be remitted to the king's mercy. Lest an accused might, through misfortune, fail of finding necessary compurgators and suffer innocently, as a last resort he might appeal to heaven, through prescribed ordeals, to establish his innocence.

In the growth of superstition and the sinister interests in the clergy administering ordeals, this method of trial became a primary, affirmative proceeding in many cases, instead of an alternative in extreme necessity, in the administration of the law. It was popular with the clergy because it recognized their professed sanctity in representing the divine will in respect to men. It might have been corrupt in gathering large gifts to the church, or the minister who presided at the ordeal, where the accused was declared innocent by the priest's favorable report of the results of such trial. For we are not to presume but that fire would burn, and water if heated might burn, or if cold might drown, both the innocent and guilty alike; but he who conducted the operation could save either at his will. The iron might not be heated to burn, or, if it were, the burning might be short of warranting a judgment of *guilty*. In fact, the life, limb, and fortune of an accused was, in this form of trial, completely in the hands of the officiating priest. He could save his friends and be revenged on an enemy. It is to be presumed that through the policy or charity of the clergy more were saved through the ordeal than punished. It continued from the days of Ine through six centuries to the time of King John.

The Norman barons despised it as only fit for use by women and maimed and aged people, while trial by battle or duel was their favorite substitute. The ordeal was finally suppressed by the Pope, doubtless for its corrupting influence on the lower clergy, who were its administrators.

THE CLERGY AS AN ELEMENT IN THE SAXON GOVERNMENT IN ENGLAND.

In the constitution of the Saxon governments in England, the clergy, if not in rank, were in influence next to the kings, though Æthelbirht of Kent, in the oldest Saxon laws extant, contents himself with protecting the clergy in their rights and possessions, by enacting a severer penalty for offenses against them than against those of the same ranks of the secular nobility. If the property of God and the church were stolen or destroyed, the compensation was twelvefold, that of the bishop was elevenfold, a priest's ninefold, a deacon's sixfold, a clerk's threefold, etc. Compensation for causing the death of these church officers was doubtless estimated at the like relative values. But I find no evidences that the clergy, during this reign of fifty-six years ending 616, assumed or were admitted to any voice in the secular government. Hence I have said that St. Augustine must have been a man of great discretion in not claiming recognition in secular affairs.

Fifty-seven years after the death of Æthelbirht, Hlothhaire and Eadric left records of sixteen special statutes in which the clergy are not referred to.

But Wihtræd, who died after a reign of thirty-four years over the kingdom of Kent, in 725, in the twenty-eight statutes that bear his name, recites that a convention of the great men was held at Bergham-styde, at which these statutes were enacted.

" There Birhtwald, archbishop of Britain, and the king, also Gybmund, the bishop of Rochester, were present, and every degree of the church of that province spoke in unison with the obedient people. There the great men decreed, with the suffrages of all, these judgments, and added them to the lawful customs of the Kentish-men, as it hereafter saith and declareth." The views of this council, in which the clerical element specially predominated, are seen in the acts copied.

Ine, king of the West Saxons, whose reign commenced 688, and who reigned contemporary with Wihtræd, assembled a council for the revision or settlement of the laws of his kingdom, at which he recited the teaching of Cenred his father, also of Hedde his bishop, and of Eorcelwold his bishop, and all his ealdormen and the most distinguished witan (council) of his people.

The characteristic of the laws settled by this council or parliament we have noted as illustrating the policy of this government; and from their character we infer that clerical influence was conspicuous if it did not predominate in their production. These provisions appear :—

"1. We command that God's servants rightly hold their lawful rule.

"2. Let a child within thirty days be baptized. If it be not so, let him [the priest or parent?] pay a penalty with thirty shillings. But if it die without baptism, let him [the priest or parent?] make bot [or pay the penalty] of all that he has."

3. Working on Sunday is specially prohibited. If such work be done by the command of the lord, thirty shillings was the penalty. A slave by so offending was subject to scourging. A freeman became a slave or paid from his property sixty shillings. A priest so offending became doubly liable.

4. Let church-scots (or taxes) be rendered at Martinmas. In default he must pay sixty shillings, and pay twelvefold.

5. Relief from penalties to be realized on the culprit fleeing to a church. A slave by so doing saved himself from scourging.

6.   To fight within a cathedral church or minster incurred a penalty of one hundred and twenty shillings.

13.   If any one before a bishop belie his testimony and his wed (pledge), he must pay one hundred and twenty shillings.

But most of the secular laws of Ine, save as to the conditions of the people in slavery or serfdom, were in the order of wholesome secular government.

Alfred, known as the Great, came to the throne of Wessex on the death of his brother Æthelred, in 871, and died in 901.

He left extant a considerable body of laws, whose record commences with recitals from the laws of Moses, to the extent of forty-nine distinct propositions.   He then reverts to the teachings of Christ and recites the salutation and teachings of the Apostles, and also that many nations had received the faith of Christ, and ecclesiastical laws, some differing from each other, had been enacted.   And he then proceeds:—

" I then, Alfred, gathered these together and commanded many of those to be written which our forefathers held, retaining those that seemed good, and by the counsel of my *witan* rejecting others,"—referring to the laws of Ine his kinsman, of Offa king of the Mercians, and of Æthelbirht, who first among the English race received baptism.

" I then, Alfred, king of the West Saxons, showed these to all my *witan* [council of state, or parliament] and they then said that it seemed good to them all so to be holden."

Church socns, protection of sanctuary when one

was accused of crimes, was allowed by these laws.
(Sec. 2 and 5.)

To fight before an archbishop incurred a penalty of
one hundred and fifty shillings. Before another
bishop or an ealdorman, one hundred shillings.

The breaking of a pledge to the king incurred one
hundred and twenty shillings; to an archbishop,
ninety shillings; any other bishop and an ealdorman,
sixty shillings. If any one in Lent put down holy
law among the people, let him pay one hundred and
twenty shillings. (Sec. 40.)

Slaves and hired servants are excepted from the
saint days prescribed for freemen, to wit: twelve
days at Christmas, the day on which Christ overcame
the devil, St. Gregory's day, seven days before Easter
and seven days after, one day at St. Peter's tide and
St. Paul's, and at harvest the whole week before St.
Mary-mass and one day at the celebration of All
Hallows, and four Wednesdays in the four ember
weeks. To theow-men (slaves) might be accorded such
privileges and in God's name might be given, making
in all forty-two legal holydays or saint days. Neither
the preface to Alfred's laws nor the subjects to which
they relate show special reverence for the clergy, or
whether any and what part of the *witan* to which
these laws were submitted was composed of clergy-
men. But the institutions of Christianity as held in
that age were respected and provided for in many of
these laws. The secular provisions in the laws of
Alfred and Ine were most of them liberal and wise
for that age.

But while these kings like sensible men sustained
the interests of religion by hearty sanctions and sup-

port and due respect for the clergy, Edward the Elder,
who succeeded to the throne, in the few statutes he
left, now extant, scarcely did more than provide for
the secular emergencies of his kingdom, though in
his treaty with Guthrum it is provided that the two
peoples should have one God, and zealously renounce
all kinds of heathenism.

But Athelstan, who succeeded Edward the Elder in
924, was by education and temperament a narrow-
minded bigot. His code of laws was more extensive
than that of any of his predecessors.

His laws have the form of the edicts of a despot
though they claim to have been established with the
counsel of Wulfhelm archbishop and of "my other
bishops."

They read like a warrant addressed to the reeves
at each burgh or town in the kingdom, "Beseeching
in God's name and by all his saints and by the friendship of the kings that they render the tithes of live-
stock and of the year's earthly fruits. So also let
the bishops and ealdormen do. I will that the
bishops and the reeves command it to all those who
ought to obey them that it be done at the right
term " . . . "but I will grant to you your own, justly,
on this condition that ye yield to me mine and shield
both yourselves and those you ought to exhort
against God's anger and against my penalty for your
contempt and disobedience."

He also enjoins on his reeves special charities in
feeding some poor Englishman, and redeeming one
wite slave for the Lord's mercy, under the witness
of the bishop in whose jurisdiction it may be. If the
reeve omit this let him pay fine or bot in thirty

·shillings for the poor in the town.   Chap. I., Sec. 6, of these laws enacts a penalty against witchcraft equal to the penalty for murder.   Such, if denying the charge shall be tried by threefold ordeal.

Edmund, the brother of Athelstan, began to reign in the year 940.

In this king's Ecclesiastical Institutes it is stated that King Edmund assembled a great synod at London during the holy Easter tide·as well of ecclesiastics as of secular degree.   There were Oda archbishop and Wolfstan archbishop and many other bishops meditating concerning the condition of their souls and of those who were subject to them.

These institutes enjoin chastity in ecclesiastics, enjoin the payment of tithes and church scot or taxes and the like, condemn with penalties the homicide of a Christian, adultery of nuns, enjoin the repairing of churches and punishment for perjuries.

In his secular statutes the king by advice of the same great council takes cognizance of the fightings and violence, sets out a process and penalty for homicide, sustains the right of sanctuary for criminals fleeing to a church.   Other offenses are noted, and finally the enactments close with the following provisions as to marriage :—

"OF BETROTHING A WOMAN.

"1. If a man desire to betroth a maiden or a woman, and it so be agreeable to her and her friends, then is it right that the bridegroom, according to the law of God, and according to the customs of the world, first promise, and give a 'wed' to those who are her 'foresprecas,' that he desire her in such wise that he will keep her, according to God's law, as a husband shall his wife: and let his friends guarantee that.

" 2. After that, it is to be known to whom the 'foster-lean' belongs: let the bridegroom again give a 'wed' for this; and let his friends guarantee it.

" 3. Then, after that, let the bridegroom declare what he will grant her, in case she choose his will, and what he will grant her, if she live longer than he.

" 4. If it be so agreed, then is it right that she be entitled to half the property, and to all, if they have children in common, except she again choose a husband.

" 5. Let him confirm all that which he has promised with a 'wed'; and let his friends guarantee that.

" 6. If they then are agreed in every thing, then let the kinsmen take it in hand, and betroth their kinwomen to wife, and to a righteous life, to him who desired her, and let him take posession of the 'borh' who has control of the 'wed.'

" 7. But if a man desire to lead her out of the land, into another thane's land, then it will be advisable for her that her friends have an agreement that no wrong shall be done to her; and if she commit a fault, that they may be nearest in the 'bot,' if she have not whereof she can make 'bot.'

" 8. At the nuptials, there shall be a mass-priest by law; who shall with God's blessing bind their union to all prosperity.

" 9. Well is it also to be looked to, that it be known, that they, through kinship, be not too nearly allied; lest that be afterwards divided, which before was wrongly joined."

The laws of King Edgar, whose reign commenced

in 959 and continued sixteen years, recites that they
are, with the counsel of his witan, ordained in praise
of God and in honor to the king and for the behoof
of all the people.

From one to five of these laws relate to the rights
of the churches, to the payment of tithes, and church
scots, or taxes.   If tithes are not paid, the clergy
with the king's reeve are to take the tithes by force—
the tenth part; while the nine-tenths are conscripted
and divided between the landlord and the bishop, by
way of penalty.   St. Peter's pence, or a penny tax on
each hearth in the kingdom, is duly levied with penalties for non-payment.   Established festivals and
fasts as previously recognized, with soul scot to be
paid to the minster to which it is due, and every
church "grith" to stand as before established.

Then follow secular laws; these are liberal in
terms but predicated on fidelity in paying dues to
the king.

King Ethelred came to the throne in 978, and died
in 1016.

It seems there was a parliament held at Woodstock
in the land of the Mercians.

In Chap. V., laws are set out or passed both in the
ecclesiastical and lay "witan." But nearly all of
Ethelred's laws relate to the church.   In fact many of
them are simple exhortations to fidelity in the Chris-
tain life, never forgetting church grith and church
scot.   There is, however, much of the spirit of true
Christianity in these laws.   They condemn the death
penalty, as applicable to Christians, and enjoin fidelity
to Christian morals and civil order, on every rank of
the clergy and the practice of Christian charity.

They are not free from the superstitions of the age, but more liberal in spirit than most of the old Saxon laws.

Canute the Dane became king of England on the death of Edmund Ironside, A. D. 1017, and died after a reign of eighteen years, in 1035. He left extant a considerable body of laws, ecclesiastical and secular. He was known among the English as Cnut, king of all England and king of the Danes and Norwegians.

He predicates his laws on "the counsel of his *witan,* to the praise of God and to the honor and behoof of himself. And that was at the holy tide of midwinter at Westminster."

These laws enjoin, first, that above all other things they should ever love and worship one God, and unanimously observe one Christianity, and love King Cnut with strict fidelity.

There are twenty-six of these ecclesiastical laws, in tone and spirit and purpose like those sanctioned by previous kings, deprecating the condemning of Christian men to death for slight crimes. They enjoin the payment of church taxes, and especially soul scot at the open grave, the keeping of the Sabbath and appointed fasts and enjoin both clergy and people to purity of life by avoiding all licentiousness, and offenses against public morals.

Among the eighty-five secular laws there are several relating to the protection of men in holy orders as well as provisions against the vices and crimes of such. There are penalties for breaking holy day festivals and fasts. Several of these statutes are against adultery and incest and like offenses. Many secular

crimes have punishments prescribed that do not
specially illustrate the influence of the clergy in the
government, though in statute eighty-five (secular)
the exhortation, invocation, and prayer seek, especially, to identify the government with religion.

The bishops often sat as judges in the local courts,
and the presumption is reasonable that the higher clergy always had seats in the witans, the grand councils
of the nation. There is a presumption of the special influence of the clergy in the government, as they
were really the depositaries of letters and learning
of the age, and so were found a necessary agency
in giving form and expression to the laws of the
land.

The secular chiefs of the people became such by
birth and inheritance, by feats of arms, or by the
accumulation of estates, while a mass priest is said
to have become thane-worthy by his acquisition of
learning.

Besides, the clergy in themselves were an organized power, under the direction of the archbishops,
who were generally the ablest men in the kingdom.
The archbishops held councils at different times and
places from the day of Theodore to the end of Canute's reign, and the church had a more thorough system of ecclesiastical law than that of the secular
government. Its organization was better defined,
and the relative ranks and duties of the different
orders of the clergy, in their relation to the people,
were well settled.

Though these sanctioned many superstitions, and
pronounced penalties for offenses that an enlightened
Christian conscience might condemn, yet these decre-

tals gave a strong hold of power to the clergy over the people and their secular rulers.·

A single principle stated will illustrate this fact. The bishops had primary jurisdiction of ecclesiastical offenses, and where the offender was of a religious order, he could not be tried for secular crimes by the civil courts until he had been degraded from his ecclesiastical dignity, by the church authorities.

Finally, I remark generally, that in law the church and its clergy were a force and a power in the land during all those centuries. This we have already noted where the clergy were vested with the functions of ministers of the civil state. But a more significant and marked influence in the government grew out of the religious opinions and influence of the church during those dark ages. The church not only had opinions and dogmas, affirmatively expressed by its claimed paramount authority, but it had a body of ecclesiastical or common laws, which had exclusive jurisdiction over all offenses and crimes committed by or charged on the clergy. Besides, the priests were vested with certain duties, in aid of the civil state, such as presiding at trials by ordeal, church sanctuary for persons charged with crime, the administration of baptisms as required by the civil statutes. The court Christian, presided over by the bishops, claimed what is really a secular jurisdiction over marriages and divorces, wills, and descents and successions of intestate and testate estates.·· These courts came to be designated as the courts of the ordinary, in later times. They seemed to claim concurrent jurisdiction with civil courts in all matters pertaining to and growing out of the relation of the sexes. The king's courts, no doubt, took cognizance of offenses committed in these relations, and only remitted them to the ecclesiastical court when a question arose peculiar to the ecclesiastical jurisdiction. But, aside from these civil matters, a body of canon law based on the Roman civil law of the continent was brought to England by the missionaries of the Catholic church. The decretals of Theodore, Archbishop of Canterbury, from 668 to 690, promulgated these canon laws to regulate the life and duties of the higher and lower clergy, to define the penances or punishments to which they should be subjected, if guilty of defined crimes against morality, against persons, against the king, embracing as varied and extensive a list of offenses as are set forth in the civil code, but varying in prescribed punishments. In the place of *bot* or fines, imprisonment on bread and water was prescribed. This last was sometimes added to the *bot* fine or compensation prescribed by the civil statutes. These canon laws assumed that a very high standard of purity and piety was needful to the clergy, while the list of offenses indicate a very low state of morals. But real crimes were punished with less severity than offenses against the superstitions and theological dogmas of the church. In later times, offenses of the clergy, not within the bishop's mercy, requiring capital punishment, were proceeded against by deposing the clergyman from his office and then turning him over to the civil power for trial and punishment. The policy manifest on the surface of these ecclesiastical decretals was to make man holy by operation of law, while holiness itself was made to consist of doing penance, self-abnegation, and voluntary suffer-

19

ing. In a word, monasticism in all the details of its discipline was regarded as the quintessence of piety. Faith in God's grace for salvation and a state of heart inducing purity of life were excluded from the creed of these ancient worthies. With purposes seemingly the most loyal to the good order and peace of society, these church law-givers relied on fear for results, the lowest conceivable force influencing man to duty and virtue.

But notwithstanding these influences as to the actual religious condition of England during the Saxon *régime*, it is probable that religious faith was as high as was consistent with the state of knowledge and civilization in those rude ages; and it is to the credit of these Catholic missionaries that they brought letters to these pagans, that enabled them to make records of their laws and to develop the arts and knowledge of civilization. The Romans had possession of Britain four or five hundred years. These generals were trained in Roman schools, they went home and wrote histories of the conquests and governments, but when they departed not a solitary vestige of letters or learning did they leave behind. For this reason, I have doubted if any Christian teachers labored in Britain during the Roman period, for any great length of time; for in all the missionary enterprises since the Christian era began, whether Catholic or Protestant, letters have invariably been planted in the missionary fields to stay. And letters have been the root and promoters of civilization. But the object of this note is to show a dominant influence of the religion of those ages over the spirit of their laws.

STATUS OF THE CIVIL LAW AT THE CLOSE OF THE SAXON RULE, AND CLAIMS OF THE COMMON LAW.

The Roman law had peculiar theories. It took nothing by intendment. If its language did not interpret itself, it failed of force outside and beyond. A law must be made and set forth in form before it could be administered. A rescript of a statute could be had by referring a case to the emperor or the law-making power—for there were four persons or bodies of men that had jurisdiction for such judgment in a case referred to them. Affirmative or positive law must be had, or there would be a failure of justice. But when a rescript was made settling the law of a case referred, such rescript became a settled and fixed law for all future cases involving the same questions.

They held that if the law in its affirmative propositions and institutes did not reach a case, the case must be immaterial and unimportant. But if it were important, a suitable law should be made to meet it; and such law might operate sufficiently, *ex post facto*, to reach the case in hand.

On the other hand, English common law, so called, may be regarded as predicated on a fiction: that ancient England had a complete system of unwritten law adapted to every emergency and condition in the experience of the people, and that a knowledge of these ancient maxims and provisions was to be found only in the bosom of the judges or the courts.

Though this theory was not an invention but a tradition of a part of the Druid religion, whose mysteries were developed by the oracles served by pagan priests, judges, and kings, yet it gave great scope to jurisprudence, and vested a venerated authority in the judges. They held that the law was of universal application, and in cases where authorities were wanting it was the duty of the court to create a precedent applicable to similar cases to arise embracing similar facts, and to set it forth as a discovered treasure in the unwritten law. But, as we shall have occasion to show, the body of our common law, as it has found proferts in judicial decisions, is not a discovery from ancient archives, but the creation of the courts. Such origin, in the emergencies of jurisprudence, has given us the principles and forms of law from able and experienced judges, rather than from capricious sovereigns or mercenary and corrupt legislatures.

The Roman or civil law was perhaps the better adapted to popular ideas than what is known as the common law, as it presented propositions that were specific and tangible and did not rely on inferences and intendments beyond the form and words set forth in the statute. When church and state became affiliated in the governments on the continent of Europe, ecclesiastical law fell into the legal forms of the civil institutes, and both followed to a considerable extent the propagation of Christianity throughout Europe, with the possible exception of Great Britain. Ecclesiastical law in the forms and precedents it acquired on the continent was introduced into England, and in all matters within the ecclesiastical jurisdiction is pursued subordinate to the municipal law to-day, including the probate of wills and settling successions in intestate estates, these being under the jurisdiction of the bishops known as *the ordinary.*

But the distinctions between the common and the civil or Roman law were more in form than in substance.   Both were predicated on natural law and human experience and both had the same *rationale* of crime.   The civil rulers of Rome legislated for cases in hand while the judicial power in England legislated to like conclusions, under the assumed sanctions of ancient law, of which no man or mind had ever seen the profert.   Of course the characteristics of different systems would be developed through the difference in the mental habits and labors of those who developed and elaborated them, and the different standpoints from which a matter was treated.   The rule of the strict construction of the Roman law is applied to modern statutes, while the common law is treated as the air we breathe, crowding itself into every nook and corner of the judicial sphere, giving place in its claims only to positive legislation and affirmative law.

In our American jurisprudence we have both strict construction of statutes, and liberal intendments derived from developed principles in adjudicated cases.

By way of illustrating the status of these two systems of law in the United States, as I write for American readers, I insert here a brief article on the jurisdiction of the Federal courts and the rules governing their judgments.   These follow, in a sense, the civil Roman law.

The Declaration of Independence makes a profert of principles affecting the rights of man, the object and ends of government, the essential franchises of a free state, and in what bodies and individuals these ought to be invested. Thus far, this document is a part of the public law of the land, and, as modified and set out and elaborated in the Constitution of the United States, is respected by our highest courts.

Then the acts of Congress, where no local jurisdiction is prescribed within them, are to be construed and enforced under the exclusive jurisdiction of the Federal courts. But in the construction and application of acts of Congress they are neither aided nor restricted by anything extrinsic to their language and provisions.

The intendments of the laws of the United States are to be found intrinsic in each and every of those laws, and not to be affected or modified by antecedent theories or precedents. But fair and full force is to be given to the language of these laws, that they may need no extrinsic aid to realize their objects and office. "The force of the statute in such case made and provided" fills the entire scope of these laws and their powers. In adjudications under these laws the decisions of the Federal courts are the only binding authority. The Federal courts have exclusive jurisdiction in the construction of treaties with foreign governments —though it has happened that State courts have sometimes, under writs of *habeas corpus*, or otherwise, assumed to investigate the claims for the extradition of alleged criminals under treaty stipulations; but the Federal courts, or United States Commissioners, are the proper tribunals for such an inquiry. As between state and state, the surrender is made by the executive, under such inquisition as may be thought proper.

The construction of treaties can only be aided by prior treaties—if any existed—or by protocols that entered into their negotiations ; and such construction must be paramount to local or general domestic law. In cases of admiralty and maritime law, the customs recognized between commercial nations, in the absence of treaties, must determine the controversy. The only common law jurisdiction recognized by the Constitution is in the cases of criminal trials ; though trials by jury, in some civil cases, are allowed, unless waived by the parties.

In the several classes of cases named, the jurisdiction of the Federal courts would end, were it not for the jurisdiction given to circuit courts of the United States to try all issues joined between citizens of different states, though the controversy arose under local laws, and by such laws the adjudication must be controlled. Then, where parties litigant in State courts belong to different states, or one party is a corporation whose franchises extend to more than one state, or the matter of the action is one in which the Federal and State courts have concurrent jurisdiction, or the constitution and laws of the United States come in question, a writ of error may be certified from the adjudication of the highest State courts to the Supreme Court of the United States for final determination. In all such cases the law of the state where the suit arose must govern the final determination of the case. In states where the common law has been adopted, and cases happening under that and the statutes of the state come to the United States Supreme Court, these local laws must follow it to the end. But in case the writ of error is certified from the highest

court of the state of Louisiana, where the common
law has not been adopted, but the civil law is the
basis of local jurisprudence, and where peculiar local
laws, as that of "*batture*," have grown up indigenous
to the country, the local laws so prevailing, and as
settled by local jurisprudence, must control the United
States Supreme Court in its final judgments.

The Chief Justice of the United States, and his
Associated Judges, composing the Supreme Court,
are thus forced to become familiar, not only with the
body of laws and precedents peculiar to matters pertaining to the exclusive jurisdiction of the United
States Courts, cases arising under the constitution and
laws of the United States, and treaties with foreign
governments, in cases of admiralty and maritime law,
or that are affected by the law of nations; but they
must be posted in the local laws and jurisprudence of
every state, territory, and district embraced in the
nation. True, the briefs of counsel are expected to
bring before the court the peculiar laws and authorities affecting each case under consideration; but this
does not relieve the judges from the exercise of judicial discrimination, and a severe analysis of the laws
sought to be applied in determining controversies.

INTRODUCTION OF THE COMMON LAW AT THE CONQUEST.

The Saxon laws subsisted by force of their original simplicity, down to the time of the Conquest, predicated primarily on the principle laid down by Glanville, that "what pleases the prince is law, or has the force of law."

Though legal proferts only represented the will of the king, these were often proclaimed under a council of state or witan that has been called a parliament; but if a parliament it was without the modern incident of a constituency, except the king, who summoned only those whose views would respond to his will; still bringing us back to the proposition that "whatever pleaseth the prince is law." Such with all the circumlocution that can be invented was the sum and body of the Saxon laws during the six centuries in which they ruled England. In what is left of these written affirmative laws, the state of civilization, the state and condition and pursuits of the people, their prevailing vices and crimes, their methods of living, and the nature of their property,—are all significantly shown. The meager provisions as to real property is explained by the fact that all the lands in the kingdom were in theory primarily held by the king, and farmed out to the chief men, as tenants of the king, and by them sub-let to the lower orders of the people. The natural desire of those who worked the estates, to retain the benefits of their betterments for their children, tended to disintegrate the great landed estates. But this force was to a great extent subdued by the aristocracy. So, at the time of Alfred, *boc* or book lands, held by charter and chiefly by the nobles, were alone descendible to heirs. The *folc* lands were the common lands of the crown or the thanes, open to leases to the people.

While I have no doubt that convenient customs might arise in matters between citizen and citizen and one rank and another of the people in matters relating to property, employment, and business, or in matters pertaining to personal rights and the domestic relations, I believe, as elsewhere stated, these customs could not in their specific details be the subject for memory, in future generations. They will survive only by force of natural law, subsisting in all nations.

The instincts of propriety in the relation of the sexes is common to the race in all countries. The veriest pagan needs no instruction on this point. Pagan moralists have commended chastity, and condemned impurity, whenever and wherever the history of man has found a record. So property, its use and ownership, when it is the product of human skill and labor, needs no legal custom to determine to whom it ought to belong. *Mine* and *thine* are significant terms all over the world.

Hence the assumption that what we praise as the common law had its origin in Britain in the Roman period, from the invasion of Julius Cæsar to near the end of the fifth century, is not only absurd, in the experience of nations in like barbarous conditions, but without a shadow of proof. As I have said elsewhere, the records or archæology of the Roman period give no intimation of law or courts, beyond the arbitrary edicts of the military commanders. If they had customs we know not what they were. If books or writings were in the land they have perished. The London wall with rubble stones and flag-tie stones in alternate layers is still there, in parts, laid in Roman cement of that period. And I think excavations have brought to light the mosaic marble floors of some old barbaric Roman mansion; but letters and laws are not among the recovered treasures. If customs existed among the Roman-Britons, their transmission through the barbarism of the six hundred years of the Saxon *régime*, as these pedantic egotists of the old law pretend, would be more of a miracle than Joe Smith's recovered plate of the Book of Mormon.

The fact is, as I have stated elsewhere, letters and laws in the development of a country go together; without writing no body of laws can be perpetuated, or without the force of natural law to reproduce the like under like conditions. Who knows anything of the jurisprudence of New Netherlands, and the colony of New York? We know, indeed, that the Honorable Daniel Horsmanden was a noted judge of the common pleas in the city of New York, but where is the evidence of his legal ability? What are the cases he decided? Did he respect the old Dutch placards of the conquered Dutch province? or was he a stickler for the common law of England?

If the people ever had knowledge to answer these inquiries, in the absence of a record, such knowledge has gone with its generation. If judicial deliverances of a distinguished magistrate have thus died out from the knowledge of the people in less than two hundred years, where is our faith to follow a myth, claimed as ancient common law, back through the ages for near two thousand years?

"But," says our reader, "the common law is an existing fact. It is the body of the judicial records of the courts. Its maxims have been compiled, its precedents established, and it is with us to-day as the pervading atmosphere of all our jurisprudence. And where did it come from?"

Your statement is true, and the answer to your inquiry is the very subject of my inquiry. But at the outset, as I have stated, I find no evidence of the existence of the common law distinct from natural law previous to the advent into England of William the Conqueror in A. D. 1066.

The Conqueror made a rescript of the old Saxon laws with little change or amendment. But he did not accept them as a system on which to predicate the jurisprudence of his government. He organized the chief courts of the kingdom on the model of the Norman courts of his government on the continent. Even the law language of the Saxons and Danes was repudiated and a barbarous French dialect was made the judicial language of the courts. William created the office of the chief justiciar, and his associates, constituting the court of king's bench, or the king's hall. The judges appointed to fill these offices were his Norman favorites, as ignorant of the laws and customs of England as they well could be. Most of them were ecclesiastics thoroughly read in what was known as the Roman civil law, and the canon laws predicated on it and following the same rules of construction and administration, though varying in penalties and remedies.

Lord Campbell, in his " Lives of the Chief Justices of England," tells us that Odo, the natural half brother of the Conqueror, was the bishop of Bayeux in Normandy and was made the first chief justiciar of England—to establish the king's hall, by the agency of which the Norman jurisprudence was to be introduced into England, and the Norman domination perpetuated.   Like many ecclesiastics at that time, he had been made familiar with the Roman civil law— the feudal system as well as the canon law. ("Campbell's Lives of the Chief Justices of England," Vol. i., page 5.)

The next chief justiciar was William Fritz Osborn, a Norman knight.

Geoffrey, bishop of Constance, was appointed justiciar for a special occasion.

On the fall of Odo, William DeWarriner and Richard De Benefacter were appointed chief justioiars, seemingly with a common jurisdiction.   Both were bred in Normandy, were soldiers and favorites of the crown.

One other chief justiciar is mentioned as appointed by William the Conqueror during his reign of twenty-seven years, William De Carilefo or Hanilagho, a pious priest—abbot of St. Vincent in Normandy— made bishop of Durham, and afterwards chief justiciar.   He was also chief justiciar under the reign of William Rufus.

Afterwards one Ralph Flambord, an infamous character, was made chief justiciar in 1095.

The first justiciar in the reign of Henry I. was Robert, bishop of Salisbury, who rendered the office more odious than it had ever been before.   He was first a village curate, in Normandy. The only other chief justiciar of much note during this reign of Henry I. was Ralph Bassett, son of one of the companions of the Conqueror. He seems to have been an infamous, cruel, and corrupt judge.

Under Stephen, Henry, afterwards crowned king as Henry II., was appointed justiciar, and actually sat as chief justiciar of the court of king's bench for some months. On the accession of Henry II. to the throne, he appointed as chief justiciar, Richard De Luci, a powerful baron of a distinguished Norman family. This judge was an enlightened and independent magistrate. It is said he went about administering justice all over the kingdom, and to him we are chiefly indebted for the "Constitutions of Clarendon," by which a noble effort was made to shake off the tyranny of Rome, and which were adopted as the basis of our ecclesiastical polity at the Reformation. (Campbell's Chief Justices, etc., Vol. i., page 18.) Afterwards De Luci became a monk and died in the monastery he had founded.

His successor was Robert, Earl of Leicester. The only case recorded of his adjudication was that of the Ex-Chancellor Thomas à Becket.

The next conspicuous figure as chief justiciar was Ranulph De Glanville, whose earliest writings extant on the common law we shall presently consider.

I have thus cited from Lord Campbell's notices of the leading magistrates of England for a hundred years after the Conquest. These were Normans by birth or descent—proud of their foreign origin, and wedded to foreign ideas and institutions; and sneering at the very language of the country. The feudal system was brought in with the Conquest, and military tenures were sought to be made the only title to the lands in the kingdom. The tillers of the soil were sought to be reduced to villeinage or slavery, and the laws had a natural repugnance to old opposing customs if such subsisted. In fact to the time of De Luci the justiciars seem to have given themselves no opportunities to know what notions of justice and right subsisted among the common people of the country. This judge and Glanville made judicial itineraries through the kingdom. In these provincial adjudications, they acquired a knowledge of the people—of their habits· and pursuits, their conflicting interests and the infelicities and hardships of their conditions.

If there were customs and legal traditions they would learn them when pleaded in excuse or defense of charges preferred against them. But these judges, Roman civilians in the law as they were, as against the conflicting allegations of parties in interest, could not determine whether an alleged custom had influenced transactions complained of, or not, or whether the alleged custom had long subsisted, or if it was a statement invented for the occasion by one of the parties litigant. The difficulties in such controversies would impose the duty on the court of determining if the alleged custom existed or not, and what effect it should have, if any, on the matters in controversy. In such a case the wisdom of the judge would determine finally as to the custom and its legal effect in the administration of justice. So in future like cases, inquiry need not be extended, as to the antiquity of the custom, beyond the last finding of the court. In this view, the great body of the common law, so called, may have been the results of judicial legislation, making up the great body of judicial reports, and no man knows or can know, whether a judicial decision had any antecedents in custom or not. It was in fact born in form and features from the judge's brain.

These Norman judges, clerical or otherwise, were distinguished civilians in the civil Roman law, and comprehended the defects of that law to meet all cases that might arise in the administration of justice. And they knew further, that these defects in the civil law were supplied by the law-making power in Rome, in the form of rescripts in cases under advisement, that such rescripts became settled law for all succeeding like cases. But these civilian judges in England had no special law-making power available to meet the emergencies arising in their adjudications. So they adopted the fiction of old antiquated customs, in making a judgment, without law, as justice seemed to require. If customs should be proved, they only superseded the judicial legislation; but in the absence of all custom, the judgment, such as it might be, stood all the same.

Then those judges that had been trained as ecclesiastics were still more familiar with canon law, made up of positive rules and regulations to govern the church—its clergy and membership—and that took nothing by intendment. The high functionaries of the church could grant dispensations or pardons; but only the Pope or the church in council could alter the law. These decretals were similar in all Catholic countries, with adaptations to meet special conditions in particular nations. They had been

familiar to the clergy in England from the days of
Archbishop Theodore.   With such a system of laws
with literal proferts, mere customs in civil life would
command little respect from ecclesiastical judges.
And when the church became a dominant power
in the state, the authority of secular customs would
command little regard.   So these Norman judges
would be more likely to follow, in their decisions, the
spirit and theory of the canon law, than any civil
customs claimed to exist among the people.   Hence
the small progress which the common law, so called,
from the then very recent beginnings, had made at the
time of Glanville.   In fact it is reasonable to believe
that De Luci, the immediate predecessor of Glanville,
was the first justiciar who admitted the notion of
customs into his decisions.

The theory that judicial decisions without positive
law were based on customs "so old that the memory of man runneth not to the contrary," saved the
judges from the displeasure of jealous kings, for their
seeming usurpation of legislative power.   But there
is another theory on which these judges might have
proceeded, in their decisions, based on the proposition, "That which pleaseth the prince has the force
of law."   The justiciars sat in the king's hall.   They
represented the sovereign; their acts were the acts of
the king, their judgments were the judgments of the
king, so that the judgments they rendered were the
judgments of the king and had the force of law.
The lack of antiquity in "the unwritten laws of
England" is more than suspected by Lord Campbell
as above, page 25, when he says, "Glanville actually
details to us the practice of *aula regis* (king's hall) in

20

which he presided, furnishes us with a copious supply of precedents of writs and other procedure then in use, and explains with much precision the distinctions and subtleties of the system which in the fifth Norman reign had nearly superseded the simple juridical institutions of our Anglo-Saxon ancestors."

Then Glanville in his preface says, indicating the state of the common law, so called, at that time: "To reduce in every instance the laws and constitutions of this realm into writing, would, in our times, be absolutely impossible, as well on account of the ignorance of writers, as of the confused multiplicity of the enactments. But there are some well established rules, which as they more frequently arise in court it appears to me not presumptuous to put into writing, to assist the memory and for general reference." The ignorance of the writers and the multiplicity of the enactments show the chaos of the law that only the incisive mind of an independent judge could use or refer to, to any purpose. This confused material for judicial solution could well have accumulated during the then one hundred years of the Norman kings.

In Reeves's History of the Common Law, Vol. i., p. 485, the author says: "The work of Glanville compared with the Anglo-Saxon law is like the code of another nation; there is not the least feature of resemblance between them."

William of Malmesbury says, the clergy supplying the lawyers, they would naturally have recourse to the law with which they were best acquainted; the civil law and the canon law, which was founded thereupon. In other words they would have recourse to the Roman law modified in matters ecclesiastical by the canon law, the Roman church and its law being established and recognized by the state. Hence the recognition of that law in the laws of the Conqueror, *laws of Henry I.*, which formed the basis of the great treatises of Glanville and Bracton, the foundation of our common law. Note p. 488, Reeves's History, Vol. i.

With these preliminary notes, I proceed to give an abstract of Glanville's treatise.

GLANVILLE.

Glanville was lord chief justice of England in the reign of Henry II., having attained that honor in 1180. He was slain in the Crusade war in 1190. It appears between those dates he wrote a treatise, not on the laws of England as usually supposed, but chiefly on the forms of judicial procedure in certain enumerated matters. The provisions of existing laws in the pleas considered are incidentally brought out, giving much insight into the status of the laws of England at that time.

Mr. Beames, the translator of Glanville's treatise, says: "Our author in general confines himself to such matters only as were the objects of jurisdiction in the *curia regis* and divides his work into fourteen books, the two first of which treat of the writ of right when originally commenced in the *curia regis* and of all its stages,—the summons, essoins, appearance, pleadings, duel or grand assize, judgment, and execution. The third speaks of vouching to warranty, which, with the two former books, comprises a lucid account of the proceedings in a writ of right for the recovery of land. The fourth book is employed upon rights of advowson; the fifth upon villeinage, and the sixth upon dower. The seventh treats upon alienation, descents, successions, wardship, and testaments. The eighth is upon final concords and records in general. The ninth is upon homage, relief, fealty, services, and purprestures. The tenth treats of debts and matters of contract; and the eleventh upon attorneys. Having thus disposed of actions commenced originally in the *curia regis* (king's court), our author in his twelfth book speaks of writs of right when brought in the lords' court; and the manner of removing them from thence to the county court and *curia regis*, which leads him to mention some other writs determinable before the sheriff. In his thirteenth book he treats of assizes and disseisins. The last book is wholly taken up in discussing the doctrines of pleas of the crown."

Glanville in his preface commences with the remark copied by Bracton, Fleta, and "The Regiam Majestatem":—

"The regal power should not merely be decorated with arms to restrain rebels and nations making head against it and its realms, but ought likewise to be adorned with laws for the peaceful governing of its subject and its people."

He commends the judgments of the courts, since each decision is governed by the laws of the realm, and by *those customs* which, founded on *reason* in their introduction, have for a long time prevailed:—

"For English laws, *although not written*, may as it should seem, and that without any absurdity, be termed laws (since this itself is a law: That which pleases the prince has the force of law). I mean those laws which it is evident were promulgated by the advice of the nobles and the authority of the prince concerning doubts to be settled in their assembly."

The pleasure of the sovereign being made the basis and force of law, although copied from the Roman code, has been pronounced the very basis of despotism. As Houard cites or remarks about Glanville, "The text of our author proves that after the Conquest the English received from William the Bastard the same maxims that we until then had followed.in regard to the exclusive right which our kings had always exercised of making the laws." ("Customs of Normandy," Vol. i., p. 378.)

But this proposition was not all flattery to the sovereign. It was expressed by the then chief justice of England, really in aid of the judicial authority of the court as representing the king, in justification of the creation of precedents to meet emergencies in the administration of justice. If the king could create laws his justices sitting in his seat could do the same thing within their functions and jurisdiction. Lord Mansfield once claimed that in his judicial administration he created more law than both houses of parliament. The fiction in such decisions, of reproducing old customs or maxims "whose origin was so long ago that the memory of man ran not to the contrary," was, as is elsewhere said, in a measure to repel any suspicion by the sovereign of usurpation of power on the part of his judges.

Glanville wrote only of matters which became familiar in the practice of his court. The enumerated list of his subjects was comparatively meager, leaving a wide field of unsettled law, where the wisdom of the judges must *create* the precedent or allow justice to fail. Customs and maxims will for a time acquire currency in any community, but unless these find a written record few of them will survive the changes of time or fail of change or abrogation by the conquest of a nation by a different race of people. The conclusion is reasonable that the great body of what was in Glanville's time known as the common law of England, came in with William the Conqueror. As we have said, the judges on the king's bench were as the king on his throne, and when the emergency was discovered, they created the rescript or precedent, to control that and all future like cases. In this review of Glanville as to the forms of proceedings which make up the bulk of his treatise, it will be sufficient to say, they indicate a well organized court in all its branches, and a careful liberality towards parties who made default in pleading or attendance; allowing them to excuse themselves for absence or defaults, by essoins or excuses for absence or defaults; and to repeat these, or others, for three or four different, or successive, court days, before judgment would be entered by default. The judgments, when obtained, were executed by warrants issued to the sheriff, in the name of the king.

Trials by battel and by ordeal still prevailed. The former, limited to land cases, was still a matter of election by the parties, though the hearing of the grand assize was commended by Glanville in preference to the brutal practice of single combat.

But the methods of judicial procedure are of interest in the course of our discussion only as they illustrate the laws of the period. Hence we proceed to note such·of these laws as were recognized by Glanville, as being then current and important. He recognizes these offenses as triable only in the king's court :—

"The crime which in legal phrase is termed that

of *Læse Majesty*, as the death of the king or a sedition moved in the realm or army ; *the fraudulent concealment of treasure-trove ;* the plea concerning the breaking of the king's peace, homicide, burning, robbery, rape, the crime of falsifying, and such other pleas as are of a similar nature. These crimes are either punished capitally or with the loss of member."

Note that mutilation, if resorted to as a penalty at all, was not a common penalty among the Anglo-Saxons. King Canute enacts its infliction (Cnut's Laws, 30) in some incorrigible cases.

In all these enumerated crimes, fines were imposed and forfeiture of goods, and where the crime was against the king, personally, the life of the culprit was put in the king's mercy. But the conquerors of the kingdom resorted to severer penalties to crush out the patriotism of the people, or their attachments to their former rulers. Though Athelstan, one of the most bigoted of the Saxon kings, excluded from punishment theft by a child under twelve years old, where the property stolen was less than twelve pence, William the Conqueror is said to have excluded the punishment of death for any crime, but ordered that the eyes of the offenders should be plucked out, or their limbs amputated. It is said that he caused to be put out the eyes of his own brother, who had rebelled against him.

A vicious proposition is laid down as law by the *Regiam Majestatem,* commenting on *læse majesty* [treason]; that the accused might be punished, not only for the *crimes* but also for the *intent* and *purpose*. Charges of theft came within the jurisdiction of the sheriff's or county courts. Scuffles and blows, in case of the neglect, by the lords' court, were cognizable in the sheriff's court; unless the accuser charged the offense as committed against the king's peace.

In the king's court, only, could be tried all questions concerning baronies, advowsons of churches, questions of condition, dower when the woman has been entirely debarred from receiving it for breach of fine made in the king's court, concerning the performance of homage and the receiving of reliefs, and concerning purprestures. This last was formerly predicated on wrongful obtrusions on the crown lands, or erecting such structures there as manifested a purpose of pleading fraudulently some royal grant. In other words, a purpose to steal the land.

The special jurisdiction of the sheriff's court was over these matters: Pleas concerning the right of freehold when the court of the lords was proved to have failed doing justice; the plea concerning villein-born, provided a special commission or writ was issued from the king in each instance to try them.

The sheriff's court seems to have had jurisdiction of all minor matters, not above enumerated, and both original and appellate jurisdiction in matters triable in inferior courts.

THE GREAT CHARTER, WITH NOTES AND COMMENTS.

INTRODUCTION.

In Glanville we have the course of judicial procedure in his time, or rather in his own court, and subject matters which had judicial cognizance. The laws, as he states, were quite unsettled, and the vicious principle he asserts as the *rationale* of law, that " whatever pleases the prince is law," would sanction many irregularities and oppressions on the part of the government, in fact, would justify absolute despotism. In Magna Charta we have the first profert or statement of the relative rights and duties of the several members of the state as then constituted, from which limitations of the monarchy and the rights of the citizen should afterwards be determined. In fact, this charter embraced the outline of the common law, as developed during near two centuries after the Conquest. We have preferred the Great Charter of King John to that of Henry III., as being earlier in origin and historically more important. Our copy is from Rapin's History of England, or as given us by the translator of his history, which was written in French. This charter is brief, not much longer than our Declaration of Independence. But it was such a departure from the despotic authority claimed by the kings and enforced by king and clergy, that it would seem to have marked the birthday of Freedom in England, though the Freedom so born was a helpless, feeble child. Whatever of liberty was in the charter was accepted in form as the *free gift* of the sovereign, though everybody knew the concessions were coerced by the refractory, turbulent barons. Of the method of nursing this child of humanity, by the courts, we shall speak further on.

At the origin of this famous charter, England, with its people, constituted both a country and a kingdom. The church, the state, the head men and dignitaries in each of these departments, were recognized as constituting and representing constituent elements of a great commonwealth. This charter had the force of a compact between parties competent and having adequate means at command to carry out its provisions and regulations. And beyond this, its provisions rested not alone on the supposed physical strength of the forces operating in the policy and political interests of the times, but in a claim of authority from existing laws, and a jurisprudence inherited from the past. But this charter, in the provisions it embraces, claims, we do not say how justly, to be a transcript of ancient laws; and that so far as those laws have died out from human memory, and perished from the records of time, the charter itself has always been treated as ultimate and original authority. It is, in fact, treated as the text of the British constitution, limiting the powers of the crown, and regulating the powers and duties of the coördinate branches of the government.

THE CHARTER.

John, by the grace of God King of England, Lord of Ireland, Duke of Normandy and Aquitaine, and Earl of Anjou: To the Archbishops, Bishops, Abbots, Earls, Barons, Justiciaries, the Foresters, Sheriffs, Governors, Officers, and to all Bailiffs, and other his faithful subjects, greeting:

Know ye that we, in the presence of God, and for the health of our soul, and the souls of our ancestors and heirs, to the honor of God, and the exaltation of holy church, and amendment of our kingdom, by the advice of our venerable fathers, Stephen, archbishop of Canterbury, primate of all England and cardinal of the holy Roman Church; Henry, archbishop of Dublin; William, bishop of London; Peter of Winchester, Joscelin of Bath and Glastonbury, Hugh of Lincoln, Walter of Worcester, William of Coventry, Benedict of Rochester, bishops; and Master Pandulph, the Pope's sub-deacon and ancient servant brother; Aymeric, master of the temple in England; and the noble persons,—William Mareschal, Earl of Pembroke; William, Earl of Salisbury; William, Earl of Warren; William, Earl of Arundel; Alan de Galoway, constable of Scotland; Warin Fitz-Gerald, Peter Fitz-Herbert, and Hubert De Burgh, seneschal of Poictou; Hugo de Neville, Matthew Fitz-Herebert, Thomas Basset, Alan Basset, Philip De Albiney, Robert de Roppele, John Marescall, John Fitz-Hugh, and others, our liege men,—have in the first place granted to God and by this our present charter confirmed for us and our heirs forever.

"And others, our liege men." It is usually held that all the people of the kingdom were designed to be embraced in the provisions

of this charter. But, in fact, the term liege men, as here used, embraces only such as held estates of the crown on condition of certain service and duties. It is true that some of its provisions are made to extend to servants and villeins, in mitigating the severity of penal judgments; but scarcely in a form to give such classes a standing in court, as against the barons, to whom they owed fealty and allegiance. Their grievances in this relation could scarcely be redressed except on information and in the name of the sovereign.

The great principle on which this charter has been beneficial to the people is its judicial application to the relative rights and duties of the superior and the subordinate classes of society. If the king may not oppress his barons and the nobility, so the nobility should be restrained from acts of injustice and wrong toward their vassals; and restraints upon unjust and illegal authority should be enforced as against the superior in favor of the humblest subject of the realm, and the maintenance of peace and justice, as between equals of every grade of society from the highest to the lowest, is justified and provided for. It is in this view that the doctrines of equal rights for each and every member of the civil state has found a prime analogy in Magna Charta and has been incorporated as bearing the force of an acknowledged authority in our Declaration of Independence, and in our national and state constitutions. The American theory, combining the idea of sovereign in the people aggregate, and of subject as pertaining to each individual, would claim all of individual duty that is beneficial to the government, and interpose every wholesome restraint upon unjust or arbitrary authority in behalf of the humblest member of society.

I. That the Church of England shall be free and enjoy her whole rights and liberties inviolable. And we will have them to be so observed, which appears from hence; that the freedom of elections, which was reckoned most necessary for the Church of *England*, of our own free will and pleasure we have granted and confirmed by our charter, and obtained the confirmation from Pope Innocent III., before the discord between us and our barons, which charter we shall observe and do will it to be faithfully observed by our heirs forever.

I. "*That the Church of England shall be free*," etc. The Church of

England at that day was Catholic, and affiliated with the Church of Rome. Jurisdiction was claimed over it by the Pope; and for centuries the contest was kept up with the head of the Romish Church, whether the Pope had the sole power of all ecclesiastical appointments for England, or whether his duty was limited to the spiritual office of consecrating such as were selected by the local churches or recommended by the king. The people believed in making the appointment of the clergy a local or, at farthest, a national franchise; and this article of the charter pledges the power of the king to sustain them in this right, as against the arbitrary and despotic claims of the See of Rome. The interest here contended for was not a technical or nominal interest merely, but one vital to the country. For the ecclesiastical revenues of the kingdom before and after that time had been disposed of by the popes, through simony, to graceless foreigners, who never domiciled in the country and who farmed out the duty of teaching the people to ignorant pauper curates, who would require the least support, and hence take the least money out of the enormous revenues of the church that found their way abroad, never to return. But here was a law admitted to be binding on the king and the people, excluding foreign interference, whether by Pope, potentate, or prelate, with ecclesiastical appointments and elections.

The analogies of this provision, when properly applied, insure religious freedom, not only in England, but in all other countries. For the rights that are essential to a national church for its preservation and progress are no less essential to a local religious community in any country. The reason of this primary law of religious liberty goes equally to sustain the rights of the humblest of churches, as those of a national ecclesiastical establishment. And it was so intended, for the Church of England at that time embraced all the real or nominal Christians in the realm, and the feeblest of the local parishes by this provision would be protected.

II. We have also granted to all the freemen of our kingdom, for us and our heirs forever, all the underwritten liberties to have, and to hold, them and their heirs of us and our heirs.

II. *"We have granted to all freemen,"* etc. At the origin of Magna Charta there was a vast population in England, not embraced in this provision. Villeins and servants, and generally those who *wrought* at trades or at hand labor in the cultivation of the soil, were not esteemed within the grant of *privileges* herein guaranteed. But in our country, those who in England are below the advantages herein guaranteed are counted as freemen. The proposition is made the basis of our nationality: "That all men are created equal, that they are endowed by their Creator with certain inalienable rights, that among these are life, *liberty*, and the pursuit of happiness." In this regard the principles of Magna Charta are not brought down to the masses of our people, but our political and national emancipation has brought us up within the scope of the original force and application of those principles.

III.   If any of our earls, or barons, or others who hold of us in chief by military service, shall die, and at the time of his death his heir is of full age and owes a relief, he shall have his inheritance by the ancient relief; that is to say, the heir or heirs of an earl for a whole earl's barony, by a hundred pounds; the heir or heirs of a baron, for a whole barony, by a hundred pounds; the heir or heirs of a knight, for a whole knight's fee, by a hundred shillings at most; and he that oweth less shall give less, according to the ancient custom of fees.

IV.   That if the heir of any such be under age, and shall be in ward, when he comes of age, he shall have his inheritance without relief or without fine.

V.   The warden of the land of such heir who shall be under age shall take of the land of such heir only reasonable issues, reasonable customs, and reasonable services; and that without destruction and waste of the men or things [upon the estate]: and if we commit the guardianship of those lands to the sheriff, or any other, who is answerable to us for the issues of the land, and he make destruction and waste upon the ward lands, we will compel him to give satisfaction, and the land shall be committed to two lawful and discreet tenants of that fee, who shall be answera-

ble for the issues to us, or to him whom we shall assign.
And if we give or sell the wardship of any such
lands to any one, and he makes destruction or waste
upon them, he shall lose the wardship, which shall be
committed to two lawful and discreet tenants of that
fee, who shall in like manner be answerable to us, as
hath been said.

VI.   But the warden, so long as he hath the wardship of the land, shall keep up and maintain the
houses, parks, warrens, ponds, mills, and other things
pertaining to the land, out of the issues of the same
land ; and shall restore to the heir, when he comes of
full age, the whole land stocked with ploughs and
carriages, according as the time of wainage shall require and the issues of the land can reasonably bear.

III., IV., V., VI.   Under the system of landed estates then established in England, the sovereign representing the nation or its government was regarded as the primary owner of the soil, subject to
such subordinate interests therein as had become vested by royal
grant or by operation of law.   The subjects holding lands were
regarded as *tenants*, holding immediately, or mediately through intervening estates, of the king.   Hence, the guardianship of infant-
heirs and of their estates pertained to the crown, or to the lord of
whom the land was more immediately held.   In the several provisions contained in these articles relating to guardianship of wards
of the crown and of their estates, it is noteworthy that no provision
for the maintenance or education of the ward out of the land
seems to have been contemplated.   What became of the ward in
the mean time, during his minority, must be inquired after elsewhere than in these provisions.   For the issues and profits of the
land the guardian was answerable to the king as well as for the
duty of keeping up the estate.   These guardianships were sold by the
crown to the persons offering the most for them, subject to the condition of keeping up the estate.   The only benefit realized by the
ward was the provision against *waste* in the farming of his estate,
by the guardian, and exoneration from paying the *relief* or *succession tax* provided for in Article III.   The reason why the crown
claimed the income from these estates was, that they were held on

the tenure of military service, and that the crown might have to pay for a substitute for such service during the minority of the ward. Or rather this, the estate being held on the condition of military service, when no person was in being capable of the service, the estate for the time reverted to the crown, and was temporarily farmed for the king. In the mean time the estate was to be kept up, that when the heir came in possession, he might not be embarrassed by the burden and expense of repairing the estate, to the prejudice of his efficiency in discharging his military duties to the government.

With us, military service is a *personal* obligation of the citizen, and is in no manner charged by law on his estates. Lands are subject to taxation, like other property, for the civil and military expenditures of the government. But the possession of real property confers no rank on its owner, and imposes no obligation not chargeable on the holder of other kinds of property. Though the right of eminent domain to take and use land for a public purpose after the payment of a just compensation therefor, to be ascertained as provided by law, is an incident of every kind of title to lands known to our laws, it is held to be a reservation in all land patents and grants—in favor of the state.

VII. Heirs shall be married without disparagement [so as that before matrimony shall be contracted those who are nearest to the heir in blood shall be made acquainted with it].

VII. "*Heirs shall be married without disparagement.*" Leaving Coke's definition of disparagement, as in the note, we may remark that in no matter of human interest has the world been so overgoverned as in that of matrimony. If marriages were in all cases and in all countries effective in restraining and controlling the manners of society in the premises, a supervising management of the affair by older and experienced friends of the parties might well be provided for by law. But, as a general rule, the more the laws seek to direct or restrain the sexes in entering into this relation, so essential to civilization and human progress, the greater is the corruption of manners likely to be found in society. The laws of France forbid the marriage of children without the consent of their parents, until they come to the age of twenty-eight years. But it is noted by intelligent writers, that before such age is attained most of the young men have become the patrons of infamy and most of the daughters are sold to shame. Mere conventional and

21

mercenary interests in marriage seldom lead to a happy married
life. There are doubtless duties which friends owe to their unmar-
ried relatives in respect to this matter, but these duties should end
before infringing on the personal liberty of the one party or the
other.

VIII. A widow, after the death of her husband,
shall forthwith and without any difficulty have her
marriage and her inheritance; nor shall she give anything for her dower or her marriage or her inheritance which her husband and she held at the day of
his death. And she may remain in the capital mes-
suage or mansion-house of her husband forty days
after his death, within which time her dower shall be
assigned.

VIII. Dower was an estate created by operation of law in pur-
suance of public policy. It was a compensation to some extent of
the disabilities imposed by law on the wife during coverture. It was
also an assurance against the widow's becoming a charge on the
parish, burdened as she might be with the care and rearing of young
children. The prospect of actual benefit on the decease of the husband, from her provident and economical care of his estate, would
operate as an inducement to fidelity in her care for the husband's
estate during his life. And, inasmuch as she might have by such
care and industry added to the value of such estate, common justice would award her some compensation in the shape of dower.
The law, as defined in this charter, did not limit dower to the estate of which the husband *died* seized, but extended it to any lands
of which the husband had an estate of inheritance in possession at
any time during coverture. The phrase, " which her husband and
she held at the day of his death," was not intended to limit dower to
such estate. But she was endowed beyond this. In this particular
she was entitled to have her dower free of charge or duty. In several
of the United States dower is limited by statute to the estates of
which the husband *dies* seized, as in Vermont and in Connecticut.

The widow's *quarantine* is protected by law in most of the United
States.

IX. No widow shall be distrained [compelled] to
marry herself, so long as she has a mind to live with-

out a husband. But yet she shall give security that
she will not marry without our assent, if she holds
of us; or without the consent of the lord of whom
she holds, if she holds of another.

IX. Laws in restraint of marriage, though very ancient, never
should be regarded with favor. The scope for moral and Christian
influence embraces the suitable marriage and settlement of one's
children and family friends; but the law has done its proper work
when it inhibits incestuous and adulterous marriages under penalties as for crimes, and defines the proper evidence of a legal marriage. The restriction of judgments of divorce for infidelity against
the remarriage of the party proved guilty in the action, under the
existing laws of the state of New York, has been the subject of
frequent and grave discussion with our legal and moral writers. The
restriction is sustained by the highest religious authority; and yet
it is a question, if every moral precept contained in the Bible were
sought to be enforced by a civil statute, if the morals of the community would be improved thereby. It becomes doubly absurd,
when the statute singles out parties with whom morality has never
had an influence and endeavors to aid the Bible in enforcing its theological precepts. God has not deferred the execution of his will in
matters of morals and conscience to human governments and their
penal enactments. The ordinances of baptism and the Lord's Sup-
per might as well be enforced by civil statute as any other of the
positive institutions of the gospel. Yet who believes that the cause
of Christian morals would be thereby promoted?

Though the continuance of the marriage relation for the joint
lives of the parties is an idea inhering in the very nature of marriage, yet a marriage conforming to what is quoted as the very law
of Christ may take place while a former husband or wife is still
living. And this is copied by the laws of the state of New York
allowing the party to a divorce suit who makes a judicial record of
personal innocence, and proves the other party guilty of adultery,
to marry at his or her discretion. But while Christ asserted the nature of marriage as illustrated in the creation of the primitive pair in
Eden, he admitted that there might be exceptions as to an innocent
party. The method of effecting divorces under the Mosaic code by
the husband giving a bill to his wife, without the intervention of
any ecclesiastical or civil court, doubtless led to great abuses and
corruption of manners eminently entitled to the condemnation of
Christ. The practice was reprehensible in every view. Yet a
probable result of the practice on the wife so put away as expressed

in the same connection should be instructive, "Whosoever putteth away his wife for any cause save fornication causeth her to commit adultery ; and whosoever marrieth her that is put away committeth adultery."

The moral probabilities that the wife, innocent to that time of all crime, would, if so divorced, commit adultery, show how little could be effected by mere law for the safeguard of a woman so circumstanced that only the highest considerations of moral duty in her heart could restrain her from wantonness. This thought suggests the intrinsic difficulty of framing human laws that assure a probable influence for good over human passions and manners. Our laws of divorce restraining the remarriage of parties proved to have been guilty of adultery, assume one of two positions ; that open continued adultery is a better example for public morals than that the association of such with the opposite sex should be sanctioned with the forms of marriage and the surroundings of domestic life ; or it must be assumed that the decree of a civil court will be effectual to restrain the man or woman who is alleged and adjudged to have trampled on all the higher sanctions and influences of morality. But the office and scope of a high moral principle as affecting mankind is one thing and a law adapted to all classes and conditions of men is another. Moses found a law of divorce a necessary part of his civil code, while Christ found a higher morality necessary to be maintained in a school of ethics and morals than was found practical under the Mosaic ritual. So civil laws must everywhere be framed and adapted to all the conditions in which we find men, socially, morally, and physically, who are to be subject to their operations.

In respect to the restrictions on marriage by the laws of the state of New York of those against whom judgments of divorce are obtained for their infidelity, we may observe that the state of public morals is scarcely improved by these restrictions. Suits for divorce are quite as common in this state in proportion to its population as in other states where a more consistent and rational policy prevails. Women of the town are not fewer, and those patronizing them are not in less proportion, than elsewhere. Husbands or wives are not more faithful to their conjugal vows than elsewhere and the utility of our divorce laws is not shown in their restraints on licentiousness.

Marriage after divorce will not make a person the worse, while the domestic interests and influences of a home and household have reformed thousands from moral degeneracy and an irregular and vicious life.

X.   Neither we nor our bailiffs shall seize any land or rent for any debt, so long as there shall be chattels of the debtor upon the premises sufficient to pay the debt, nor shall the sureties of the debtor be distrained, so long as the principal debtor is sufficient for the payment of the debt.

XI.   And if the principal debtor fail in the payment of the debt, not having wherewithal to discharge it, then the sureties shall answer the debt, and if they will they shall have the lands and rents of the debtor until they shall be satisfied for the debt which they paid for him; unless the principal debtor can show himself acquitted thereof against the said sureties.

X., XI.   This is still the rule of law as well in Great Britain as the United States.   Slight modifications charging responsibility on sureties on the mere default of the principal, without imposing the necessity of exhausting legal remedies against the principal before proceedings are commenced to charge the surety, now obtain in all cases affected by the principles known as the law merchant, which seeks quick transactions and ready returns as well as certainty in commercial responsibility.   In other cases suretyship follows in its liabilities special conditions in contract, taking them out of the general provisions of law.   Under our statutes, generally the obligations of the surety are perfected on the default of the principal and notice of such default to the surety.   Afterwards a compromise may be had with the principal or sureties or either of them without discharging the other parties, the doctrine of the statute being that the obligations of each of the parties is perfect, on being regularly charged for the entire debt.   The remedies of sureties against the defaulting debtor do not attach to land in the state of New York, unless a mortgage by way of indemnity is held thereon, or a judgment has been obtained as for moneys paid to the debtor's use.

XII.   If any one have borrowed anything of the Jews, more or less, and dies before the debt be satisfied, there shall be no interest paid for that debt, so long as the heir is under age, of whomsoever he may

hold.   And if the debt falls into our hands, we will
take only the chattel mentioned in the charter or instrument.

XIII.   And if any one shall die indebted to the
Jews, his wife shall have her dower and pay nothing of
that debt; and if the deceased left children under
age, they shall have necessaries provided for them
according to the tenement (or real estate) of the deceased, and out of the residue the debt shall be paid;
saving however the service of the lords.   In like
manner let it be with the debts due to other persons
than the Jews.

XII., XIII.   Laws discriminating against classes of community
are but the counterpart of laws establishing aristocractes.   For if
the jurisdiction exists to legislate classes out of their rights the
same jurisdiction may bestow distinction and partial and discriminating benefits on other classes.   Leaving the Jews out of these two
sections, and the discrimination for the widow and children is within
the principles recognized by the laws in most of the United States.

In Vermont, in the case of insolvent estates having assets, the
Judge of Probate may award out of the personalty such reasonable
sum as will provide for the support of the widow and minor children under seven years of age, in preference to the claims of the
general creditors of the estate.   In New York such allowance is
restricted to specified articles and other assets to the value of $150.
Exemptions of specified articles from levy or execution is predicated
on the same principle—the reasonable humanities of the law.
These exemptions work no injustice to the creditor so long as the
law gave notice of the risk, before the creditor parted with his property.

XIV.   No scutage or aid shall be imposed in our
kingdom, unless by the common council of our kingdom, except to redeem our person, and to make our
eldest son a knight, and once to marry our eldest
daughter; and for this there shall only be paid a reasonable aid.

XIV. Our present term "*tax*" answers to the word "*scutage*" (escuage) in the better defined and matured systems of free governments. For "the great council" we may substitute "*parliament*" or legislature or any more immediate representative body of the people and we will have the force of this section in its application to the theory of a free government. While thus the rights of those who were to be charged with the burdens of taxation were to be considered, emergencies might arise when immediate relief should not be deferred to the slow process of summoning a parliament, as if the king were taken captive where a ransom alone could restore him to his people; and, in cases in the known experience of the government where the dignity of the government would otherwise be affected, the people might be charged to a limited extent without special act of parliament. Our own state and national governments in the practical necessities of their administration are not always saved the necessities of using the public credit and charging the people without the form of previous legislation. The spirit of our statesmanship however looks with a jealous care to the extraordinary use of our public credit without prior special authority. And where the emergencies of war and provisions for public defense have forced informal use of the public credit the prerogatives of the people are sought to be preserved by a formal authority for levying a tax and a liquidation of such special expenses under the law, I believe it is generally held that those trusting their money to a public executive do so at their own risk as to future legislative sanction.

The violation of the principle of Magna Charta embraced in this section by the British government as against its American colonies was made a chief issue in the contest for our independence. For, reasoned our colonial statesmen, if the king could not by his prerogatives impose arbitrary taxes on his subjects at home, why should he with the aid or in combination with those subjects impose arbitrary taxes on us where we have no representation?

XV. In like manner it shall be concerning the aids of the city of London; and the city of *London* shall have all its ancient liberties and free customs, as well by land as by water.

XVI. Furthermore, we will and grant that all other cities and boroughs and towns and ports shall have all their liberties and free customs, and shall

have the common council of the kingdom concerning
the assessment of their aids, except in the three cases
aforesaid.

XV., XVI. The franchises of the city of London to lay its own
taxes was practically a condition precedent to the *enjoyment* of its
liberties as a commercial town. If arbitrary exactions and forced
loans were to be allowed the government, all other liberties and
franchises would be rendered nugatory and valueless.

But the franchise as to imposing its own taxes rendered the others
material aids to commercial prosperity. The taxing clause as to the
other towns and boroughs seems to have been omitted for the reason that they were small towns and never had been made the special sources of public revenue. The prerogative of the crown to
impose special taxes on them had never been claimed or asserted as
an incident of the civil administration of the government in the time
of peace, while the king was inhibited from imposing taxes on cities,
towns, etc.; to parliament was reserved the right to lay special
taxes on any one of these, except the city of London. This jurisdiction on the part of our state legislature exists in the state of
New York. To the boards of supervisors, quasi legislators of the
counties, is remitted the general duty of levying taxes. But the legislature is the ultimate authority in using the taxing power; so the
annual tax levy of the city of New York is generally enacted by the
legislature to save any question of jurisdiction or regularity.

XVII. And for the assessing of scutages we shall
cause to be summoned the archbishops, bishops, abbots, earls, and great barons of the realm, singly by
our letters.

XVIII. And, furthermore, we shall cause to be
summoned, in general by our sheriffs and bailiffs, all
others who hold of us in chief at a certain day; that is
to say, forty days before their meeting, at least, to a
certain place; and in all letters of such summons we
will declare the cause of the summons.

XVII., XVIII. These articles indicate the extent of the franchises that were then esteemed to represent the kingdom,—archbishops, bishops, abbots, earls, and great barons of the realm, and

such others as held lands in chief of the crown. Though popular liberty was without any specific representation in this preliminary parliament, yet the conflict and adjustment of various interests, brought together from different orders in society and different locations in the kingdom, tended to mitigate severity in the civil administration and to remove, to some extent, the restraints and burdens which crushed out popular impulses.

An aristocratic government is not, necessarily, oppressive or despotic, when it happens to represent antagonistic forces and interests. Thus the Dutch Republic of two centuries ago is regarded as the freest government in Europe, though it had no shadow of popular franchise in its constitution, its "*states general*" being made up of the executive head of the nation and representatives of municipal and borough corporations. The beneficial interests secured by the people, under such governments, result on the principle of the old adage, "When rogues contend, honest men get their dues."

In experience, it is found that popular liberty has the best guaranties for its continuance where the elective franchise is extended to all who are affected by the measures and policy of the government, and who will honestly exercise it for the public good.

XIX.   And summons being thus made, the business shall proceed, on the day appointed, according to the advice of such as shall be present, although all that were summoned come not.

The XIXth article seems to have been inserted to render the action of the great council certain, when convened; putting it out of the power of the few to prevent its action by absenting themselves, and preventing the king from dissolving the sitting on pretense of the absence of members.

XX.   We will not for the future grant to any one, that he may take aid of his own free tenants, unless to redeem his body, and to make his eldest son a knight, and once to marry his eldest daughter; and for this there shall only be paid a reasonable aid.

XXI.   No man shall be distrained to perform more service for a knight's fee, or other free tenement, than is due from thence.

XX., XXI. A part of the *XIVth* article is here applied to the relative ranks and conditions in the kingdom below the king, and suggests a construction of the law in behalf of the weaker as against the stronger members of the state. To the honor of English jurisprudence this beneficial adaptation of the law to the lowest members of a community has developed the great body of what is now known as the common law of England in the interests of humanity and justice. And still, with the labor and progress of centuries, the attempts to crganize a reasonably free government in England without a popular franchise has been a failure. The extension of the franchise has hitherto served as an index of the progress of national emancipation.

The arbitrary exaction of money by the lord from his subject beyond established custom is herein forbidden.

XXII. Common pleas shall not follow our court, but shall be holden in some certain place. Trials upon the writs of *novel disseisin,* and of *mort d'ancestor,* and of *darrein presentment* shall be taken, but in their proper counties, and after this manner; we, or (if we shall be out of the realm) our chief justiciary, shall send two justiciaries through every county four times a year, who, with the four knights chosen out of every shire by the people, shall hold the said assizes in the county, on the day and at the place appointed.

XXIII. And if any matters cannot be determined on the day appointed to hold the assizes in each county, so many of the knights and freeholders as have been at the assizes aforesaid shall be appointed to decide them as is necessary, according as there is more or less business.

XXII., XXIII., provide for the early and convenient administration of justice in a plan adapted to the then condition of the people. Our circuit courts are still organized somewhat on the plan herein suggested. The uniform administration of justice throughout the country was then, as now, a thing desired. And this would be more readily attained by the same judge sitting in different counties. Besides, a few experienced and learned judges would be able to administer justice with a better intelligence and a flexible adaptation to different cases than could reasonably be expected from a mere local magistracy. Defaults could be entered before the local judges, and matters of minor importance could be disposed of.

XXIV. A freeman shall not be amerced for a small fault ; but, according to the degree of the fault, and for a great crime in proportion to the heinousness of it, saving to him his contenement, and after the same manner a merchant, saving to him his merchandise.

XXV. And a villein shall be amerced after the same manner, saving to him his wainage, if he falls under our mercy. And none of the aforesaid amercements shall be assessed but by the oath of honest men of the neighborhood.

XXVI. Earls and barons shall not be amerced but by their peers, and according to the quality of the offense.

XXVII. No ecclesiastical person shall be amerced but according to the proportion aforesaid, and not according to the value of his ecclesiastical benefice.

XXIV., XXV., XXVI., XXVII. Amercements and fines are not held synonymous. The latter is fixed by statute, while the former is, in the discretion of the court, within the restrictions and reasons of law. Though the latter are regarded as most merciful to offenders, yet, in experience, it is doubtful if amercements are not frequently most oppressive and unreasonable.

Amercements were inflicted not so much with respect to the character of the offense as to the rank, condition, and ability to pay of the offender, though the character of the offense seems to have had some respect in the sentence.

What is known as trial by jury seems to have been contemplated in these articles, though without any certainty as to number of such jurors, or method of their organization, or the proceedings to be had before them.

The reservation of certain things essential to life, and useful to public industry, even as against punishments for crime, was the result of public policy, but the criminal after punishment should be cast on society as a vagabond or a pauper. Yet the provision was humane as a mitigation of the evils that might follow punishment.

The exception in the case of an ecclesiastical person was a concession to the church in its jealousy for its revenues, and on the theory that the benefice was at all times the property of the church, and that the "*incumbent*" was only the administrator of its charities. But with us this law has expired, as the reasons sustaining it do not exist.

XXVIII.   Neither a town nor any person shall be distrained to make bridges over rivers unless anciently and of right they are bound to do it.

XXVIII.   An estate might be held on condition that the tenant should keep in repair a certain bridge. This duty being in the place of rent, those for whose benefit the bridge was to be kept up might distrain for the default. So, if towns had maintained a bridge whose convenience to the citizens had induced them to settle in the town or vicinity, the town could be compelled to continue the bridge. But otherwise, the bridge, as a part of the king's highway, must be maintained out of general revenues, or by tolls, as might be provided by law.

XXIX.   No sheriff, constable, coroner, or other our bailiffs shall hold pleas of the crown.

XXIX.   These were inferior officers, and the dignity of the crown might be compromised in their assuming to represent its judicial functions. But the better reason for this is found in the fact that pleas of the crown, so called, were in the nature of indictments for criminal offenses, and the sentence in such cases was to be executed by some one of these officers named. Hence would arise the singular anomaly of a court by its personal hands executing the sentence which it had pronounced, which would operate as a hindrance to the due administration of justice.

XXX.   All counties, hundreds, wapentakes, and tithings shall stand at the old rents without any increase except in our demesne lands.

XXX. This article is intended to keep the rents due the government for lands held under its various grants and tenures at a fixed and settled rate, and not leave the holders to capricious, exorbitant, and oppressive exactions. As a practical provision it secured to the use of the tenant his betterments and improvements without being taxed therefor, though this provision in its terms seems to relate to public burthens to be exacted of the communities therein enumerated. But its principle is eminently beneficial when applied to the relation of landlord and tenant as individuals. The opposite policy has a fitting illustration in the present condition of Ireland. Irish landlords are charged with raising the rent on their tenants from year to year and that they make every improvement put on the soil by the tenant a reason for increasing the exactions. And such practice is even said to be extended to all cases where the tenant may indulge in a new blouse coat at Christmas. The quarter sale charged by the patroon on the alienation of manor estates in New York, by the tenant, was equally absurd and unjust.

The demesne lands of the crown were an exception to this rule, as in theory they were in the possession of the sovereign, or in the lord as his representative, and not charged with any continuous estate in 'the tenant. The king as owner in such case was entitled to control the possession and make any disposition of the estate he might judge proper. These lands were occupied by the lord representing the king and not sublet to tenants, and any exactions as to them would fall on the lord, who was able to bear them and would so discharge obligations arising from his intimate relation to the government.

XXXI. If any one that holds of us a lay fee dies, and the sheriff or our bailiff show our letters patent of summons concerning the debt due to us from the deceased, it shall be lawful for the sheriff or our bailiff to attach and register the chattels of the deceased, found upon his lay fee, to the value of the debt, by the view of lawful men so as nothing be removed until our whole debt be paid, and the rest shall be left to the executors to fulfill the will of the deceased. And if there be nothing due from him to us, all the chattels shall remain to the deceased; saving to his wife and children their reasonable shares.

XXXI. The preference of debts of decedents, due the government, is a part of our own revised statutes. In the payment of debts, those entitled to preference under the laws of the United States must be first paid; then taxes assessed on the estate of decedent in his lifetime, etc. But with us, the executor or administrator is an officer of the government, as well as trustee of the legal representatives of the deceased; so that in ordinary cases there is no occasion for the intervening of special warrants in the hands of sheriffs or bailiffs.

XXXII. If any freeman die intestate his chattels shall be distributed by the hands of his nearest relations and friends, by view of the church, saving to every one his debts which the deceased owed.

XXXII. This provision is scarcely changed, save in the manner of its execution, by administrators etc., and the further provisions of our statute to charge the lands of decedent with debts, after exhausting his personal estate, and for a sale of lands to pay such debts.

XXXIII. No constable or bailiff of ours shall take corn or other chattels of any man unless he presently give him money for it or has respite of payment from the seller.

XXXIII. It was a part of the covenants of this charter that the king should respect private property, and if it should be necessary to resort to such property to meet any pressing want, the same should be fairly paid for at the time of the taking, unless the owner consented to give credit. The principle contained in our constitution and laws is but a re-enactment of this article; so as to articles XXXVI. and XXXVII.

XXXIV. No constable shall distrain any knight to give money for castle guard, if he himself shall do it in his own person or by another able man, in case he shall be hindered by any reasonable cause.

XXXV. And if we shall lead him or if we shall send him into the army, he shall be free from castle guard for the time he shall be in the army, by our command.

XXXIV., XXXV. This very rational provision seems to have been often disregarded in times prior to *Magna Charta*, in violation of the plainest principles of common justice, that a person should not be taxed to pay for a service which he himself was personally performing, or if otherwise in the army, he was detained from his castle.

XXXVI. No sheriff or bailiff of ours or any other shall take horses or carts of any for cartage.

XXXVII. Neither shall we nor our officers take any man's timber for our castles or other uses, unless by the consent of the owner of the timber. [See note under XXXIII.]

XXXVIII. We will retain the lands of those convicted of felony but one year and a day, and then they shall be delivered to the lord of the fee.

XXXVIII. The precise reason for this seizing the estate of a felon for a year and a day is not so clear, unless it were by way of indemnity for the legal costs of prosecuting the offense. But this, if a penalty, would be at the expense of the lord of the fee, and seemingly remote from justice.

Our laws have taken good care that indictments for felony shall not profit the informer or the state, though fines for less crimes are sometimes divided with informers.

XXXIX. All wears [weirs] for the time to come shall be demolished in the rivers of Thames and Medway and throughout all England except upon the sea coast.

XXXIX. The English law in this particular is scarcely followed in any state in America. The rule here is *free hunting* and *free fishing*. Yet in the progress of society the rearing of fish in private ponds has come to be protected by law; and laws for the preservation of fish in running streams and rivers by limiting the methods and seasons of fishing, and of game by prescribing the seasons of the year when game may not be killed, are passed by several of our state legislatures. Weirs even to run water to a mill are only allowed in England where the right has been established by prescription. Weirs were allowed on the sea coast either for securing of fish or perhaps for tide mills, on the theory that what might be so acquired from the sea could not interrupt the chances of others, to their damage, as weirs across running streams would probably do.

XL. The writ which is called *præcipe* for the future shall not be granted to any one of any tenement whereby a freeman may lose his cause.

XL. This seems to have been a summary writ to restore possession of lands to one who complained that he had been unjustly ousted. But it was in no manner conclusive as to the title to the lands. And this provision of the charter is to preserve to the person, put out under the summary writ, his day in court to try his title to the lands. Analogous to this is the provision of our laws granting new trials as of course in ejectment suits.

XLI. There shall be one measure of wine and one of ale through our whole realm, and one measure of corn; that is to say, the *London quarter;* and one breadth of dyed cloth and russets and haberjects; that is to say, to ells within the testa. And the weights shall be as the measures.

XLI. Exactitude in weights and measures regulated by a uniform standard is of the first importance to the harmony and peace of a people. Without such standard, commerce could neither be initiated nor carried on. It matters less what the standard and its details may be, provided it is fixed and continuing the same. Yet the interests of commerce are now seeking an international standard of weights and measures and money that shall be uniform in all countries adopting it.

XLII. From henceforward nothing shall be given or taken for a writ of inquisition from him that desires an inquisition of life or limbs, but shall be granted *gratis* and not denied.

XLII. The office of this article is now answered by the writ of habeas corpus, or anticipated by preliminary examinations of accused parties by justices of the peace or coroners before their commitment for trial.

XLIII. If any one holds of us by fee farm or socage or burgage, and holds lands of another by military service, we will not have the wardship of the heir or land which belongs to another man's fee by reason of what he holds of us by fee farm, socage, or burgage. Nor will we have the wardship of the fee farm, socage, or burgage, unless the fee farm is bound to perform military service.

XLIV. We will not have the wardship of an heir, nor of any land which he holds of another by military service, by reason of any petit sergeanty he holds of us, as by the service of giving us daggers, arrows, or the like.

XLIII., XLIV: Wardship in that day was usually exercised over the estate for the benefit of the guardian, free of any claims for account by the ward, and under one pretext or another the estates of infant heirs had been subject to ruinous waste by the agents of the crown. In this article the king covenanted against arbitrary seizures of such estates and deferred his rights to the incident of legal title recognized by law; to wit, a claim on the estate for military service.

XLV. No bailiff for the future shall put any man to his law upon his single accusation, without credible witnesses produced to prove it.

XLV. In compliance with this article it is still the rule of criminal law embraced in the constitutions of most of the American states, that prosecutions in criminal cases shall only be had on indictments, and the accused shall be furnished with a copy of the indictment with the names of witnesses relied on to prove the charge. Malicious prosecutions by public officers, and perhaps for mercenary motives, was the evil sought to be suppressed.

22

XLVI. No freeman shall be taken or imprisoned, or disseised, or outlawed, or banished, or in any wise destroyed, nor will we pass upon him or commit him to prison unless by the legal judgment of his peers or by the law of the land.

XLVI. This article is sufficiently familiar as a part of our own subsisting constitutional law and it needs no comment.

XLVII. We will sell to no man, we will deny no man, nor defer right and justice.

XLVII. The corruption of public justice by bribery and fraud is evidently not of modern origin, and the violation of this article of Magna Charta, I am sorry to say, is not unknown to the history of English jurisprudence.

XLVIII. All merchants shall have safe and secure conduct to go out of and to come into England, and to stay there ; and to pass as well by land as by water, to buy and sell by the ancient and allowed customs, without any evil tolls except in time of war, or when they shall be of any nation at war with us.

XLVIII. The domicile of foreign merchants in England, and their free transit to and from the kingdom in times of peace, were, by this article, made a part of the public policy of the government. It seems to have been discovered at that early day that commerce was an important interest of the country, and that it would only flourish by such guaranteed freedoms to its agents and representatives.

XLIX. And if there shall be found any such in our land, in the beginning of a war, they shall be attached without damage to their bodies or goods, until it may be known unto us, or our chief justiciary, how our merchants be treated in the nation at war with us, and if ours be safe there they shall be safe in our land.

L. It shall be lawful for the time to come for any

one to go out of our kingdom and return safely and securely by land or by water, saving his allegiance to us, unless in time of war by some short space for the common benefit of the kingdom ; except prisoners, and outlaws, according to the law of the land, and people in war with us, and merchants who shall be in such condition as is above mentioned.

XLIX., L. Where merchants of various nations had so interchanged their residences it might operate as an act of humanity, at the commencement of a war, to make them hostages for the conduct of their own governments towards English merchants abroad.

The same liberties and means of enforcing reciprocity by the government is also extended to others than merchants.

LI. If any man holds of any escheat, as of the *Honor of Wallingford, Nottingham, Bologne,* Lancaster, or of other escheats which are in our hands, and are baronies, and dies, his heir shall not give any other relief or perform any other service to us than he would to the baron if the barony were in possession of the ·baron; we will hold it after the same manner the baron held it.

LI. It seems to have been a policy of the nobles to prevent the consolidation of large estates in the crown; or to prevent undue advantage and profits being taken by the sovereign from accidents or contingences affecting baronial estates.

LII. Those men who dwell without the forest from henceforth shall not come before our justiciaries of the forest upon summons, but such as are impleaded or are pledges for any that were attached for something concerning the forest.

LII. The forests were peculiar estates of the crown, being woodlands, appropriated to the rearing and preserving of game. Peculiar courts seem to have been erected, having jurisdiction of all matters pertaining to these forests. It often happened that these justiciaries sought to exercise their judicial functions over such as were not within their jurisdiction, to give a show of claim to the frequent attempts to extend the law of the forests over private estates held by a title vested entirely different from the demesnes of the forests. The first object of this article was to restrict the crown estates to their ancient prescription, and also to commit the rights of the citizen to the experience of the ordinary courts and not to such as might be presumed ignorant of all questions not arising under game laws or laws of the forest.

LIII. We will not make any justiciaries, constables, sheriffs, or bailiffs, but what are knowing in the law of the realm and are disposed duly to observe it.

LIII. An intelligent administration of justice with strict regard to existing laws is essential to the welfare of any nation. A knowledge of law and a disposition to be governed thereby are here made prerequisite qualifications of a judge.

LIV. All barons who are the founders of abbeys and have charters of the king of England for the advowson, or are entitled to it by ancient tenure, may have the custody of these when void, as they ought to have.

LIV. *"Advowson"* was the right to nominate an incumbent to a clerical benefice. But this right could only be exercised when there was a vacancy. The incumbent, when inducted into office, was nearly independent of the patron. At any rate he was amenable, in his clerical duties, only to the ecclesiastical authority. When there was no incumbent, then the patron had the custody of the parish, living, or abbey, until he presented a new incumbent for the place, who was duly installed therein.

LV. All woods that have been taken into the forests, in our own time, shall forthwith be laid out again, and the like shall be done with the rivers that have been taken and fenced in by us, during our reign.

LVI. All evil customs concerning forests, warrens, and foresters, warreners, sheriffs and their officers, rivers and their keepers, shall forthwith be inquired into, in each county, by twelve knights of the same shire, chosen by the most creditable persons in the same county and upon oath, and within forty days after the said inquest be utterly abolished so as never to be restored.

LV., LVI. The object of restricting the king's forests to their old prescribed bounds is herein affirmatively declared. In this, two objects were sought: first, the protection of private landed estates against encroachments by the crown; second, a respect to the necessary political economy, requiring the use of land in raising food for the people, instead of to the mere amusement of the sovereign.

LVII. We will immediately give up all hostages and engagements delivered unto us, by our *English subjects*, as securities for their keeping the peace and yielding us faithful service.

LVII. The giving up of hostages was an essential requirement of the barons to render the great charter of any avail in the protection of their rights. Mutual confidence between ruler and people was sought by this charter, at least in theory; and the retention of hostages by the king to coerce the good behavior of the barons would have been entirely incompatible with the objects of the charter.

LVIII. We will entirely remove from our bailiwicks the relations of Gerard de Athyes, so as that for the future they shall have no bailiwick in England. We will also remove Engelard de Cygony, Andrew, Peter, and Gyon from the chancery, Gyon de Cygony, Geoffrey de Martyn and his brothers, Philip Mark and his brothers and his nephew, Geoffrey, and their whole retinue.

LIX. And as soon as peace is restored we will send out of the kingdom all foreign soldiers, crossbowmen and stipendiaries who are come with horses and arms to the injury of our peace.

LVIII., LIX. A government controlled by foreigners or those in the interests of a foreign country and sustained by foreign mercenary troops can never be a free government. If all its measures were just and sound, the repressing influence it would exercise on the spirit of a people would be fatal to national enterprise and prosperity; it was one of the grievous complaints of our Declaration of Independence that Great Britain looked to our future military coercion and subjugation by stationing here what to us were essentially foreign troops. In this declaration our fathers were sustained by these articles of the great charter. As Englishmen yielding allegiance to English law they were not rebels but patriots.

LX. If any one has been dispossessed or deprived by us, without the legal judgment of his peers, of his lands, castles, liberties, or rights, we will forthwith restore them to him; and if any dispute arises upon this head, let the matter be decided by the five and twenty barons hereafter mentioned for the preservation of the peace.

LX. The theory of the divine right of kings, or that kings can do no wrong, is herein, and in subsequent articles, effectually contradicted. That the law is superior to the executive in a government is asserted, insomuch that the rights of the government to its property in possession might be inquired into, in a lawful court or a recognized tribunal.

LXI. As to all those things of which any person has, without the legal judgment of his peers, been dispossessed or deprived, either by King *Henry* our father, or our brother King *Richard*, and which we have in our hands, or are possessed by others, and we are bound to warrant and make good, we shall have a respite, till the term usually allowed the croises; excepting those things about which there is a suit depending, or whereof an inquest hath been made by our order before we undertook the crusade. But when we return from our pilgrimage, or if we do not perform it, we will immediately cause full justice to be administered therein.

LXII. The same respite we shall have for disafforesting the forest which *Henry* our father, or our brother *Richard*, have afforested; and for the wardship of the lands which are in another's fee, in the same manner as we have hitherto enjoyed those wardships, by reason of a fee held of us by knight service; and for the abbeys founded in 'any other fee than our own, in which the lord of the fee claims a right. And when we return from our pilgrimage, or if we should not perform it, we will immediately do full justice to all the complainants in this behalf.

LXI., LXII. The crusades in that age were held to bear with them the exigencies of war, to the extent that private justice must defer its claims to the conclusion of a military contest. This provision finds its analogy in the common practice of nations, to defer their obligations to their citizens to the times of peace; on the ground that the citizen is equally bound with the government to hazard all for the life of the government, and the further consideration that the government might be so crippled by an unsustained war as to put it out of its power to discharge its private obligations.

LXIII. No man shall be taken or imprisoned upon the appeal of a woman for the death of any other man than her husband.

LXIII. Whatever might have been the purpose of this article, it has scarcely an analogy in modern criminal jurisprudence. To save the sex from the painful commingling with the administration of criminal law would doubtless be the pretense for this article. But that this provision would not facilitate the escape of criminals from justice, in many cases, is not so certain. The article is dubtless predicated on the disabilities of women recognized by the common law, and that are now only being mitigated but not entirely set aside.

LXIV. All unjust and illegal fines and all amercements imposed unjustly and contrary to the law of

the land, shall be entirely forgiven; or else be left
to the decision of the five and twenty barons, hereafter mentioned, for the preservation of the peace, or of
the major part of them, together with the aforesaid
Stephen, archbishop of *Canterbury*, if he can be present, and others whom he shall think fit to take along
with him; and, if he cannot be present, the business
shall, notwithstanding, go on without him. But, so
that if one or more of the aforesaid five and twenty
barons be plaintiffs in the same cause, they shall be
set aside, as to what concerns this particular affair, and
others be chosen in their room, out of the said five
and twenty, and sworn by the rest to decide that
matter.

LXIV. The only incident in this article not within the notes on
LX. is the provision that a party to a controversy should not sit in
judgment on his own case. A then existing abuse of the forms of law
appears to have been intimated as requiring this special provision.

LXV. If we have disseised or dispossessed the
Welsh of any lands, liberties, or other things without
the legal judgment of their peers, they shall immediately be restored to them. And if any dispute arise,
upon this head, the matter shall be determined in the
marches by the judgment of their peers; for tenements in England, according to the law of *England;*
for tenements in Wales, according to the law of Wales;
for a tenement of the marches, according to the law
of the marches. The same shall the Welsh do to us
and our subjects.

LXV. Recognition is here expressed of the local law of a province differing from the laws of a kingdom or empire. After all the
fight against the Irish contest for home rule the laws of England
have professed to respect local customs, as well as city and borough
ordinances, as a part of the laws of the land, as our United States

courts decide appeals to them by the laws of the state where the controversy arose. A local legislature in Ireland would not be a novelty under English law.

LXVI. As for all those things of which any Welsh-man hath, without the legal judgment of his peers, been disseised or deprived by King Henry our father, or our brother King Richard; and which we either have in our hands, or others are possessed of, and we are obliged to warrant it, we shall have a respite till the time generally allowed the croises; excepting those things about which a suit is depending, or whereof an inquest has been made, by our order, before we undertook the crusade. But when we return, or if we stay at home and do not perform our pilgrimage, we will immediately do them full justice, according to the laws of the Welsh and of the parts aforementioned.

LXVII. We will without delay dismiss the son of Llewelin and all the Welsh hostages and release them from the engagements they entered into with us for the preservation of the peace.

LXVIII. We shall treat with Alexander, king of the *Scots*, concerning the restoring of his sisters and hostages and his right and liberties, in the same form and manner as we shall do to the rest of our barons of England; unless by the engagements which his father William, late king of *Scots*, hath entered into with us, it ought to be otherwise; and this shall be left to the determination of his peers in our court.

LXIX. All the aforesaid customs and liberties which we have granted to be holden in our kingdom, as much as it belongs to us towards our people, all our subjects, as well clergy as laity, shall observe, as far as they are concerned towards their dependents.

LXVI., LXVII., LXVIII., LXIX. A sound policy in a government towards a comparatively remote part of the kingdom is herein enforced, requiring the extension to such a province and its people of the same legal guarantees and rights as were established for the rest of the kingdom. The release of hostages was a condition precedent to the establishment of the internal peace of the nation. The unjust detention of persons convicted of no crime, as a means of coercing obedience by their friends at home, in the light of modern days, would, of itself, produce a rebellion and make the subjects the enemies of their government. The closing provision of Article LXIX. was probably more than the barons bargained for, but once in the charter it has been working the emancipation of the lower classes from that day until now. It was doubtless appreciated in those evil times, that the public peace and stability depended on the contentment of the different orders of society with their situations and relations, while the oppressions and tyranny of the king had organized such a formidable civil war against him the subordinates of the barons might be equally restless, under like treatment from their superiors. It was an hour for gratitude on the part of the barons when their retainers had aided them in the brilliant victory they had obtained over the king. But this article did not enfranchise a single vassal nor scarcely give them a standing in court to enforce their rights by judicial aid; still we have here warrant for redressing the wrongs of the humblest in the kingdom when judges of enlightened benevolence found opportunity to administer justice in the spirit of equity.

LXX. And whereas for the honor of God and the amendment of our kingdom and for quieting the discord that has arisen between us and our barons, we have granted all the things aforesaid; willing to render them firm and lasting, we do give and grant our subjects the following security; namely, that the barons may choose five and twenty barons of the kingdom, whom they think convenient, who shall take care with all their might, to hold and observe and cause to be observed the peace and liberties we have granted them, and by this our present charter, confirmed. So as that if we, our justiciary, our bailiffs or any of our officers, shall, in any case, fail in the performance of them towards any person, or shall break through any of these articles of peace and security, and the offense is notified to four barons chosen out of the five and twenty aforementioned, the said four barons shall repair to us, or our justiciary, if we are out of the realm, and laying open the grievance shall petition to have it redressed without delay ; and if it is not redressed by us, or, if we should chance to be out of the realm, if it is not redressed by our justiciary, within forty days, reckoning from the time it has been notified to us, or to our justiciary if we should be out of the realm, the four barons aforesaid shall lay the case before the rest of the five and twenty barons, and the said five and twenty barons, together with the community of the whole kingdom, shall distrain and distress us all the ways possible ; namely, by seizing our castles, lands, possessions, and in any other manner they can, till the grievance is redressed according to their pleasure ; saving harmless our own person and the persons of our queen and children. And when it is redressed they shall obey us as before.

LXXI. And any person whatsoever in the kingdom may swear that he will obey the orders of the five and twenty barons aforesaid in the execution of the premises and that he will distress us jointly with them, to the utmost of his power; and we give public and free liberty to any one that will swear to them and never shall hinder any person from taking the same oath.

LXXII. As for all those, our subjects, who will not of their own accord swear to join the five and twenty barons in distraining and distressing us, we will issue our order to make them take the same oath as aforesaid.

LXXIII. And if any one of the five and twenty barons dies or goes out of the kingdom or is hindered any other way from putting the things aforesaid in execution, the rest of the said five and twenty barons may choose another in his room in their discretion, who shall be sworn in like manner as the rest.

LXXIV. In all things that are committed to the charge of these five and twenty barons, if when they are all assembled together they should happen to disagree about any matter, or some of them when summoned will not or cannot come, whatever is agreed upon or enjoined by the major part of those who are present shall be reputed as firm and valid as if all the five and twenty had given their consent, and the aforesaid five and twenty shall swear that all the premises they shall faithfully observe, and cause with all their power to be observed.

LXXV. And we will not by ourselves, or others, procure anything whereby any of these concessions and liberties be revoked or lessened, and, if any such thing be obtained, let it be null and void; neither shall we ever make use of it either by ourselves or any other.

LXXVI. And all the ill will, anger, and malice that hath arisen between us and our subjects, of the clergy and laity, from the first breaking out of the dissensions between us, we do fully remit and forgive. Moreover all trespasses occasioned by the said dissension from Easter in the sixteenth year of our reign, till the restoration of peace and tranquillity, we hereby entirely remit to all, clergy as well as laity, and so far as in us lies do fully forgive.

LXXVII. We have, moreover, granted them our letters patents, testimonial of *Stephen* lord archbishop of *Canterbury*, *Henry* lord archbishop of Dublin, and the bishops aforesaid, as also of Master *Pandulph* for the security and concessions aforesaid.

LXXVIII. Wherefore, we will, and firmly enjoin, that the church of England be free, and that all men in our kingdom have and hold all the aforesaid liberties, rights, and concessions, truly and peacefully, freely and quietly, fully and wholly, to themselves and their heirs, in all things and places forever, as is aforesaid.

LXXIX. It is also sworn, as well on our part as on the part of the barons, that all the things aforesaid shall faithfully and sincerely be observed.

Given under our hand, in the presence of the witnesses above named, and many others, in the meadow called Running Mead between Windelfore and Stanes, the fifteenth day of June, the seventeenth year of our reign.

Articles LXX. to LXXIX. embrace no special principle of law but only provide for the organization of a power in the state, consisting of twenty-five barons, nearly independent of the sovereign, to see that the charter was duly kept and its provisions fairly enforced. This was a sort of council of state, or house of lords, whose authority the king bound himself to respect. And he also bound himself in these articles to other measures essential to the perpetuity of the liberty and franchises designed to be vested by the charter.

The dominant principles controlling the rights of individuals and of society find abundant expression in this charter, showing the people had attained in their conceptions some intelligence of law and justice. And we have a right to conclude that their best views on these points found expression in the charter. But the people, as parties to this compact, were scarcely represented below the barons, though the king enjoined, as if by malice, that the barons should respect the charter in their treatment of their inferiors. But whatever in the charter infringed or modified the prerogatives of the crown had no precedent. These provisions were begotten and born of the civil war which led to the adoption of the charter. When this charter was established, it was less than forty years after Ranulph De Glanville, the chief justiciar of England, lays down the proposition that "whatsoever pleases the prince is law." Under this charter a king might be a very respectable executive—as many have been since that day—in governing his people by law instead of by his arbitrary will. True statesmanship can only govern well by force of established law.

The pretended desire of the barons for the revival of the laws of Edward the Confessor was only the cover to force the king to adopt and grant special franchises and liberties to the barons which Edward in his time never thought of. They were bound to be protected against the arbitrary power of the monarchy; and they scarcely concerned themselves, in drawing the charter, if St. Edward ever saw the like or not. Our copy in translation of St. Edward's laws, as compiled under the direction of William the Conqueror, justifies the remark of Hume that he did not see any special excellency in these laws, that the people should be so vehement for their restoration.

The following articles are not contained in form or substance in the charter of King John but are in the third charter of Henry III. and are numbered as below.

XVI. No bank shall be defended from henceforth but such as were in defense in the time of King Henry our grandfather by the same places and the same bounds as they.

This article qualifies the doctrine of riparian ownership of the borders of rivers, and it makes the use of such right to depend on ancient prescription. The rights of riparian ownership are always subordinate to the rights of the public in navigable waters; but here is a reservation as to the public right of fishing and access to the water for other uses.

XXXII. No freeman from henceforth shall give or sell any more of his land, but so that of the residue of the lands the lord of the fee may have the service due to him which belongeth to the fee.

It seems to have been the custom to sublet the whole or portions of estates held of the lord; but this was found prejudicial to the certainty of realizing the service or rent due to the lord.

And hence this provision operated to the benefit of the lord, and as a restriction on the tenant. If the tenure and nature of the estates in the land were beneficial and just, then the restriction was equally just.

XXXIII. All patrons of abbeys which have the king's charters of England of advowson or have old tenure or possession in the same shall have the custody of them when they fall void as it hath been accustomed and as is afore declared.

The ambition of the prelates to exclude secular persons from any voice in church affairs, even as to its temporalities, was noted, in the history of that remote age, as a point of great danger to the liberties of the kingdom. And as most of the religious houses were built by secular patrons the custom of presentation by the patron of the clergyman who was to enjoy the living, or the inmates and beneficiaries of these houses or foundation, such custom established as by covenant the *secular* right reserved in these grants to the patron.

XXXV. No county court from henceforth shall be holden, but from month to month; and where greater time hath been used there shall be greater; nor any sheriff or his bailiff shall keep his turn in the hundred but twice in a year and nowhere but in due place and accustomed; that is to say, once after Easter, and again after the feast of St. Michael. And the view of frank pledge shall be likewise at the feast of St. Michael, without occasion, so that every man may have his liberties which he had or used to have in the time of King Henry our grandfather, or which he hath purchased since. The view of frank pledge shall be so done that our peace may be kept, and that the tithing be wholly kept as it hath been accustomed; and that the sheriff seek no occasion and that he be content with so much as the sheriff was wont to have for the view-making as in the time of Henry our grandfather.

This provision seems to have been intended to promote the regular and orderly administration of justice, that the sheriff should not for any pretense hold courts or inquests to increase his fees and exactions from the people.

XXXVIII. Reserving to all archbishops, bishops, abbots, priors, templars, hospitalers, earls, barons, and all persons, as well spiritual as temporal, all their free liberties and free customs which they have had in times past.

And all these customs and liberties aforesaid, which we have granted to be holden within this our realm, as much as appertaineth to us and our heirs we shall observe; and all men of this our realm, as well spiritual as temporal (as much as in them is), shall observe the same against all persons in like wise.

And for this, our gift and grant of these liberties, and of others contained in our charter of liberties of our forest, the archbishops, bishops, abbots, priors, earls, barons, knights, freeholders, and other our subjects have given unto us the fifteenth part of all their movables. And we have granted unto them, on the other part, that neither we nor our heirs shall procure or do anything whereby the liberties in this charter contained shall be infringed or broken; and if anything be procured by any person contrary to the premises, it shall be had of no force nor effect. These being witnesses, Lord B., archbishop of Canterbury; E., bishop of London, and others.

Thus is shown that the parties to this charter as to all others might be the subjects of compassion in their weakness, to be protected against oppression and wrong. But of these lower classes this charter neither exalted them in rank or position nor enfranchised them in their rights. It is, as I have remarked before, only by a judicial accommodation of the doctrines of Magna Charta to the circumstances of the people of no rank that it has become the broad foundation of English popular liberty.

CONCLUSION.

So we have shown, by the most ancient and available records, the growth and development of law within the realm of England, down to the enactment of the great charter in A. D. 1215. And to our own satisfaction, at least, we have shown that the common law, so called, had no organization as a system prior to the reign of William the Conqueror. It is a maxim of the common law that every man is to be esteemed *innocent* until he is *proved guilty ;* while the Anglo-Saxon rule was that every man accused of crime must *clear himself* by his own oath of innocence, while the oaths of eleven others (compurgators) certified that they believed he told the truth.

Our theory of the origin of the common law is that it consisted in a modification of the administration of the civil law, by Norman judges. To this there is no counter-evidence. In support of this theory, we have no authentic proof that the common law was previously known. If customs existed, the very machinery was wanting to define them, or to give them a profert and a record. If customs had a judicial cognizance under Saxon laws, the fact is not recorded ; nor would it have been tolerated, unless as growing out of some law admitted by the sovereign. Otherwise every such adjudication would have gone to impair the prerogatives of the crown, as to which the kings were exceedingly jealous.

In further support of our theory, we cite the fact from Professor Carl Güterbock, of the University of

Königsberg, Germany, as translated by Brinton Cox, Esq., that a considerable portion of Bracton's treatise on the Customs and Laws of England was copied substantially from the civil law. Bracton, like several other justiciars of England, was educated as a clergyman, and was familiar with the civil and canon laws, and became, as a judge, familiar with the common law, which had grown as a system during the two hundred years of the reigns of the Norman kings. If the judges, in their circuits, discovered any customs that had influenced suitors in their contracts and transactions, they predicated their judgments upon them, and thus gave them a record. But if no custom was shown the judge made a *ruling*, all the same, that stood in the place of a custom, and in the judgment became a precedent in the common law unless superseded by a statute or overruled by the court. The remark before cited is in point here: Lord Mansfield, who understood this subject well, remarked to a friend that, in his judicial work, he *created* more law than both houses of parliament.

We have accomplished our task in showing the agency by which the common law came into existence. Its elaboration as a system is of less interest in this country, where we have no landed aristocracies, and few paramount and subordinate estates, which have been the chief subjects of adjudication in England. Our titles to lands are simplified by statute, and nearly every important interest has been made the subject of legislation; so that we rarely resort to common law, save to enforce a principle of legal morality, to aid in the construction of a statute, or to uphold as authority the decisions of our courts. In fact, so voluminous and varied has been our legislation, that a compilation of the body of our statutes would form a code more elaborate and comprehensive than the Code Napoleon. Our legal profession are opposed to such a code, for fear it would not have the liberality of construction claimed by the common law. But this objection is predicated on a *distrust* of the compass of thought and of liberality of views of our judges. We can see no objection to the enactment of such a code, with declared liberal intendments, provided it left the previous statutes and the common law, of force to cover its imperfections. The great error of our legislature in passing the Throop code of civil procedure is the repealing act, where beneficial statutes are set aside and no provision in this code furnishes equal facilities.

But the body of the common law, as the history of a science, is worthy the attention of any thoughtful student, or any civilian of independent thought and reason. There is a body of thought and intellectual force in the writers of the old text books of the law, remarkable for the age when they were produced. Glanville wrote of the courts and forms of judicial procedure, and, to some extent, of subject matters of adjudications. Bracton also wrote of the forms of procedure, but enlarged the scope of his investigation, and so increased the topics discussed that his work gave him the position of the father of the common law. Fleta and Britton copied from Bracton, with some matters that claimed the personal attention of the writers. The grand *Coutumier de Normandie* seems to have been compiled to prove a harmony between the new system of the common law and the law of the province on the continent upited with England by the Conquest. With these general expositions of law and jurisprudence, to guide suitors and the courts, the results of judicial work, and hence the growth of the common law, were found in the Year Books kept up through several reigns. Lyttleton wrote on land tenures, in the fourteenth century, but with so much obscurity that Lord Coke thought to do the public a service by an extended commentary on his definitions, near two centuries afterwards. So that Coke-Lyttleton has been an authority in English courts ever since.

Of Coke as a law writer we have before spoken. He was unquestionably a man of extensive reading, for his day; but in his law writings he so mixes in family histories with legal authorities and expositions, that it seems to have been his purpose to show a higher attachment to aristocracy than to the science of law. In prosperity, while in favor with the crown, he was both a toady and a parasite. But in disgrace and retirement, his revenge on the government found expression in advocating the rights of the people, and in forcing measures through parliament, of which he continued to be elected a member; establishing many important popular rights in permanency.

Blackstone, whose later commentaries have been more generally read, in this country, will soon be superannuated by legislation superseding the common law, though as an archive of heavy materials gathered from a broad field it will still be a useful text book in the history of the law.

If the common law as a system is still to prevail in this country, it will be a useful service to the profession to eliminate from English cases such doctrines and principles as have been adopted in this country, from such as find no recognition by our courts. It is possible this end may be reached by the adoption of a civil code, or our lawyers may believe with Glanville that "this is impossible, through the multiplicity of the enactments, and the ignorance of the writers."

FINIS.

INDEX TO THE SAXON LAWS.

ABBREVIATIONS.

Ecclesiastics and foreigners not to be wronged. Ed. & G. 12.
Edward's laws.
>   Historical note of. Ed. C. 35.
>   Ratified by William the Conqueror. Ed. C. 34.
Emancipation. Wd. 8.
Evil men to be driven out of the country. Ethd. vi. 7, 36.
Excommunicated. Ethd. v. 29.

Fœthe, punishment of man-slayer. Egr. Sec. 7.
False charge. Egr. ii. 4 ; Ct. Sec. 16.
Fasts and festivals. Ed. & G. 8; Alf. 43; Egr. i. 5; Ethd. v. 14–20 ;
>   vi. 22–25; Ct. Eccl. 16, 17; Ct. Sec. 47, 48; Wd. 14, 15; Ed. C.
>   1, 2.
Feeding an offender. Ethd. iii. 13.
Fencing.
>   Close. Ine 40.
>   Meadows. Ine 42.
Fidelity.
>   In Christian life. Ct. Eccl. 18–23 ; Ct. Sec. 11, 69, 85.
>   To church duty. Egr. Sup. 1.
Fighting.
>   Before an alderman in the gemot. Alf. 38.
>   Before a bishop. Alf. 15.
>   In a ceorlish man's flet. Alf. 39.
>   In the king's house, etc. Ine 6.
Fight-wite and man-bot not to be forgiven. Edm. Sec. 3.
Flyma. Ethd. iii. 10.
Folk-right. Egr. Sec. ii. 1.
Forfang. Æthn. iv. 6.
Forsteal, open opposition to God and the king. Ethd. v. 31; vi. 38.
Fostering a foundling. Ine 26.
Fraud. Ethd. v. 24, 25.
Frith, protection, safety.
>   Ed. E. 4.
>   Of the king, or king's protection. Ethd. ii. 3 ; vi. 13.
Frith-borh or frith-borg, security for public peace. Ed. C. 20.

Gemot.
>   Failing to attend. Æthn. i. 20
>   Term of. Ed. E. 11.
Gesithcund-man, thane ; what he may take on his journey. Ine 63.
God-bot. Ethd. vi. 51, 52.
Governor. Ed. C. 32.

King's frith not well kept. Æthn. iv.
King's grith—pledge of protection. Æthn. iv. 5.—Price of. Ethd.
    iii. 1.
King's hall, Fighting in. Alf. 7.
King's household, Fighting in. Ct. Sec. 60.
King's rights. Ct. Sec. 12, 14, 15.
King's security, Breaking of. Ct. Sec. 59.

Lame may be helped. Ed. & G. 10.
Land.
    Boc-, Title to. Alf. 41.
    Owners must cultivate certain portion. Ine 64–66.
Landless men. Æthn. i. 8.
Land-rica to seize cattle whose owners are not shown. Ethd. iii. 5.
Law, Submission to. Ethd. v. 4, 20, 32, 33; vi. 31, 32.
Laws.
    Of God to be loved and obeyed. Ethd. vi. 30.
    To be just. Ct. Sec. 1, 38, 70.
London.
    Citizens of, not to entertain. Ed. C. Sup. 2.
    Foreign merchant in. Ed. C. Sup. 8.
    Lieutenant governor of, restricted. Ed. C. Sup. 4.
Lord.
    Attachés changing to another. Alf. 37.
    Going from without leave. Ine 39.
    Plotting against. Æthn. i. 4.
    Responsible for his men. Ct. Sec. 31.
    Running away from. Ine 39; Alf. 37; Ed. E. 10.
Lordless men to seek a lord. Æthn. i. 2; iv. 1.

Manslaughter and murder. Æthb. 5–8, 13, 20–26, 30, 86; H. & E.
    1–4; Ine 5, 16, 21, 23, 24, 34, 35, 54, 76; Alf. 8, 9, 13, 21, 27–31;
    Alf. & G. 2, 3; Ed. E. Sec. 1; Ed. & G. 12; Æthn. iv. 6; Ethd.
    ii. 5; v. 25; Ct. Sec. 39–41, 57; D. S. 5; Ed. C. 15, 16.
Mass days, Celebration of. Alf. 43.
Misdemeanors. Æthb. 2, 3, 18, 24, 33, 73, 88; Ine 29; Alf. 19.
Money and measures. Æthn. i. 14.
Monks.
    Made custodians of cattle. Alf. 20.
    Must be attached to some minster. Ethd. v. 5, 6; vi. 3.
Moses' laws, Extracts from. Alf. Eccl. 1–48.
Mund-bryce and ham-socn. Edm. Sec. 6.

Navy. Ethd. v. 27; vi. 33, 34.

INDEX TO TERMS EXPLAINED IN FOOT NOTES.

GLOSSARY.

The meaning of the terms found in the Saxon Laws stated in the following table is gathered as far as practicable from a glossary annexed to the text of the translators. Where they have stated several meanings, that is selected, for brevity, which is thought best to accord to our copy of the text where the words occur. In the translation from which we copy, there occurs a large number of Saxon words copied literally in the text without explanation or definition. Where a reasonable meaning could be inferred from the connection of the word in the sentence into which it is copied, such meaning is stated in the following table. I have not the scholars of antiquity or of ancient Saxon literature as critics, which the English translators obviously feared. If in any instance I have blundered, my readers are not worse off than if I had left them the bald old obsolete Saxon term or phrase.

Æwdas : men standing in the oath with an accused, compurgators.

Ceap-gild : price of cattle.

Church-socn : protection to an accused fleeing to a church.

Dooms : judgments, decrees, laws.

Drihtin-beah : a sort of atonement to the king for slaying a person.

Drinc-lean : a contribution, aid by the tenant to his lord.

Feoh-bot : relating to coining money.

Feorm : rent in kind, portion of the crop.

Flyma : tramp, vagabond, outlaw, one who has run away from justice.

Forfang : fee for pursuing thieves.

Forfongen : rescuing cattle from a thief.

Frith : peace, freedom from molestation, power of granting protection.

Frith Gegilda : freedom or protection to the members of a guild.

Frymth or Fyrmth : harbor, or entertainment to any one.

Ful : judgment against.

Fyrd : campaign, camp, war.

Fyrd-wite : fine for non-attendance on military duty.

Grith : freedom or protection by the king or high officer through the actual putting forth of force to that end; a keeping for the purpose of safety.

Had-bryce : injury to persons in holy orders.

Handhabenda : having a thing in hand.

Hlaford : a tribute.

Hordere : treasurer.

Hynden : ten men of a guild called together on matters pertaining to the guild.

Lad : exculpation, purgation.

Lah-cop : a certain due to the king.

Lah-slit : penalty under Danish law.

Land-cop : purchase of land.

Leod-geld : 200 shillings, value of a person.

Loc-bore : women wearing long hair indicating rank.

Lyblac : arts kindred to witchcraft.

Mœg-bot : Fine or damages to a kindred.

Mœg-burg : kindred, family.

Mancuses : coins, money.

Manung : precinct of the reeve or sheriff.

Morth : pertaining to the guilt of murder.

Morth-dœd : assassination.

Orige : appearing openly.

Socn : sanctuary, place of refuge.

Stœth : station or place designated.

Thrall : a state of bondage.

Tun : homestead, cottage, town, or castle ; house and surrounding lawn.

Walreaf : despoiling the dead.

Wer-fœthe : compensation for a homicide paid by the slayer.

Wer-tyhtle : accusation involving the penalty of the wer.

Wite-rœden : a particular fine.

Wit-word : a sort of knowledge.

Wlisc : resident Welshman.

Lightning Source UK Ltd.
Milton Keynes UK
UKOW06f1935100917

308919UK00006B/52/P